Associated Labor and Production in the Age of Barbarism

Henrique Tahan Novaes

Associated Labor and Production in the Age of Barbarism

Education Beyond Capital

CAPES

palgrave macmillan

Henrique Tahan Novaes
Faculty of Philosophy and Sciences
São Paulo State University - UNESP
Marilia
São Paulo, Brazil

ISBN 978-3-031-51182-0 ISBN 978-3-031-51183-7 (eBook)
https://doi.org/10.1007/978-3-031-51183-7

This Palgrave Macmillan imprint is published by the registered company Springer Nature Switzerland AG
The registered company address is: Gewerbestrasse 11, 6330 Cham, Switzerland

Paper in this product is recyclable.

Foreword

Among the many challenges present in the fight to supersede capitalism, there is a huge imperative for the *class-that-lives-off-of-labour*: the need to reinvent a *new way of living*.

This is because, since the Paris Commune's original, embryonic and exceptional experiment, the subsequent experiences that developed after the Russian Revolution couldn't bring forth effective implementation of *autonomous, self-determined and associated work*.

On the contrary, what we saw, throughout the twentieth century (especially with the tragedies of the system known as "real socialism"), was the maintenance of *hierarchical structures of command and control on labour* that, little by little, was suppressing all attempts that sought to move forward in the direction of a structured social formation, based on the *free association of male and female workers*, to reiterate Marx.

And this is exactly the central point of reflection present in Henrique Tahan Novaes's book. Just as much a result of personal investigation, as it is a collective study, the book's concerns are varied and relevant and can be summarised accordingly:

How to conceive of labour in its pendular dialectic that oscillates between *vital activity and alienated work*?

What were the contributions of the labour councils, the factory committees and the cooperatives in the history of the worker's struggle since the beginning of the Industrial Revolution?

What were the main advances and limitations present in the practices that prioritised self-governance?

Coming from the study of diverse experiences carried out by *occupied or recuperated factories* (a term used by the labour movement in Brazil and Argentina), what was able to progress in regard to *self-governance*?

What made them flourish, advance and also regress?

Was it possible to practice effective forms of *associated work*?

Based on some of their experiences, what contributions could the social movements of the Global South offer, with an emphasis on the actions taken throughout four decades by the Landless Workers' Movement (MST) in Brazil?

Given all of these experiences, what seeds of (self)education could effectively flourish? Which ones have shown vitality and force?

Moreover, during the Workers' Party's first terms in government in Brazil (2003–2016) were there gains that remained? And, conversely, what were some of the main causes of their collapse?

In a reality in which *capitalism's system of social metabolism* (Mészáros, *I., Oltre Il Capital,* Edizioni Punto Rosso, 2016) has been accentuating its destructive tripod in relation to *nature, work* and to *humanity*, how will it be possible to advance *self-organisation* of labour and the construction of a *new way of life*?

Regarding *nature*, it's about immediately stopping the destruction and thus, seeking instant recovery, since global warming, fossil fuels, pesticides, GMOs, mining, forest fires, agribusiness, etc., have been directly responsible for the environmental destruction and, for this very reason, should definitely be eliminated.

In regard to *work*, the precarisation, *exploitation*, *despoilment* and *expropriation,* as well as the destruction of labour rights that were won in many labour struggles have been the rule and not the exception, especially since the growth of uberised and platformatised digital work, occurring during one of capitalism's periods of structural crisis. This obliges us to restore it to its *vital*, *self-determined* essence, and one that is based on *available time.*

Just as capitalism's system of antisocial consumption destroys nature and work, the construction of a new system of truly humane and social metabolism will only be able to come about by fighting against the destruction of humanity that depends on labour to survive—against all of the forms of class, gender, race and ethnic oppression.

This book by Henrique Tahan Novaes has been a gift in its contribution to this crucial topic of our time. With a perspective from the Global South, it reflects on the lived experiences through the perspective of the world of associated work in its clashing which aims to overcome the system of capitalism.

Ricardo Antunes
State University of Campinas
São Paulo, Brazil

Preface for the English and Italian Editions

We have entered into the Era of Barbarism. Around the world, there are land grabs on a devastating scale, privatisations, globalisation of hunger and of unemployment, with capitalism trampling down on workers. In Brazil, after the meagre social-liberalism of the Workers' Party that generated more work and resulted in a few rights to those "at the bottom", the already fragile and restrictive democracy was suspended by Michel Temer, and won an even larger momentum with Jair Bolsonaro's counter-reforms.

The "waves" of the dictator, removal of rights, closing of factories, commodification of life, outsourcing and sub-contracting of labour, progression of agribusiness and de-industrialisation in the last 40 years have devastated Latin-American indigenous peoples. In contrast, as a product of the resistance of a portion of workers, associated work experiences where male and female workers encounter new forms of decision-making, producing, using the surplus and means of production that emerged and have been arising within the core mode of capitalist production, regardless if it is still very little and still rather small in terms of quantity.

The World of Associated Work, with its wealth and misery as well as its contradictions, progress and limits, is portrayed in this book through the vantage point of recovered factories in Brazil and Argentina—from the experiences of cooperations and the cooperativism of the Landless Movement, from the experiences of the "murtirão" (mobilization of a group of people, paid or otherwise, that executes a service that benefits the larger community) and the homeless work cooperatives.

We believe that, at least to some degree, they demonstrated the possible and urgent need to change the nature of work. They are forms of working that, on their onset, alter labour and possess an emancipatory potential, but also reproduce a sort of deterioration of labour and indirect subordination to capitalism.

In the same context of the advancement of the World of Associated Work, experiences in Education have emerged in Latin America beyond the realm of capitalism. In the very recovered factories, besides self-learning on the job, schools were created that altered both the content and educational framework. With regard to the fight for self-determination and food security, and against destructive production, we observed the creation of agroecology schools from the Landless Movement. They made a critique of the use and possession of land of the so-called "green revolution" while at the same time theorising and practising agroecology. The agroecology schools also give the students new ways of organising life in the schools and within the settlements, through centres, committees and general assemblies that question government-taught technocracy and practice self-governance within the schools.

The fruit of my research with friends who are devoted to the movement or study these themes, this book addresses the new world that insists on coming forth, staring down the old world of capitalism that insists on crushing workers, commercialising life, destroying the conditions of existence on the land, unemploying, underemploying and hijacking everything that is still public.

* * *

This book was published in March of 2018 in Brazil by the Publishing company Lutas Anticapital (Anticapitalism Fights). In 2022, it was published in Spanish by the publishing company Callao (Argentina); and will it be published by Editora Ediciones desde abajo (Publishing from below Publisher—Colombia), Quimantú (Chile) in 2024.

It is highly likely that the World of Associated Work and its alternative forms of education—which in this book I call education beyond capitalism (Mészáros, 2002)—found more "fertile" land in Latin America than in that of Europe and the United States.

Latin America hasn't been able to free itself of neoliberalism, let alone capitalism. At the exact moment in which I write these words—a far-right president has been elected in Argentina (Javier Milei). While the political scene in Argentina is heated, Brazil is even more ablaze, with record temperatures close to 44.8° Celsius.

The lack of a radical and far-reaching alternative on the part of the political left (Mészáros, 2002) has brought about a sort of peculiar election "pendulum" in the Southern Cone: neoliberal parties won the elections and implemented their neoliberal dos and don'ts in the 90s. The political left in power (Lula, Kirchner, etc.) was elected and made small positive reforms but it was recently superseded by the right or the far-right (Macri, Temer, Bolsonaro, La Calle Pou). Fernandez's election in Argentina and Lula's return to Brazil generated and will generate very meagre reforms that didn't create and won't create an electorate "identity" for these presidents. The response to Argentinian constituency was very clear. Don't vote for candidates on the political left in Argentina, but rather for those right-wing extremists—those who are truly "revolutionaries" and "anti-system". Evidently, we have to reference the new types of coups and the immense media machine that concocts far-right politicians who are supposedly against the "political class" and who will supposedly resolve social issues.

In this political scenario where there is a lack of anti-capitalist theory and praxis on a large scale that radically changes capitalism's order, the world of associated work acquires an "exotic" character, even though we can't write off its role in teaching, as a tool of the working class to change the "here and now" reality of a part of the working class, in a context where capitalism is in the offence.

Marx once said that workers' cooperatives are the first rupture in the old structure, even if they reproduce all of the flaws of the old structure. The World of Associated Work isn't insignificant, but in the absence of more substantive shifts in society, it tends to make up a marginal role in financialised capitalism.

While observing these limits, we intend to analyse both the positive and negative aspects (Mészáros, 2002) of the experiences of associated production and alternative education of the Latin-American social movements.

We believe that the deepening of barbarism has only allowed capitalists to create superficial solutions to severe problems created by the mode of capitalist production. Severe socio-environmental issues are being "solved" interestingly enough with an expansion of neoliberal policies and with environmental "solutions"—on the part of the transnational corporations—which don't even scratch the surface of capitalism's destructive progression.

In turn, the expansion of neoliberal educational policies has produced illiteracy and precarity "within" public services, by providing services for private companies that commercialise education and devour public funds.

This book, modestly, intends to contribute to the debate for a radical and far-reaching alternative to the theory of democracy of the councils and of education beyond capitalism. Concurrently, it intends to help elucidate the contradiction regarding the world of associated work and of the educational experiences of the social movements: their achievements, contradictions and limits.

In one way or the other, it also contributes to the socialisation of the theory of transition by István Mészáros, one of the main Marxists at the end of the twentieth century.

* * *

The translation of this book was made with support from the Post-Graduate Program in Education (PPGE) from UNESP (State University of São Paulo)—statue of Publications of Books in English—CAPES/PPGE UNESP Marília.

I would also like the thank the patience, cordiality and camaraderie of the translators Toni Infranca and Diogo Saraiva. I would also like to thank my friend Ricardo Antunes for the preface, the publisher Editora Punto Rosso (in Italy) and the publisher Editora Palgrave. Enjoy the read!

São Paulo, Brazil
November 2023

Henrique Tahan Novaes
On the hottest recorded day
in the history of Brazil

Introduction

The Wealth and Misery of the World of Associated Labour and An Education Beyond Capital in the Age of Barbarism

This book is a collection of articles written by myself and by researchers Douglas Silva, Erika Alaniz, Fabiana Rodrigues, João Henrique Pires, Lais Santos and Maurício Sardá de Faria. Some of this research has already been presented at conferences, as is normal in our field, or in book chapters. For this book, the texts have been revised and expanded, eliminating repetitions where possible and necessary, and merging parts in order to provide the reader with a more organic book.

This book presents articles or chapters written over the last 7 years, as a development of the research I carried out with the support of FAPESP during my master's and Doctoral studies (UNICAMP), as well as the first results of the research funded by FAPESP for the 2015-16 biennium (process 2014/19013-8), as Professor at Unesp-Marília.

* * *

Everything indicates that we have entered the age of barbarism. Capitalism has absolutely nothing left to offer humanity. Proof of this is the increase in illiteracy and functional illiteracy, the destruction of the environment, the increase in unemployment and underemployment on a global scale and the destruction of workers' rights.

There are processes of "slummification" and "condoisation". Land theft and the murder of landless squatters, indigenous peoples and quilombolas are also prominent phenomena in the Age of Barbarism.

The commodification of education, health and the few public projects that existed in the state also symbolises the end of the "civilising" phase of capitalism. Finally, we have the complete commodification of life. Capitalism, or rather the socio-metabolism of capital, may take 500–600 years to "fall", and this will depend on a sociopolitical revolution permeated by the constant and coordinated struggle of the most diverse anti-capitalist social movements. Overcoming a society that produces commodities and alienated labour is the prize at stake.

The age of barbarism has opened a new cycle of struggles for workers around the world. The capital-controlled media do not show us, but from China to Uruguay, from California to Russia, numerous anti-capital struggles are emerging.

The chapters presented here are the direct and indirect result of the research that I and my friends have carried out on the world of associated labour, on the alienation and embryos of alienation from work of Latin American social movements. They are also the fruit of my research on destructive production, agroecology and the embryos of an education beyond capital, which I began in my doctoral thesis.

If associated labour is an educational principle, it means that workers, by organising themselves to produce, are experiencing—in statu nascendi—new social relations that to some extent anticipate how anti-capital labour can organise itself, while reproducing the "defects" of the capitalist mode of production and indirectly subordinating themselves to capital.

We believe that associated labour has enormous potential to educate workers in a new form of social control. It also entails the need to create systematic spaces for education and/or training that will help us to educate the future.

Capitalist production in the age of barbarism, essentially destructive of human beings and nature, has proved ineffective and inefficient in solving the problem of world hunger. On the contrary, the "green revolution" has stimulated a growing concentration of land ownership and increased unemployment in the countryside, and has also led to the expulsion and displacement of peasants, increased allergies and cancer and generated a new phase of "primitive" accumulation that has not yet been fully described by academics.

Social movements, intellectuals, political parties and NGOs have spoken out about the harmful relationship between agribusiness, synthetic fertiliser, pesticides, transgenic seed and tractor industries and the capitalist state. The resistance of social movements to the advance of the "green revolution" has led to the creation of numerous landless settlements with agroecological principles, fairs, "public policies" and, above all, the creation of agroecological centres and schools. These educational experiences, still little known in Latin America, have led us to study and now socialise what we have found, especially in the state of Paraná.

* * *

To present this debate, we have divided the book into 10 chapters.

Chapter 1 introduces the discussion of work as a vital need and an analysis of alienated work. This is followed by a brief analysis of the ontology of social being, that is, the difference between humans and other animals. In the second section, we describe alienated labour within the framework of capitalist society, where workers are alienated from themselves, the products of their labour, their relationship with other human beings and with nature. In the third section, we briefly outline ways of overcoming the alienation of labour, based at least in part on our research into anti-capitalist social movements. They led us to believe in the need to foster associated labour and school spaces beyond capital.

"Workers' Councils and The Limits of Cooperativism: The Contribution of István Mészáros" is the title of Chapter 2. We note that Mészáros argues that workers' councils must fulfil the role of effective material mediators between the old order and the desired socialist order. He warns that as long as the vital control functions of socio-metabolism are not effectively occupied and exercised autonomously by associated producers, as opposed to being left to the authority of a separate control group, that is, a new type of personification of capital, labour itself will continue to reproduce the power of capital against itself, maintaining it materially and thereby extending the domination of alienated wealth over society. Similarly, Mészáros shows us the limits of cooperativism in a society where the strategic centres of control are fully in the hands of capital.

Chapter 3—Factory committees: an attempt at self-management in the midst of a dictatorship? It was written by myself and Prof. Maurício Sardá de Faria. We look at the formation of factory committees in Brazil in the context of growing workers' struggles from the 1950s to 1968. Our hypothesis is that the Factory Committees were formed as embryos of workers' self-management struggles in Brazil, which were quickly stifled by the intensification of the military dictatorship in 1968 and then by the restructuring of the productive sector.

The exhaustion of the "civilising" phase of capital and the historical need for educational projects beyond capital are discussed in Chapter 4. In the first part of the chapter, we characterise the world counterrevolution and the exhaustion of the "civilising" phase of capital. We briefly discuss the growth of child labour, the violence of structural unemployment, the return of slave labour and, last but not least, the violence of underemployment and alienated labour.

The second part of the chapter begins with a brief look at the manifestations of barbarism in Brazilian schools and the misery of São Paulo's education policy. It then defends the historical need for an education beyond the capital.

Chapter 5 provides an overview of urban-associated labour in Brazil, showing the positive and negative sides of self-management in the productive microcosm. We try to explore the positive and negative sides of associated labour based on the experiences of worker-owned enterprises, collective efforts and associations in civil construction, as well as in garbage collection associations and urban popular cooperatives.

Chapter 6 is called "Cooperation and cooperativism of the MST in São Paulo: an analysis of the actions of the capitalist state that block the educational potential of associated labour". I wrote it together with João Henrique Pires and Douglas Silva. We note that the State of São Paulo offers a privileged vantage point from which to observe the restructuring of the countryside and the (im)possibility of an agrarian reform aimed at creating the conditions for the development of cooperative, cooperativist and agroecological agrarian reform settlements. The first half of the chapter provides a brief historical overview of the political economy of the countryside in the state of São Paulo, with special emphasis on São Paulo's autocratic traits. The second part shows the limits and contradictions of cooperation and cooperativism in MST settlements in the face of the new agribusiness offensive in the state. The chapter concludes with some final considerations.

Chapter 7 discusses associated labour as an educational principle and schooling. To do this, we have rescued our research on Brazilian and Argentinean Recovered Factories and how these experiences raise the debate on education, schools and training in social movements.

In Chapter 8, Erika Alaniz and I look at the experience of the National Centre for Training in the Solidarity Economy to show the contradictions of the self-managed education of the solidarity economy movement.

Chapter 9, entitled ""Green Revolution", Agroecology and the MST Agroecology Schools", was written by myself, João Henrique Pires and Lais Santos. In it, we criticise the so-called "Green Revolution", and show attempts to build an alternative production proposal, the so-called agroecology, as well as the bountifulness and contradictions of the agroecological schools.

"Notes on social movements and education: challenges of the struggle between capital and labour in the Brazilian reality" is the title of Chapter 10. It was written by Fabiana Rodrigues and myself. In it, we make some observations on the relationship between social movements and education in light of the particularities of Brazilian capitalism. It is based on the understanding that social movements are an expression of class struggle. However, there are different theoretical explanations for the existence of these movements and the way they develop. Therefore, a summary of the different theories of social movements is presented first. Then we work on a specific understanding of social movements as an expression of the contradictions between capital and labour in the capitalist mode of production. Based on this understanding, the third part of the text discusses the relations between social movements and their educational potential in the specificity of Brazilian capitalism.

Through the socialisation of our production, we believe that the reader will have access to the results of collective research on the world of associated labour and the embryos of education beyond capital. I sincerely hope you enjoy reading this book!

2017 Henrique Tahan Novaes

Contents

About the Author

Henrique Tahan Novaes is an Economist who graduated from the Araraquara campus of UNESP (2001) and has a master's degree (2005) and a doctorate (2010) in Scientific and Technological Policies from the University of Campinas (UNICAMP). His dissertation was the embryo of the book "The fetish of technology - the experience of recovered factories" (Popular Expression-Fapesp, 2007 and 2010, 3rd edition by Lutas Anticapital Press, also published in Argentina).

His doctoral thesis became the book Reconnecting an interrupted wire: The relationship between University and social movements in Latin America (Expressão Popular-Fapesp, 2012, 2nd edition by the Lutas Anticapital Press, also published in 2016, in Argentina). He has also written the book "The world of associated labour and embryos of education beyond capital" (The world of associated labour and embryos of education beyond capital) (Lutas Anticapital Press, 2018).

He has also been a professor at the School of Philosophy and Science at UNESP, in the city of Marília, since 2011, and a professor at the Graduate Studies Program in Education since 2013. He is the coordinator of the Itinerant Enhancement Course "Social Movements and Contemporary Crises, seen in the light of the classics of Critical Materialism" (9 editions). Coordinated the Post-Middle Courses in Agroecology (2014-2016) and the Technical Course in Agriculture and Livestock Raising, integrated into the high school programme, with emphasis on agroecology and agroforestry (2019 to present). Coordinator of the Post-Graduate Program in Education at UNESP Marília. hetanov@gmail.com

Abbreviations

ABC Paulista	The ABC Paulista is a group of municipalities on the outskirts of São Paulo: Santo André (A), São Bernardo (B) and São Caetano (C)-ABC
ANTEAG	National Association of Workers in Self-Management Companies
CEBs	Ecclesial Base Communities
CFES	Centre for Training in Solidarity Economy
CFES	Nacional—National Centre for Training in Solidarity Economy
CIPA	Committee to Prevent Accidents
CNBB	National Brazilian Bishops' Council
CUT	Single workers center (syndicate)
EBEM	Brazilian Meeting on Education and Marxism
ERTs	Worker-recovered Companies
FAPESP	Public foundation in the State of São Paulosupport research projects in higher education and research institutions
GMOs	Genetically modified organisms
MST	Landless Rural Workers Movement
NGOs	Non-governmental organizations
OTAs	Associated Labor Organisations
PACs	Alternative Community Projects
PLANFOR	National training plan
PNQ/Proesq	National Qualification Plan - Special Qualification Projects
POS	Political opportunity structure
RFs	Recovered Factories (RFs)
RMT	Resource Mobilization Theory
SEBRAE	Brazilian Support Service for Micro and Small Businesses

Sedex	The Brazilian Mail Service's express service
Sudene	Superintendency for the Development of the Northeast
TPM	Theory of Political Mobilization
UEL	State University of Londrina
UNISOL	Center for Cooperatives and Solidarity Enterprises
UNISINOS	University of Vale dos Sinos

CHAPTER 1

Labour as a Vital Need and Alienated Labour: Contributions to the Debate on the Relationship Between Labour and an Education Beyond Capital

Introduction

This chapter aims to reflect on labour as a vital need for human beings and on alienated labour in the capitalist mode of production. This is an introductory chapter on the subject, aimed mainly at education workers. As far as possible, we have tried to simplify the debate, but as the subject is complex, this has not been possible in some passages.

In the first section, we carry out a brief analysis of the ontology of the social being, that is, the difference between human beings and other animals. The second section describes alienated labour in the frameworks of capitalist society, where workers are alienated from themselves, the products of their work and their relationship with other human beings and with nature. In the third section, we conducted a brief outline of ways to partially overcome the alienation of labour based on our research on anti-capital social movements. They lead us to believe in the need to foster associated labour and school spaces beyond capital. We close the chapter with some conclusions.

H. Tahan Novaes, *Associated Labor and Production in the Age of Barbarism*, https://doi.org/10.1007/978-3-031-51183-7_1

The Ontology of Social Beings: The Difference Between Humans and Other Animals

Marx (1996) and Lukács (2010) focused on the particularities of human beings in relation to other animals and nature. For them, work is the foundation of being human, the essence of the human being. It is the authentic foundation of a human community (Infranca, 2005).

Infranca (2005) states that work is the original phenomenon that allows the passage from organic being to social being. Marx distinguishes the human being from animals with the following aspects: unlike animals, the human being is the only animal species in which vital activity is conscious (Lukács 2010), and is guided to an end (known as the teleology of work).[1] In other words, human beings are the only species that can plan (prior ideation) before performing. Only we conceive our work before executing it. In Marx's own words (1996, p. 22):

> [...] what distinguishes the worst architect from the best bee is that the former built the comb inside his head, before building it in wax. At the end of the labour process, a result is achieved that already existed at the beginning of work in the labourer's imagination, and therefore as an ideal. (Marx 1983, pp. 149–150)

If other animals reproduce only by instinct, human beings can work consciously, produce tools, "regulate" nature and, at the same time, transform themselves. Moreover, only human beings are educated, only they develop, only they find answers to problems that arise and only they have unlimited educational needs.

Many historians studying the question of work have sought to carry out an "archaeology of labour", that is, to verify, throughout history, how human beings created their instruments of work, the means of production of life, which, concomitantly, transformed nature and transformed themselves.

For Marx (1996), what differentiates the human being from other animals is that only the human being is a "tool maker". In addition, he

[1] Lukács (2010) sees work as a specifically human category. The metabolism of other animals with nature is always characterized by passive adaptation, genetically determined according to changes in environmental conditions. The human being promotes active adaptation. We create the material conditions for our own reproduction.

notes that animals such as bees, beavers, and ants erect nests, hives, etc.[2] But the animal:

> produces only what is absolutely necessary for themselves or their offspring; they produce only in one direction, while man produces universally; they produce only under the domination of immediate physical necessity, while man produces when he is free from physical necessity and only produces truly in the freedom of such necessity; the animal produces only for themselves, while man reproduces all nature; their product belong immediately to their physical body, while man is free from his product. Animals build only according to the pattern and necessity of the species to which they belong, whereas man knows how to produce according to the pattern of each species and knows how to apply the appropriate pattern to each object; thus, man also builds in accordance with the laws of beauty. (Marx 2004, p. 117)

It is worth noting that, in order to unravel the difference of the capitalist labour process from the previous historical phases of humanity, Marx analysed the emergence of machine manufacturing (in the 1st Industrial Revolution). He sought to unravel the fetish of commodities through the theoretical-historical demonstration of the capitalist labour process, making clear that it is concurrently a process that produces use values and also surplus value.[3]

Reconstituting the labour process to verify whether there is a process of exploitation of labour—whether through absolute or relative surplus value—is a fundamental task not only to understand the mechanisms of exploitation and alienation in capitalism, but also to find ways to overcome it.

Bringing this debate to the present day, many researchers and documentarians have denounced the exploitation of labour and the growth of labour analogous to slavery in the clothing, construction and oil industries, sugarcane fields, and others. It is very difficult to find a

[2] For a didactic introduction on the difference between humans and other animals, see the film *Ilha das Flores* (1989).

[3] To learn more about the manifestations of alienation before Big Industry, see Mészáros (2006).

sector that escapes this trend in capitalism under the hegemony of financial institutions.[4] Vasapolo (2005), Linhart (2007), Hirata (2002), and Antunes (2008) have shown the growth of child labour and female labour in this new phase of flexible accumulation, driven by the hegemony of financial capital, in which Taylorism-Fordism, Toyotism, complex labour and labour analogous to slavery coexist with underemployment and unemployment, and outsourcing, through which the "modern" and "backward" sectors of the economy are structured.

Alienated Labour

> As a matter of routine, we are insulted. When the boss gets angry, he swears at us, calling us bitches, pigs, sluts; we have to endure all this with resignation, without reacting [...] Officially, we work from seven in the morning to three in the afternoon (with a salary of less than two dollars a day), but we often have to work mandatory overtime; sometimes – especially if there is an urgent request to be delivered – until nine in the evening. As tired as we are, we can't go home. We received an extra payment of 200 rupees (10 cents USD) [...] We walk to the factory from our homes. Inside the factory, it's very hot. The shed has a metallic roof, and there's not much room. It's all very crowded." There are more than 200 people working there, most of them women, but there is only one bathroom for the whole factory [...] After work, when we get home, we have no strength to do anything but eat and sleep. (Seabrook 1996, apud Harvey 2005, p. 88)

The account above, made by two sisters who are factory workers in India, is a typical example of alienated labour within the framework of flexible accumulation, that is, of the "return" of slave-like labour.

The phrase in which Marx (1996, p. 77) observes that "as soon as no physical or other compulsion exists, labour is shunned like the plague" is well known. Workers only feel close to themselves outside of work and outside of themselves at work. Work gains airs of forced, compulsory, imposed labour, a hateful activity, which generates suffering, becoming a source of torment. It is not the satisfaction of a need, but only a means to satisfy needs outside it (Marx 2004; Antunes n/a; Lima Filho 1996).

[4] See, for example, the films *The Corporation* (2002), *Mondays in the Sun* (2002), *China Blue* (2005), *Conterrâneos velhos de guerra* (1984), *Blood Diamonds* (2006) and *The Full Monty* (1997).

Under the dominance of capital, labour is a source of suffering, and torture is a mere activity for survival with no social sense (Lukács 2010; Mészáros 2002). This, however, does not mean that this specific type of work is eternal and present in every moment of human history. Marx (2004) not only recognised the negative aspects of work in capitalism but noted that we human beings can build a new mode of production in which work is focused on our holistic development and the satisfaction of our needs.[5] In this society, labour will no longer be alienated, being controlled according to the needs of freely associated producers.

Daniele Linhart (2007) characterised the ambivalence—which we are calling positivity and negativity—we all have in relation to work in two sentences: "One cannot live without work: work gives meaning and value to free time and life. Work prevents us from living, from enjoying life; it ruins life; one does not have enough time to live" (Linhart 2007, p. 42).

In the introduction of the collection *Trabalho e Emancipação [Labour and Emancipation]*, published by Publisher Expressão Popular, Ricardo Antunes reached similar conclusions:

> In the long history of human activity, marked by an incessant struggle for survival, for the achievement of dignity, humanity and social happiness, the world of work has been vital. It was through work that individuals, men and women, distinguished themselves from animals. Marx's famous distinction between the "worst architect and the best bee" is that the former conceives of the work they are going to do, while the bee works instinctively. This mark has made human history a monumental achievement, rich and full of paths and detours, of alternatives and challenges, of steps forward and steps back. Without work, everyday life would not reproduce itself. However, when human life is limited exclusively to work, it becomes a painful effort, imprisoning individuals and flattening them to a single dimension of their being. If, on the one hand, we need human work and

[5] For this discussion, see *Beyond Capital* where Mészáros poses the question of the "communal system". In Latin America, José Mariátegui is one of the intellectuals who has very aptly joined this debate from the standpoint of Andean societies and the transformations necessary in Latin America for the construction of "American Indian socialism" without necessarily having to go through capitalism. The book *The Class Struggle in Russia* gathers practically the last writings of Marx. In it one can see that for Marx "primitive" societies must not be destroyed by capital in order to achieve progress. They could "jump" from one stage to another without necessarily having to destroy old social relationships.

> its emancipatory potential, we must also refuse labour that exploits, alienates and destroys the happiness of a social being. These two sides of the work process – a phenomenon which creates but also subordinates, emancipates and alienates, humanises but degrades, liberates and enslaves – are essential to the study of work in our world and our lives in this troubled 21st century, in which the greatest challenge is to give meaning to human work while also endowing our life outside of work with meaning. (Antunes s/d)

The symptoms of negative labour can be seen in the horror of degrading work in the framework of capitalist exploitation, in disinterest in work, in absenteeism, in suicides, in job turnover rates and in struggles and demands for free time, control of work, self-management, etc.[6]

According to Antunes (2008, p. 144),

> Something that should be a basic purpose of the human being – their realisation *in* and *by* work – is perverted and impoverished. The work process becomes a means of subsistence. Labour-power becomes, like everything else, a commodity, the purpose of which comes to be the production of commodities. What should be the human form of individual achievement is reduced to the sole possibility of subsistence of the dispossessed.

At the same time, life without work leads to anguish. Workers with no work feel like pariahs like they're empty. After all, what is the meaning of life for an unemployed worker? For a young worker who is tirelessly looking for a job with a formal contract and can't find any?

Ricardo Gleyzer, an Argentinian filmmaker, captured the relationship between alienated labour and unemployment, expressing this human drama with the title of his film *"They kill me if I don't work and if I work they kill me"* (Gleyzer 1974). On the other hand, a life full of social meaning in "productive" work and outside of work can only really take place in a communist society.

[6] To learn more about the symptoms of labour alienation in Taylorism, see Braverman (1987); in Toyotism, see Tragtenberg (2005), Oliveira (2006) and Antunes (2008). Two classic films, among others, address the alienation of work: *The Working Class Goes to Paradise* (1976) and *The Companions* (1964). Not even continuous-flow industries (breweries, oil, etc.)—where the transformation of matter does not depend on the skill and dexterity of workers—escape this reality.

There are many emergent struggles fighting for the de-alienation of labour, which—*in statu nascendi*—partially surpass alienated labour, but evidently faces limits to overcome it completely.[7]

In the following passage, Daniele Linhart (2007) makes numerous connections between life without work and the organisation of life in the nineteenth and twentieth centuries:

> By bringing workers together in the same workplace, capitalist industrialisation destroyed their home and family environment. Time and space were structured according to the hours and places in which wage labour took place. This process produced a void around areas which concentrated labour. The absence of a large part of the population during working hours was institutionalised through types of housing (dormitory neighbourhoods in the peripheries, workers' cities, popular housing, housing projects, among others) and the organisation of leisure (most entertainment events happen after working hours, gaining airs of a reward after effort; the "after-work" period alternates with work). In these conditions, not working, or rather not executing an activity in a workplace, implies a long daytime wait, most of the time. One waits for people to return from work and for the world of leisure, or simply "free" time, to happen. (Linhart 2007, pp. 42–43)

For Marx (2004), the phenomenon of alienation can be understood in its four aspects: the worker's relationship with themselves, with the product of their work and their relationship with other human beings and with nature (Mészáros 2006; Agazzi 2000).[8]

In his Economic and Philosophic Manuscripts, Marx recognises that the key to all alienation—be it religious, legal, moral, artistic, political or economic—is alienated labour, the alienated form of man's

[7] See, for example, the articles gathered in the collection organized by Rodrigues, Novaes and Batista (2012).

[8] In everyday life, an alienated person is a person who is not aware of current affairs, some with "their head in the clouds", who's "hallucinating" or "uninformed" about what is happening in the world. The word is also used when transferring a good or asset to another. In the 1990s, for example, we had numerous campaigns "against the alienation of public assets." A car is alienated to a bank until we pay all the instalments. Machado de Assis wrote a great exploration of alienation in the sense of "madness" in the short story *The Alienist*, where a doctor, in the name of science, arrested practically all the "crazy" people of the city, including, at the end, himself.

practical activity (Mészáros 2006). In his book *Marx's Theory of Alienation*, Mészáros (2006) produced an excellent analysis, reconfiguring and updating Marx's thinking on this topic. We draw the reader's attention to the didactic development of the four aspects of alienation addressed by Mészáros: economic, debated in Chapter IV, political, addressed in Chapter V, ontological and moral, debated in Chapter VI, and aesthetic, discussed in Chapter VII.

In other words, for Marx, alienated labour reflects not only the relation of workers to themselves and to the product of their labour, but also their relation to other human beings and to nature. In the words of Mészáros:

> the alienation of humanity, in the fundamental sense of the term, means loss of control: its embodiment in an external force that confronts individuals as a hostile and potentially destructive power. When Marx analysed alienation in his 1844 manuscripts, he pointed out its four fundamental aspects: the alienation of human beings from nature; from their own productive activity; from their species, the human species; and from one another. He stated emphatically that this is not a "fatality of nature," but a form of self-alienation. In other words, it is not the feat of an all-powerful natural or metaphysical external force, but the result of a certain type of historical development, which can be positively altered by conscious intervention in the process of transcending the self-alienation of labour. (Mészáros 2002)

In the same vein as Mészáros, Netto and Braz (2008) accurately summarised the debate on the alienation of labour in the following passage:

> In certain social-historical conditions, the products of human labour and imagination cease to appear as objectifications that express the humanity of humans – they can even appear as something that, beyond their control, comes to control them as a power that is superior to them. Under these conditions, objectifications impose themselves on humans as external and transcendent instead of revealing themselves as the expression of their vital social forces. In other words: the actual relationship between humans and their work, which is the relationship between creator and creature, appears reversed – the creature comes to dominate the creator. This inversion characterises the historical phenomenon of alienation. It is indeed a historical phenomenon because, although it is characterised by its truly huge permanence, encompassing a variety of historical eras, the social conditions in which it takes place are neither eternal nor natural – they are conditions

that can be overcome in the course of historical development. (Netto and Braz 2008, pp. 44–45)

From this point of view and using Mészáros's (2006) terms, we can conclude that political alienation means loss of control of fundamental decision-making bodies and that political de-alienation means the "return" of political power to the workers. In a nutshell, fundamental decision-making power has been alienated by large corporations, the capitalist state (state bureaucracy, schools, etc.), bureaucratised unions and by rulers who perform the vital functions of reproduction of the socio-metabolism of capital.

Alienation in the *act of production* (labour process), alienation as the result of the product of labour, and alienation from the self and human civilization were explored by Marx in the *Economic-Philosophical Manuscripts*, *On the Jewish Question*, and in the *Capital*. Let us remind ourselves that his thoughts on commodity fetishism seem precisely to show that the relationship between things is actually a relationship between human beings that,

> [...] escaping their control, control them as a power that is superior to them. Under these conditions, objectifications impose themselves on humans as external and transcendent instead of revealing themselves as the expression of their vital social forces. In a word: between humans and their works, the real relationship, which is the relationship between creator and creature, appears reversed – the creature comes to dominate the creator. (Netto and Braz 2008, p. 42)

For Marx (2004, p. 82):

> [...]this estrangement is shown not only in the result [product of his labour], but also, and especially, in *the act of production*, within the *productive activity itself*. How could the worker be alienated (*fremd*) from the product of his activity if in the very act of production he was not alienated from himself?

In the words of Netto and Braz (2008, p. 45):

> [...] alienation is characteristic of societies in which the social division of labour and private ownership of the fundamental means of production take effect, societies in which the product of a worker's activity does not belong

to them, in which workers are expropriated – that is, societies in which there are certain forms of exploitation of man by man.

To illustrate the alienation of producers in relation to the products of their labour, it is always useful to remember that, for Marx (2004, p. 122): "The mineral trader sees only the commodity value of a mineral, but not its beauty and peculiar nature. For the mineral producer, the mineral has no mineralogical sense at all", it is only an exchange value.[9] The alienation of the labour process occurs basically with the emergence of the specifically capitalist mode of production, that is, with the emergence of machine manufacture, where knowledge is expropriated by capital and transferred to an "automatic system of machines".[10]

The Positive Overcoming of the Alienation of Labour Entails a Need for the Flourishing of Associated Labour and an Education Beyond Capital

Mészáros (2002) posits that positive transcendence of the alienation of labour could occur in a long and complex process of struggles for the modification of work activities, characterised by the promotion of "discontinuities in continuity" within a revolutionary project. It is worth emphasising the revolutionary project because the author argues that profound social change requires a qualitative leap.

The need for "[...] conscious global social control of the conditions of human self-realisation" is essential for human beings to break "the tyranny of the material base" (Mészáros 1993, p. 201). The author proposes that Workers' Councils and other forms of mediation should take on the role of performing "genuine planning". Let us remember that Councils have the potential to mediate and emancipate by rationally solving workers' vital existential problems, their daily concerns with housing and work, and the main issues of social life according to their basic needs as a class (Mészáros 2002; Ness and Azzellini 2011; Martorano and

[9] To learn about the concepts of use value and exchange value, see Marx (1996), in addition to Netto and Braz (2008).

[10] As this is a rather introductory chapter, we cannot discuss all the dimensions of labour and alienated labour in depth. For further details, see Mészáros (2004), Netto and Braz (2008), Ranieri (2001), Musto (2014) and Iasi (2006).

Pinheiro 2013). We cannot overemphasise that in Workers' Councils and other forms of mediation, workers are educating themselves to exercise new social relations. Therefore, they are part of an educational structure beyond the capital.

According to Mészáros (2002), as long as the vital control functions of socio-metabolism are not effectively "returned", occupied and exercised autonomously by associated producers but left to the authority of separate control personnel (i.e., a new type of personification of capital), work will continue to reproduce the power of capital against the workers themselves, materially maintaining and thus extending the domination of alienated wealth over society (Mészáros 2002, p. 601).

Regarding the embryos of political and economic de-alienation, we could mention the case of the Recovered Factories (RFs) (Faria 2011; Henriques 2013), where one can find practices which begin to overcome the capitalist division of labour between those who plan and those who execute, between those who work and those who control the means of production. In Novaes (2011, 2013), we developed some of these ideas. Here, it is necessary to summarise them. Even within the limits of a labour process that involves countless production chains and countless factories, RFs try to overcome the "structural hierarchy of capital" within their microcosm (Mészáros 2002); in short, they try to reunify *homo faber* and *homo sapiens*. Decisions are made in democratic assemblies; workers rotate in strategic posts and positions are revocable.

Actions are taken to reach an increased knowledge of work processes in the factory, allowing us to state that they partially overcome the alienation of labour, while still preserving some of its elements.

In the late 1920s, Gramsci witnessed the struggles for the formation of workers' councils in Turin, leading him to theorise about the pedagogical role of workers' councils in anti-capital struggles. For him, the factory councils were a "wonderful school". It is precisely from this line of thinking that the title of this section is derived: we believe that associated labour is extremely pedagogical, but it is obvious that it does not single-handedly exhaust the role of education in a possible and necessary transition beyond capital.

Some Recovered Factories (RFs) overcame a part of the divisions of capitalist labour to the extent that knowledge, which was retained in the hands of some, began to be socialised. The dependence on the "foreman engineers" and the complex work carried out by them has been modified to some extent.

In the most advanced cases, the overcoming of the wage system is outlined through the principle: "[...]from each according to his ability, to each according to his needs" (Marx 2012, p. 216). In other cases, there is a closer approximation of withdrawals ("wages") and the creation of funds, either to support the struggles of other workers or to allow some workers to access university or to improve year-end earnings, etc. From this point of view, this embryonic stage of the overcoming of the wage system and the creation of workers' funds are responses connected to what Mészáros (2006) calls economic alienation.

However, it is important to highlight the case of an RF in Argentina, where a fund was created to improve the withdrawal of workers who had higher expenses with children. This reminds us of the principle of "substantive equality", developed by Mészáros based on the writings of François Babeuf and Karl Marx. To develop his argument, Mészáros resorted to the following paragraph by the French socialist Babeuf::

> Equality must be measured by the capacity of the worker and the needs of the consumer, not by the intensity of work or the quantity of things consumed. A man endowed with a certain degree of strength, when he lifts a weight of ten pounds, works as much as another man with five times his strength who lifts fifty pounds. He who, to quench a burning thirst, drinks a large mug of water, enjoys no more than his comrade who, less thirsty, drinks only one glass. The aim of communism is equality of work and pleasure, not things to be consumed and tasks performed by workers. (Babeuf, apud Mészáros, 2007, p. 42)

Certainly, this principle does not exhaust the challenges posed, but we believe that it helps guide the struggles of movements that combine issues of class, gender, ethnicity and age/generation, materialising the principle of substantive equality. In this regard, we must remind the reader of a case reported by our friends at the Usina Collective—a group of architects and social scientists who advise social movements. They said that, in a joint effort, at first they thought of dividing the work "equally" among all members. Soon, they realised that there were elderly people, people who had been stroke victims and workers with other problems who could not perform heavy work "equally". From this observation, Babeuf's above-mentioned principle is relevant: "a man endowed with a certain degree of strength, when he lifts a weight of ten pounds, works as much as another man with five times his strength who lifts fifty pounds" (apud Mészáros 2007, p. 42).

Even in the most advanced cases, the cooperative workers of the RFs do everything they can to avoid establishing statuses differentiating workers, that is, they fight for everyone to be cooperated. It is important to highlight this fact because we will see below that a reasonable share of RFs is hiring outsourced workers—in our point of view, a symptom of their degeneration. This allows us to state that, in these experiences, associated labour becomes an educational principle.

Even though they are part of the commodity-producing system, many associated labour experiences organised by social movements have the decommodification of society as their goal, that is, a society without profits, without capital accumulation, where goods are produced to satisfy human needs.[11]

Last but not least, we can highlight that the Bossless Factory Zanón and, to some extent, Flaskô—an occupied factory—are bringing together "class-aware" workers, which can be interpreted as an attempt to unify portions of the Argentinian working class that have goals laying beyond the capital. We can already say that FaSinPat Zanón is one of the few RFs that has not succumbed to accommodation and degeneration. It remains alive and well and its struggle is renewed every day. All these principles exercised daily in the RFs are pedagogical and will be fundamental in the struggle for the de-alienation of work.

When thinking about the challenges to be faced in constituting an emancipatory education, Mészáros (2005) understands that it is necessary to create horizontal workers' organisations—with a view to de-alienating work—linked to an educational system that overcomes processes that would internalise them into capital. Only a different process of internalisation can contribute to the transcendence of what Mészáros (2002) calls the socio-metabolism of capital, which reproduces itself in all dimensions of life. Thus, the existence of collective ownership of the means of production is not enough, not least because, as Marx (2009) observed in his

[11] Recent research in Latin America has shown growing dissatisfaction with the advance of control of people's lives by transnational corporations, whole populations being kicked out of their lands in the name of progress and GMOs, the profit of tolls and the scandal of privatizations, the absurdity of the price and quality of the subway and bus systems, banks' profit margins and many other such phenomena. See, for example, Sevá Filho (2019) and Pinassi and Mafort (2012) and the manifestos of some anti-capital social movements.

critique of Proudhon, commodity production can remain intact and the wage system, the role of managers and competition can be perpetuated in new forms. It does not hurt to repeat that what is being discussed is the meaning of work or, more generally, the resumption of control of the product of work, of the work process, of oneself and of human civilization by human beings.

So far, we have focused on the political and economic aspects of alienation. Mészáros (2006), Vázquez (2009) and Fátima Cabral (2012) attribute a fundamental role to aesthetic education for human development. Within the complex production and reproduction of alienated life, the cultural industry promotes conservative art, which generates huge profits and domination. It keeps its consumers alienated. To cite an example: "for the non-musical ear the most beautiful music has no meaning" (Marx 2004).

In the meantime, revolutionary art, while partially "de-alienating" its producer, helps human beings to develop their ears, their hands, and their eyes. Partially de-alienated, because—as we have seen—the complete de-alienation of human beings can only take place in a society governed by freely associated producers.

From the point of view of aesthetic education, one of the fundamental tasks of schools linked to emancipatory struggles is to prepare the hands, the ears, the brain and the eyes, that is, the human senses to produce revolutionary art and "capture" the great works of humanity. Let us remember that, for Marx (2004), there must be a complete emancipation of all human qualities and senses.

With regard to the school space itself, we outline in the pages below what would be the foundations of an Emancipated Labour School:

a) The exercise of self-management at school: rotation of functions, collective habits, and self-management. This principle is based on the pedagogy of self-organisation and the creation of new social relations in school, that is, the form of the school forms those in contact with it. (Pistrak et al. 2009; Tragtenberg 2006; Dal Ri and Vieitez 2008; Freitas 2009, Novaes and Castro 2011; Nascimento 2011);
b) Self-management of the educational system, including all the spheres currently alienated from teachers, employees, students, and the "community". In this regard, it is enough to remember the

power of the central administration in shaping the curriculum, salary policy, career plan, system supervision, evaluation, etc.

c) Performing socially necessary work (cleaning, cooking, gardening, etc.) (Pistrak et al. 2009; Shulgin 2013);
d) Preparation for the struggle and insertion in the struggles of the current time, linking the school with its social environment (Pistrak et al. 2009; Novaes 2012);
e) Use of a "method" of thematic complexes/holistic studies, with a view to understanding the socio-metabolism of capital under a totalising, dynamic perspective which examines contradictions, combining totality and particularity (Pistrak et al. 2009; Lukács 2010);
f) Aesthetic education: preparation for the understanding and construction of non-market culture (Mészáros 2006, ch. 13; Cabral 2012; Hilsenbeck Filho 2012; Vázquez 2009);
g) Physical education to develop the human body;
h) Study of history from a materialist point of view and rescue of the Brazilian Theory of Revolution (Rodrigues 2013; Lima Filho, Macedo 2011);
i) Exercising emancipated work, that is, the school must prepare for collective and de-alienated work (Mészáros 2002; Pistrak 2002; Bruno 2004; Vieitez and Dal Ri 2001);
j) Socialisation of historically accumulated knowledge so that workers can understand the "scientific foundations of work" (Lombardi 2011; Saviani 2008; Ramos 2010; Dagnino 2008). At the same time, carrying out a review of capitalist science, that is, how science and technology are not neutral, carrying out an *inventory* and *filtering* of the productive and destructive forces created by capital and developing technoscience for human emancipation, with a view to the complete de-commodification of society and self-government by freely associated producers (Dagnino 2008; Novaes 2012; Caldart 2013; Rolo 2012).

In Conclusion ...

We saw in the pages above that, for Marxism, the key to understanding capitalism is the labour process alongside production relations.

Taking a step back, understanding the previous historical forms and thinking about other forms of work organisation are fundamental steps to understanding the uniqueness of the human being (ontology of the social being), as well as the possibility/need to overcome alienated work. We have seen that within the framework of capital, whether in "real capitalism" or "real socialism", workers do not decide what to produce, how to produce or for whom to produce.

Mészáros (2004) believes that the transcendence of alienated labour is the most urgent theme in this new millennium. He defends the need for universalisation of work as a vital activity of the human being (positivity of work). Certainly, when he refers to the universalisation of work, he means that we must all work, as long as it is unexploited work, work that enriches us as human beings. He presupposes that in this case work has the characteristics of meaningful activity, producing use values aimed at satisfying human needs and not stultifying labour, degrading labour, producing commodities aimed at the expanded reproduction of capital. Mészáros (2002) also refers not to a formal egalitarianism, but to substantive equality "[...] from each according to their abilities, to each according to their needs" (Marx 2012, p. 216).

We believe that only through the unified struggle of the anti-capital social movements (Rodrigues et al. 2012) and within a revolutionary project can we transcend alienated work and alienating life.

In opposition to the expansionist order of capital, we have the emergence of new ways to organise production created by workers, in which associated labour is an educational principle and debates on how to build an education beyond capital are held.

Only an education that is guided by the principle of Associated/Non-Alienated Labour in production and social life as a whole and that lends itself to the revolutionary task of human emancipation through the reorganisation of material and cultural life can overcome the socio-metabolism of capital.

Bibliography

Agazzi, D. L. Trabalho e alienação no paradigma marxiano: uma discussão teórica e uma reflexão sobre a sua aplicação no capitalismo contemporâneo. 2000, 317 f. Tese (Doutorado em Economia), FEA – USP, São Paulo, 2000.

Antunes, R. Adeus ao trabalho? 15. ed. São Paulo: Cortez, 2008.

Antunes, R. Apresentação da coleção *Trabalho e Emancipação*. São Paulo: Expressão Popular, s/d.

Braverman, H. Trabalho e capital monopolista. Rio de Janeiro: LTC, 1987.

Bruno, L. Estudos sobre poder político, ideologia, trabalho e educação. 2004. 512 f. Tese (Livre-Docência), FE – USP, São Paulo, 2004.

Cabral, F. Arte para pensar a vida e educar os sentidos. In: MENDONÇA, S. G. L. et al. (Orgs.). Marx, Gramsci e Vigotski: aproximações. Araraquara, SP: Junqueira & Marin, 2012. pp. 377–398.

Caldart, R. Desafios do vínculo entre trabalho e educação na luta e construção da Reforma Agrária Popular. Goiânia, 36ª Reunião Anual da Anped, GT Trabalho e Educação, 2013.

Dagnino, R. Neutralidade da ciência e determinismo tecnológico. Campinas: UNICAMP, 2008.

Dal Ri, N. M.; Vieitez, C. Educação democrática e trabalho associado no Movimento dos Trabalhadores Rurais Sem Terra e nas fábricas de autogestão. São Paulo: Ícone, Fapesp, 2008.

Faria, M. S. Autogestão, cooperativa, economia solidária: avatares do trabalho e do capital. Florianópolis: Editora em Debate, 2011.

Freitas, L. C. A luta por uma pedagogia do meio: revisitando o conceito. In: Pistrak, M. M. A escola-comuna. São Paulo: Expressão Popular, 2009, pp. 8–100.

Harvey, D. A produção capitalista do espaço. São Paulo: Annablume, 2005.

Henriques, F. C. Empresas Recuperadas por Trabalhadores no Brasil e na Argentina. Doutorado (Planejamento urbano e regional). UFRJ, Rio de Janeiro, 2013.

Hilsenbeck Filho A. O MST e o Teatro – potencialidades pedagógicas. 2012. Obtido em: http://passapalavra.info/2012/11/66247. Retirado em 15/11/2012.

Hirata, H. Nova divisão sexual do trabalho? São Paulo: Boitempo, 2002.

Iasi, M. Ensaios sobre consciência e emancipação. São Paulo: Expressão Popular, 2006.

Infranca, A. Trabajo, individuo, historia: el concepto de trabajo em Lukács. Buenos Aires: Herramienta, 2005.

Lima Filho, P. A. Os devoradores da ordem: exclusão social no capitalismo incompleto. In: Galeazzi, M. A. (Org.). Segurança alimentar e cidadania: a contribuição das universidades paulistas. Campinas, SP: Mercado das Letras, 1996. pp. 45–77.

Lima Filho, P. A.; Macedo, R. A poeira dos mitos: Revolução e contrarrevolução nos capitalismos da miséria. In: BENINI, É.; SARDÁ DE FARIA, M. S.; NOVAES, H. T.; DAGNINO, R. Gestão pública e sociedade: fundamentos e políticas públicas de economia solidária. São Paulo: Outras Expressões, 2011. pp. 150–182.

Linhart, D. A desmedida do capital. São Paulo: Boitempo, 2007.

Lombardi, J. C. Educação e ensino na obra de Marx e Engels. Campinas: Alínea, 2011.
Lukács, G. Prolegômenos para uma ontologia do ser social. São Paulo: Boitempo, 2010.
Marx, K. A miséria da filosofia. São Paulo: Expressão Popular, 2009.
Marx, K. Crítica do programa de Gotha. São Paulo: Boitempo, 2012.
Marx, K. Manuscritos Econômico-Filosóficos. São Paulo: Boitempo Editorial, 2004.
Marx, K. O capital. 3. ed. São Paulo: Abril Cultural, 1983, volume I.
Marx, K. O capital. São Paulo: Nova Cultural, 1996, volume I.
Mészáros, I. Para além do capital. São Paulo: Boitempo, 2002.
Mészáros, I. A educação para além do capital. São Paulo: Boitempo, 2005.
Mészáros, I. A teoria da alienação em Marx. São Paulo: Boitempo Editorial, 2006.
Mészáros, I. Filosofia, ideologia e controle social. São Paulo: Ensaio, 1993.
Mészáros, I. O desafio e o fardo do tempo histórico. São Paulo: Boitempo, 2007.
Mészáros, I. O poder da ideologia. São Paulo: Boitempo Editorial, 2004a.
Musto, M. Revisitando a concepção de alienação em Marx. In: DEL ROIO, M. (org.) Marx e a dialética da sociedade civil. Marília: Oficina Universitária, 2014, pp. 61–94.
Nascimento, C. Experimentação autogestionária: autogestão da pedagogia e pedagogia da autogestão. In: BATISTA, E. L.; NOVAES, H. T. (Orgs.). Educação e reprodução social: as contradições do capital no século XXI. Bauru, SP: Canal 6; Londrina: Praxis, 2011, pp. 130–166.
Ness, I. Azzellini, D. (eds). Ours to Master and to Own: Workers' Control from the Commune to the Present. Chicago: Haymarket, 2011.
Netto, J. P.; Braz, M. Economia política: uma introdução crítica. São Paulo: Cortez, 2008.
Novaes, H. T.; Castro, M. . Em busca de uma pedagogia da produção associada. In: Benini, É.; Sardá De Faria, M.; NOVAES, H. T.; DAGNINO, R.. (Org.). Gestão pública e sociedade: fundamentos e políticas públicas de economia solidária. São Paulo: Outras Expressões, 2011, pp. 153–188.
Novaes, H. T. A Autogestão como Magnífica Escola: notas sobre a educação no trabalho associado. In: Batista, E. L.; Novaes, H. T. (orgs.) Educação e reprodução social: as contradições do capital no século XXI. Bauru: Canal 6/ Praxis, 2011.
Novaes, H. T. Reatando um fio interrompido: a relação universidade-movimentos sociais na América Latina. São Paulo: Expressão Popular-Fapesp, 2012.
Novaes, H. T. A miséria ideológica da política educacional paulista. Marília, mimeo, 2013.
Novaes, H. T.; Benini, É. Quem controla o Estado Brasileiro: o capital rentista e a dívida pública. In: Benini, E. A.; Faria, M. S.; Novaes, H. T.; Dagnino,

R. (orgs.) *Gestão Pública e Sociedade: fundamentos e políticas públicas de Economia Solidária*. São Paulo: Outras Expressões, 2012.
Oliveira, E. Toyotismo no Brasil. São Paulo: Expressão Popular, 2006.
Pinassi, M. O.; Mafort, K. Os agrotóxicos e a reprodução do capital na perspectiva feminista da Via Campesina In: Rodrigues, F. C.; Novaes, H. T.; Batista, E. L. (Orgs.) Movimentos sociais, trabalho associado e educação para além do capital. São Paulo: Outras Expressões, 2012, pp. 141–158.
Pinheiro, M.; Martorano, L. (orgs). Teoria e prática dos conselhos operários. São Paulo: Expressão Popular, 2013.
Pistrak, M. Fundamentos da Escola do Trabalho. São Paulo: Expressão Popular, 2002.
Pistrak, M. M. (org.) A escola-comuna. São Paulo: Expressão Popular, 2009.
Sevá Filho, A. Populações e Territórios espoliados pela ampliação recente da infraestrutura industrial capitalista: focos de luta política e ideológica na América do Sul. Marília: Lutas anticapital, 2019.
Shulgin, V. Rumo ao politecnismo. São Paulo: Expressão Popular, 2013.
Ramos, M. Trabalho, educação e correntes pedagógicas no Brasil. Rio de Janeiro: EPSJV/ UFRJ, 2010.
Ranieri, J. A câmara escura: alienação e estranhamento em Marx. São Paulo: Boitempo, 2001.
Rodrigues, F. C. MST - Formação Política e Reforma Agrária nos anos de 1980. Tese (Doutorado em Educação). UNICAMP, Campinas, 2013.
Rodrigues, F. C.; Novaes, H. T.; Batista, E. L. (orgs.) Movimentos sociais, trabalho associado e educação para além do capital. São Paulo: Outras Expressões, 2012. v. I.
Rolo, M. Ocupando os latifúndios do saber: subsídios para o ensino da ciência na perspectiva politécnica da educação. 2012. 382f. Tese (Doutorado em Educação). Rio de Janeiro, UERJ, 2012.
Tragtenberg, M. Administração, poder e ideologia. 3. ed. São Paulo: Editora da UNESP, 2005.
Tragtenberg, M. Sobre educação, política e sindicalismo. 2ª Ed. São Paulo: Editora da Unesp, 2006.
Vasapolo, L. Trabalho atípico e precariedade. São Paulo: Expressão Popular, 2005.
Vazquez, A. S. As ideias estéticas de Marx. São Paulo: Expressão Popular, 2009.
Vieitez, C.; Dal Ri, N. Trabalho associado. Rio de Janeiro: DP&A, 2001.

Film

Ilha das Flores. Direção: Jorge Furtado. Porto Alegre, 1989.
Me matam se não trabalho e se trabalho me matam. Direção de Raymundo Gleyzer. Buenos Aires, 1974. Videocassete.

CHAPTER 2

The Foundations of Self-Managed Socialism: The Contribution of István Mészáros

The Return to Self-Management, Cooperativism and Associativism in the late Twentieth Century

Workers began to feel the need for self-management the first day that they were placed in a factory against their will. In the nineteenth century, cooperativism and mutual support societies gained force as a form of resistance against unemployment, principally during the industrial revolution in England. I should note that one of the main reasons mutual support societies were created was so that workers could have decent burials.

By that time, consumer cooperatives had made it possible for workers to get good quality products at accessible prices. This is what George Holyoake said:

> What should arouse the most interest in the writer or the reader is not the brilliance of commercial activity, but the new and quickened spirit that enlivens that exchange. The buyer and the seller meet as friends; there is no cunningness on the one side, or suspicion on the other. Those multitudes of humble workers, who previously never knew if they were eating good-quality food, who used to eat adulterated food every day, whose shoes would quickly fall to pieces, whose jackets were patched together with tallow and whose wives used common fabric that was impossible to wash, now shop in the markets [the Rochdale cooperatives warehouses] as if they

H. Tahan Novaes, *Associated Labor and Production in the Age of Barbarism*, https://doi.org/10.1007/978-3-031-51183-7_2

were millionaires, and with regard to the purity of their food, they live like lords.[1]

Incipient industrial self-management occurred during the 1840s and under the Paris Commune in 1871, when the bosses abandoned their factories and the workers organised to get them operating again. In the words of one scholar:

The offices of the [Paris] Commune were... models of proletarian democracy. The workers appointed their managers, their office directors and their team managers. They reserved the right to replace them in case of unsatisfactory performance or working conditions. They set their wages and hours, and their working conditions, and even better, a factory committee would meet in the afternoons to decide on the next day's work.[2]

Similar cases were seen in 1905 in Russia and the early years of the 1917 Revolution, the Spanish Revolution, the 1919 and 1956 Hungarian revolutions and the Polish and Portuguese revolutions, involving not only workers' control of factories and coordinated production among factories but also the self-management of schools, shipyards, hospitals, housing construction and workers' control of the cities, etc. In the early years of the Russian Revolution, workers' councils (soviets) fulfilled their role but subsequently were strangled by the growing bureaucratisation of that society's strategic decision-making. According to Tragtenberg, a Brazilian intellectual who is little known in Latin America:

Nationalisation of the means of production, preservation of wages as remuneration for labour, technocratic control of the production process, and a political party with power over the State are dominant practices in the USSR, China, the Eastern European countries and Cuba. Did a revolution take place? Yes. Private ownership of the means of production was replaced by state ownership, but it is administered by the bureaucracy of a party, either socialist (SP) or communist (CP) — which became the main instrument for disciplining workers.[3]

[1] G. Holyoake, *Os vinte oito tecelões de Rochdale*, Rio de Janeiro: GB, 1933.

[2] A. Guillerm and Y. Bourdet, *Autogestão: uma visão radical*, Rio de Janeiro: Zahar, 1976, p. 22.

[3] M. Tragtenberg, *Reflexões sobre o socialismo*, São Paulo: Moderna, 1986, p. 8.

In the late 1960s, numerous anti-capitalist uprisings occurred, the most notable among them in May 1968. In Latin America, these included the 1969 Argentine rebellion known as the *Cordobazo*, factory committees in Brazil and the takeover of factories and industrial belts during the Allende government in Chile.

There are diverse cases of land collectivisation and of new, communist-led social projects in the countryside. A few examples: the collectivisation of land during the 1936–1939 Spanish Revolution; the little-known Georgist movement in the USA; the Peasants' Leagues (*Ligas Camponesas*) in Brazil, based in part on cooperativism; and much earlier, the seventeenth-century Palmares Commune, also in Brazil, operated with a certain degree of self-management for some years.

It is no coincidence that cooperativism, as part of the perspective of socialist transition anticipated by Marx, was cast aside by social democracy. Marx criticised the reformist tendencies of his era, which were already signalling towards a crisis for the potential of his ideas. This may be seen especially in his criticism of the Gotha and Erfurt programs and Robert Owen's paternalistic socialism.

As one of the rare exceptions in today's situation, in which. bourgeois revisionism predominates, the work of the thinker István Mészáros contains repeated and implacable criticism of the "socio-metabolism of capital". For some, there is a revival taking place, especially in the search for a "balance" between the errors of the Soviet experience and those of European social democracy. For Mészáros, the proposal of self-management has never died. This article focuses on the social and historical foundations of the thought of one of the advocates of self-managed Marxism: István Mészáros.

During a national conference in Lisbon on "self-managed socialism", self-management was defined as:

> ...The permanent construction of a model of socialism, in which different levers of power; the centres of decision making, management and control, and social, political and ideological mechanisms are in the hands of the producer-citizens, freely and democratically organised into forms of association created by the producer-citizens themselves, based on the principle that any organisation should be structured from the bottom up, and from the periphery to the centre, in which the practice is established of direct

democracy, free elections and the possibility repeal decisions, public offices and agreements at any time.[4]

It is no coincidence that the most radical view of self-management did not gain space in theoretical/practical debates on the solidarity economy. Nevertheless, in Brazil, articles have been published recently by authors who could be considered supporters of a "socialist solidarity economy", such as Antônio Cruz (2006), Cláudio Nascimento (n.d.), Lia Tiriba (2001), Maurício Sardá de Faria (2005),Carlos Schimidt (2008), my own works, and those of others like Bernardo (1986), Bruno (1986), José Henrique de Faria (2004), Guimarães (2004), Vieitez and Dal Ri (2001), Dal Ri and Vieitez (2008), Pinassi (2009) and Antunes (2008). They hark back to the Marxist debate on resistance cooperativism and workers' autonomy, and include revisionist tendencies, such as Bernstein's. More recently, criticism has emerged of cooperativism that is linked to "entrepreneurialism" and the cooperatives known as "*coopergatos*", which were created to get around Brazilian legislation. These authors seek to establish a "parallel" debate to that around solidarity economy, perhaps to prevent the term from becoming emptied of meaning or used by supposed or real reformist movements.

The most important connections or common points between these authors and Mészáros' work are related to the fact that they, too, view capital as the crux of a totalising relationship. That is, they acknowledge that it is insufficient to criticise only certain manifestations of capital.

I believe that Brazil's solidarity economy, at least in its hegemonic version, partially criticises capital, but not as a total social relationship. Mészáros's contribution is decisive to that, and to solidarity economy not inheriting the theoretical crises of Marxism.

However, another question emerges: Why do so many researchers of solidarity economy return to the work of Robert Owen, Charles Fourier and others, but fail to mention Marx? Perhaps the answer lies in the fact that Marx's work has always been interpreted—in our opinion, erroneously—as a simple question of the ownership of the means of production, or as an apology for the nationalisation of the means of production as a way of achieving socialism. Stalinism interpreted socialism

[4] C. Nascimento, *Autogestão e o "novo" cooperativismo*, Brasilia: Ministério do Trabalho e Emprego, 2004, p. 2.

as state ownership of the means of production and "forgot" the debate about transcending the alienation of labour.[5]

The socialist variant of the solidarity economy is apparently returning to the debate over self-management in revolutionary periods, such as the silk workers' (*canuts*) revolt in 1831 and 1834, the Paris Commune, the early years of the Russian Revolution, the Spanish Revolution and other revolutions mentioned above. When "isolated" cooperatives emerge in the absence of a social and political revolution, there are doubts about self-management as a means (a prefigurative practice) and an end (self-managed socialism). Now that we have spent several years reviewing the work of István Mészáros, we can see that he weaves implacable criticism of the "socio-metabolism of capital", and that his arguments are based on observing and overcoming alienated labour.

This article was structured as follows: it begins with a brief introduction to the work of Mészáros. It then proposes a radical criticism of private ownership of the means of production and defends cooperativism as providing a possibility for reconnecting the "snail to its shell". The need for a new division of labour—self-management as opposed to hetero-management, the role of democratic assemblies in cooperatives and workers' associations and of a new type of workers' participation in cooperatives and workers' associations, along with a new type of workers' participation in transforming society and in "overall control of the labour process by the associated producers" are addressed in the third section. Mészáros's view on the need to restructure the productive forces and socialist planning of production are addressed in the fourth and fifth sections. The "final considerations" section mentions Mészáros's criticism of commodity-producing societies and envisions the building of a society that has the goal of meeting human needs (use value).[6]

[5] István Mészáros, *Para além do capital,* Campinas: Unicamp/Boitempo, 2002.

[6] I realize how difficult it is to read Mészáros work. For interpretations by some of his followers, see, for example: R. Antunes: *O caracol e sua concha – ensaios sobre a nova morfologia do trabalho*. Boitempo Editorial, São Paulo, 2005 y M. O. Pinassi: *Da miséria ideológica à crise do capital – uma reconciliação histórica*. Boitempo Editorial, São Paulo, 2009. In Latin America, Mészáros's work seems to be more "widespread" in Brazil and Venezuela, where his work has received many awards and was constantly quoted by former President Hugo Chávez.

A Society Beyond Capital: Starting the Debate

According to the editor of his book, *Beyond Capital*, Mészáros, who now lives in England, was born in Hungary in 1930. At the age of 12 and a half, he got a job in a cargo plane factory by claiming that he was 16. He began working as an assistant to Georg Lukács in 1951 and would have been his successor at the University of Budapest, but the 1956 Soviet invasion forced him to leave the country.

It is important to emphasise that the 1956 Hungarian Revolution deeply marked the theories and life of István Mészáros. The Soviet bureaucracy severely repressed attempts to build "socialism with a human face" in that country. Researchers estimate that about 2000 people died and 13,000 were injured in Budapest, along with 700 deaths and 1500 injured in the rest of the country. Many combatants were jailed, most of them young people, and about 100 were executed by firing squad. This repression led Mészáros into exile in Italy. That was where he wrote *The Revolt of the Intellectual in Hungary* (*La rivolta degli intellettuali in Ungheria,* Turin, Einaudi publishers, 1958) about those events, a book that has yet to be translated. His experience as a worker and student in "socialist" Hungary was decisive to his understanding of education as a way of overcoming the obstacles of reality.

Lukács once said that Marxism should be re-founded. I believe that his follower, István Mészáros, is one of the authors committed to that re-founding. We could say that his criticism is very complete and unrelenting: of the mode of production of capital, demonstrating how it strengthened the dictatorship of capital in the twentieth century; of capital's theorists and apologists; of social democracy; of "real socialism", which he calls a "post-capitalist" experience, as we will see further on. He attempts to return to the unity of Marx's theory, which was split by twentieth-century Marxism, principally by developing the subject of the alienation of labour and by updating Marx's work.

Mészáros' (2002) reflections on the socialist transition are part of his proposal for formulating comprehensive change, with the goal of transcending the "social metabolism of capital". His theory seeks the qualitatively higher demands of the new historic form, post-capital (and not post-capitalist) socialism, where human beings can develop their "rich individuality". He uses the expression "post-capital" and not "post-capitalist" because, for example, while private ownership of the means of production was "extinguished" in the post-capitalist society of the Soviet

Union, giving way to bureaucratic planning, a post-capital society should extinguish all the main dynamics of the production of commodities.[7]

In his introduction to Mészáros's book, *Beyond Capital*, Ricardo Antunes observes that the Hungarian intellectual views capital and capitalism as distinct phenomena, and the conceptual identification between them is what led to the inability of all revolutionary experiences of the past century, from the Russian Revolution to the most recent attempts to build a socialist society, to overcome capital's system of social metabolism. He views capitalism as one way in which capital may be fulfilled, or one of its historic variants.

Antunes also observes that Mészáros describes the social metabolism system of capital as powerful and all-encompassing, with its core formed by a triad: capital, labour and the State—three fundamental aspects of the system, which are materially constructed and interrelated—and argues that it is impossible to overcome capital without eliminating all of its elements.[8] With no limits to its expansion, the social metabolism system of capital is evidently uncontrollable.

As we will see in the following sections, Mészáros's theory revolves around the alienation of labour and the need to overcome it. For him:

> Humanity's alienation, in the basic sense of the word, signifies a loss of control: its embodiment in an external force that individuals confront as a hostile and potentially destructive power. When Marx analysed that alienation in his 1844 manuscripts, he pointed out four main aspects of human alienation: from nature; from their own productive activity; from their species, the human species; and from each other. And he affirmed emphatically that this was not a "fatality of nature," but a type of self-alienation.[9]

[7] Idem.

[8] For example, for his criticism of the State, see I. Mészáros: *Produção destrutiva e Estado capitalista*. 2nd ed., Ensino, São Paulo, 1989 and *Para além do capita*. Editora da UnicampBoitempo, Campinas, 2002. This is a question that was not addressed in this article. Many other subjects that comprise Mészáros's complex and all-encompassing work, such as the inseparability of the military-industrial complex and the socio-metabolism of capital; the question of gender, class and individual; the national question, etc., were addressed by him in *O poder da ideologia*. Boitempo Editorial, São Paulo, 2004.

[9] Mészáros, *Marx: A Teoria da Alienação,* 4th ed., Rio de Janeiro: Zahar, 1981, p. 9.

In other words, it is not a question of an all-powerful natural or metaphysical external force, but the result of a certain type of historical development, which may be positively altered by conscious intervention in the process of transcending the self-alienation of labour.[10] Let's take a look at his critique of ownership of the means of production.

The Snail and Its Shell: A Critique of Ownership of the Means of Production

The socialist variant of the solidarity economy is based on a critique, sometimes gentle and diplomatic, of ownership of the means of production, the accumulation of capital and hetero-management. This approach views cooperativism and associativism as an amphibious formula—that is, transitory and never perfect—to create a society governed by associated producers.

One question frequently raised by researchers who are involved in workers' cooperativism and associativism is that of private property. For them, cooperativism is an intermediary form which should challenge private ownership of the means of production, even if within the structure of capitalism. Cooperativism and associativism should signify the restoration to workers of their means of subsistence. For self-managed Marxism, cooperativism partially challenges ownership of the means of production. However, one problem is clear: in the absence of a revolution that challenges the ownership of the means of production as a whole, cooperative ownership is reduced to being a marginal cell in a body dominated by large corporations.

Marx said that cooperativism, in contrast to the publicly-traded companies, had the potential to "reattach" workers to the means of production—like reattaching the snail to its shell. When he referred to changes brought about by manufacturing, he said: "In general, workers and their means of production were indissolubly united, like the snail and its shell; thus, the principal base of manufacturing was missing: the separation of workers from their means of production and the conversion of those means into capital".[11]

[10] Mészáros, *Para além do capital.*

[11] R. Antunes, *O caracol e sua concha – ensaios sobre a nova morfología do trabalho,* São Paulo: Boitempo, 2005, p. 38.

Mészáros theorised about this historical question. He believed it was necessary to acknowledge that there are clear limits to workers' ownership in a context where there is no generalisation of expropriations, and that the "expropriation of the expropriators" leaves the structure of capital intact. Although the question involves ownership of the means of production, Mészáros notes that:

> In fact, nothing is achieved solely with more or less easily reversible changes to property rights, as seen in many cases of the history of post-war "nationalizations," "de-nationalizations" and "privatizations." Legally-induced changes to property relations have no guarantee of success, even when they encompass the large majority of private capital, and that is even truer when they are limited to its bankrupt minority. What needs to be radically altered is the way the reified "micro-cosmos" of the individual workday is utilised and reproduced, despite its internal contractions, through the homogenised and balanced "macro-cosmos" of the system as a whole.[12]

What he is saying is that the fundamental question is "overall control of the process of labour by the associated producers, and not simply the question of how to subvert established ownership rights".[13]

The "expropriation of the expropriators" is just a prerequisite; it barely signifies any change at all to the essence of the question: the need for overall control over the labour process by the associated producers. That may be seen, for example, in the case of the Russian Revolution, where the means of production were affected, but capitalist production relations were reproduced in a new package.

Workers' cooperatives and associations are practical experiences in workers' self-organisation that can be fostered during a set of social transformation that aim towards transcending alienated labour.[14] However, if workers' cooperatives and associations remain separate from other struggles, they will either disappear or will survive with difficulty, but are unlikely to advance toward overall control of the labour process by associated labourers.[15] In the case of Brazil, cooperatives engaged in resistance,

[12] Mészáros: *Para além do capital*, p. 629.

[13] Mészáros: *Para além do capital*, p. 628.

[14] Ibid.

[15] Ibid.

created in the heat of workers' struggles, prefigure, or show us some of the elements of a higher form of production based on collective labour and with a social meaning, where possibilities exist for overcoming the self-alienation of labour.

The central problem is the alienation of labour in the classic sense of the term. It exists as a function of capital, and workers are dominated, above all, by working conditions over which they have no power. The crucial point is that whatever improvements are made to wage rates or retirement benefits, working conditions as such—that is, control over the pace, design, and the status of labour—remain outside of workers' control.[16]

Evidently, when immersed in the capitalist mode of production, workers' cooperatives and associations cannot carry out the complete emancipation of the working class. But they do suggest certain changes as a result of their self-managed aspects.

Interpreting Mészáros, there may be elements of self-management in agrarian reform settlements, popular cooperatives and recovered factories, but for these elements to gain force, a revolution is needed. In attempting to demonstrate the different possible forms of transformation a given phenomenon may go through—in our case, the existence of recovered factories and popular cooperatives—and without falling into a Manichean analysis, he is able to show the "lack of continuity in continuity" and "continuities in discontinuity". In other words, he points out the advances and retreats that have characterised these transformations. Through that analysis, we can demonstrate how, although they produce significant transformations, recovered factories and popular cooperatives are unable to overcome the substance of the class-based exploitation and oppression inherent to the social relations of capitalist production.[17]

Let us look at the dialectic established by Marx, when he addressed the question of cooperativism in the nineteenth century:

> At the same time the experience of the period from 1848 to 1864 has proved beyond the shadow of a doubt that, however, excellent in principle and however useful in practice, co-operative labour, if kept within the narrow circle of the casual efforts of private workers, will never be able

[16] M. Tragtenberg, *Administração, poder e ideología*, 3rd ed., São Paulo: Unesp, 2005.

[17] H. T. Novaes, *O fetiche da tecnologia – a experiência das fábricas recuperadas*, São Paulo: Expressão Popular-Fapesp, 2007.

> to arrest the growth in geometrical progression of monopoly, to free the masses, nor even to perceptibly lighten the burden of their miseries. It is perhaps for this very reason that plausible noblemen, philanthropic middle-class spouters, and even keep political economists have all at once turned nauseously complimentary to the very co-operative labour system they had vainly tried to nip in the bud by deriding it as a dreamer's utopia, or stigmatizing it as the sacrilege of the socialist. To save the industrious masses, co-operative labour ought to be developed to national dimensions, and, consequently, to be fostered by national means. Yet the lords of the land and the lords of capital will always use their political privileges to defend and perpetuate their economic monopolies. Far from promoting, they will continue to lay every possible impediment in the way of the emancipation of labour... To conquer political power has, therefore, become the great duty of the working classes.[18]

The "conquest of political power" extolled by Marx should not be understood in a mechanical way. For him, as for Mészáros, cooperativism and associativism should be inserted within a broader project for transforming society, which necessarily involves a political revolution.

To a certain extent, Marx praised the cooperatives in Rochdale, England. Note that he quoted the *Spectator* newspaper, which said that the Rochdale experience "...'showed that workers' associations could manage shops, mills, and almost all forms of industry with success, and they immediately improved the condition of the men; but then they did not leave a clear place for masters.' *Quelle horreur*!"[19] For Marx, bourgeois political economy tried to make it seem as though the capitalists of the time were practically "indispensable", natural and eternal, and cooperativism was able to demonstrate in practice that society could be organised differently, without capitalists. The following excerpt from the *Manifesto of the International Workingmen's Association* (1864) is more exact:

> But there was in store a still greater victory of the political economy of labour over the political economy of property. We speak of the co-operative movement, especially the co-operative factories raised by the unassisted efforts of a few bold "hands...." By deed instead of by argument, they have shown that production on a large scale, and in accord with the behests

[18] Karl Marx, *Instruções para os Delegados do Conselho Geral Provisório. As Diferentes Questões (1866),* Lisbon: Avante, 1990, p. 521.

[19] Marx, *O capital*, Vol. 2, São Paulo: Nova Cultural, 1996, p. 381.

> of modern science, may be carried on without the existence of a class of masters employing a class of hands; that to bear fruit, the means of labour need not be monopolized as a means of dominion over, and of extortion against, the labouring man himself; and that, like slave labour, like serf labour, hired labour is but a transitory and inferior form, destined to disappear before associated labour plying its toil with a willing hand, a ready mind, and a joyous heart. In England, the seeds of the co-operative system were sown by Robert Owen; the workingmen's experiments tried on the Continent were, in fact, the practical upshot of the theories, not invented, but loudly proclaimed, in 1848.[20]

However, as Marx stated, if cooperativism is "kept within the narrow circle of the casual efforts of private workers, [it] will never be able to arrest the growth in geometrical progression of monopoly, to free the masses, nor even to perceptibly lighten the burden of their miseries".[21] The timeliness of that criticism is enormous when applied to the variant of solidarity economy that "forgets" the role of politics in the construction of a new society. According to two important Marxist theorists on self-management:

> Readers of *Self-management: a Radical View* will be convinced without effort that, for us, self-management should be understood in a general sense, and it can only come about through a radical revolution that transforms society in all dialectically-connected aspects of the economy, politics and social life.[22]

Self-Management: for a New Social Division of Labour and a New Type of Participation in Strategic Decisions for Society

The other main foundation of Mészáros's theory is the need for self-management as opposed to what is called hetero-management. For some, self-management means the reunification of the acts of conceiving and carrying out labour—i.e. *Homo faber* becoming *Homo sapiens* again. For

[20] Marx, *Instruções para os Delegados do Conselho Geral Provisório*, p. 7.

[21] Marx, *Instruções para os Delegados do Conselho Geral Provisório*, p. 521.

[22] A. Guillerm and Y. Bourdet, *Autogestão: uma visão radical*, p. 18.

others, what distinguishes workers' self-management is the weight given to democratic assemblies (1 member = 1 vote).

This question takes us back to the current debate about what type of participation associated labourers should have in a factory and in society in general. We should distinguish the "participationism" incited by capital from "authentic participation". History shows us that the participationism proposed by capital has not diminished the power of management in capitalist enterprises. Likewise, it has not altered the control exercised by finance capital in this new stage of capitalism.[23]

Some theories attempt to expose capital's new discourse about workers' participation in factories and its contrast with teachings about human emancipation. For Hirata, Quality Control Circles (QCC) do not represent "production controlled by the workers, but are instead [informal] organisations of small groups to discuss and resolve problems identified in the workplace". She says that the QCCs are at odds with self-management proposals "by their very nature, not just in form".[24]

Efforts to achieve workers' participation, Quality Control Cyrcles, Kanban and Kaizen are all strategies used by capital to attack the symptoms rather than the causes of alienated labour. Self-management does not come from this type of participation, but from the historical struggles of the working class in the nineteenth and twentieth centuries to have democracy in production and to build a society devoted to meeting human needs.

In that sense, self-management means re-taking control over the labour process, the labour product, one's self and human civilization.[25] "Managerialist" strategies seek to "reduce" workers' participation to the narrow/simple need to increase productivity, and with that, to facilitate the reproduction of capital.

However, variants that advocate cooperativism and associativism provide a new meaning for participation "within" the enterprise through

[23] M. Tragtenberg, *Reflexões sobre o socialismo.*

[24] H. Hirata, "Transferência de tecnologia de gestão: o caso dos sistemas participativos," in R. M. Soares, *Automação e Competitividade,* Brasilia: IPEA, 1990, pp. 135–148.

[25] Mészáros, *Para além do capital.*

the building of autonomous councils, and they add the need for participation "outside of" the enterprise itself (neighbourhood assemblies, parliaments, etc.). In short, they propose workers' participation in controlling society.

We should remember that for Tragtenberg, "authentic participation" is "where most of the population, through freely-elected, articulated bodies, are in a position to direct the labour process and to participate in decisions about the purpose of production and other meaningful aspects of social life".[26] Mészáros probably would agree with that.

Participation in freely elected bodies, with rotating duties, would be extraordinarily educational for workers.[27] The need to rotate posts and for those posts to be revocable are principles that are vital for self-management. They tend to prevent the bureaucratization of self-managed enterprises such as cooperatives and prepare workers for controlling society.[28]

For a Radical Restructuring of the Productive Forces

Unlike most twentieth-century Marxist authors, Mészáros does not view technology and science, etc., as neutral; therefore, he believes that when workers "inherit" the productive forces, they should concern themselves with radically restructuring those forces. For him, the liberating power of the productive forces "remains as mere potential given the self-perpetuating needs of capital".[29] In the more specific field of technology, he says that its insertion is structured with the sole purpose of the "expanded reproduction of capital at any social cost".[30]

His interpretation of the productive forces also can be seen in his book *The Power of Ideology*, when he criticises Habermas and dialogues

[26] M. Tragtenberg, *Reflexões sobre o socialismo*, p. 30.

[27] J. Bernardo, "A autonomia das lutas operárias," in L. Bruno and C. Saccardo (coord.), *Organização, trabalho e tecnologia*, São Paulo: Atlas, 1986.

[28] This subject and others related to "education" were addressed by Mészáros in his book *La educación más allá del capital*, Buenos Aires: Siglo XXI/Clacso, 2008.

[29] Mészáros, *Para além do capital*, p. 786.

[30] R. Dagnino and H. T. Novaes, "As forças produtivas e a transição ao socialismo: contrastando as concepções de Paul Singer e István Mészáros," *Organizações & Democracia* 7 (2007): 35–57 & 54.

with Raniero Panzieri. According to Mészáros,[31] Habermas "caricatures Marx" by claiming that he "talks about neutral productive forces".[32] Based on the observations of Panzieri[33] and other authors about machines and capitalist rationality, Mészáros says that Marx knew very well that "in capitalist usage, not just the machines, but also the 'methods' and organisational techniques, etc., are incorporated into capital and confront workers as capital: as an external 'rationality'".[34] Thus, any system is "abstract and partial, capable of being utilised in a hierarchical type of organisation".[35] According to Mészáros:

> Marx would never have considered the productive forces as neutral, by virtue of their organic ties to the relations of production; therefore, a radical change in those relations, in societies that want to extirpate capital from its position of dominance, requires a fundamental restructuring and a qualitatively new course for incorporating the productive forces into socialist relations of production.[36]

In his article "Surplus value and Planning", Panzieri says that:

> ...In response to the interconnection of technology and power carried out by capital, the perspective of an alternative use (by the working class) of machinery evidently cannot be based on the pure and simple reduction of the relations of production (of ownership), in which they are considered as a shell that is destined to disappear, to a certain level of productive expansion, simply because it became too small. The relations of production are contained in the productive forces, and the latter were "moulded" by capital. That is what makes it possible for capitalist development to perpetuate, even after the expansion of the productive forces has reached its highest level."[37]

[31] Mészáros, *O poder da ideologia*, São Paulo: Boitempo, 2004, p. 519.

[32] J. Habermas, *Autonomy and Solidarity: interviews with Jürgen Habermas*, ed. Peter Dews, London: Verso, 1986, p. 91.

[33] R. Panzieri, "The capitalist use of machinery: Marx versus the 'Objectivists,'" in P. Slater, org., *Outlines of a critique of technology*, London: Ink Links, 1980.

[34] Mészáros, *O poder da ideologia*, p. 519.

[35] Idem.

[36] Idem.

[37] R. Panzieri, "Mais-Valia e Planejamento," in M. Tronti et al., *Processo de trabalho e estratégias de classe*, Rio de Janeiro: Zahar, 1982, pp. 60–87 & p. 66.

Mészáros calls attention to the fact that the "material conditions of production, as well as their hierarchical organisation, remain exactly the same on the day after the revolution as they were before".[38] In doing so, he highlights the key question we are addressing: capitalist technological forms, because of their high degree of inertia resulting from a long period of accumulation and powerful stimuli for their development, represent a significant challenge for qualitative sociopolitical change. This is why he believes that a radical transformation of the means and techniques of production is "a paradigmatic question for transition".

According to Mészáros, immediately after the "expropriation of the expropriators", it is not just the inherited material resources and production technology that remain the same, along with their ties to the given system of exchange, distribution and consumption. The organisation of labour itself also remains deeply entrenched in that hierarchical social division of labour, "which becomes the heaviest oppression inherited from the past".[39]

In arguing that the issues of division of labour, alienation and the "advance" of productive forces were addressed incorrectly, Mészáros offers powerful foundations for criticising most twentieth century Marxist interpretations of science and technology. The Marxist Left concentrated its attention on short-term tasks such as the working class taking power, state ownership of the means of production and other immediate goals related to the transitional period. This may be why it reduced the question of technology and science to mere "appropriation" of the productive forces engendered in capitalism by the proletariat, and its "best" use for building socialism.

Interpreting Mészáros, we can say that capital's domination of labour has an essentially economic nature and cannot be reduced to the question of taking power. Everything leads us to believe that qualitative transformations do not take place as a result of simple political change; instead, they are processes that involve a long period of "social revolution" through positive efforts at "regeneration".[40] But surely, Mészáros is not a fatalist and does not believe that we are at a dead end, much less that we should return to the Middle Ages and begin all over again. He

[38] Mészáros, *Para além do capital*, p. 575.

[39] Mészáros, *Para além do capital*, pp. 596–597.

[40] Mészáros, *Para além do capital*, p. 865.

analyses the question of the productive forces by placing them in their historical context and demonstrates the errors of leftists who "forgot" this problem. However, he also points to the historical possibilities of "transcending the self-alienation of labour".[41]

Socialist Planning of Production

In the introduction to his book *The Power of Ideology*, Mészáros comments that the failure of Soviet planning—adopted throughout all of Eastern Europe—and with it the end of Soviet-type systems, came about as a result of the imposition of decisions from above, by a "separate" body. In fact, even planners had to accept plans with no discussion. Moreover, the producers themselves were never really consulted, and merely participated in the annual ritual of their "enthusiastic approval". Decisions also were authoritarian in the sense that it was impossible to review and modify predictions or assumptions upon which plans were based after they had been codified, generally with very painful consequences for those involved.

However, according to Mészáros:

> Those who disregard the idea of planning by virtue of the Soviet implosion are very much deceived. The sustainability of a global order of socio-metabolic reproduction is inconceivable without an adequate planning system, administered on the basis of substantive democracy by freely associated producers.[42]

We should note that in his writings on the 1871 Paris Commune, Marx stated that:

> If co-operative production is not to remain a sham and a snare; if it is to supersede the capitalist system; if united co-operative societies are to regulate national production upon common plan, thus taking it under their own control, and putting an end to the constant anarchy and periodical convulsions which are the fatality of capitalist production – what else, gentlemen, would it be but communism, "possible" communism?"[43]

[41] Mészáros, *Para além do capital*.

[42] Mészáros, *O poder da ideologia*, p. 15.

[43] Marx, *O capital*, p. 225.

As Mészáros reminds us, "the real objective of emancipatory transformation is the complete eradication of capital as a totalising method of control of the reproductive socio-metabolism, and not simply the displacement of the capitalists from their historically specific status as 'personifications of capital'".[44]

He criticises the cooperativist Left for failing to be concerned with promoting "double attacks" on capital's socio-metabolic system. It is the "overall complex of socio-metabolic reproduction" that needs to be radically restructured, so that a qualitatively different and consciously controlled "macro-cosmos" can be created, based on the autonomous self-determination of qualitatively different "micro-cosmoses".[45]

We should note that for Marx, "the tyranny of circulation is no less wicked than the tyranny of production".[46] According to Mészáros, the exchange relationship to which labour is subjected is no less enslaving than the separation and alienation of workers from their material conditions of production. In reproducing the established relations of exchange on a larger scale, labour merely multiplies the power of alienated wealth over it. He continues, "The sad story of cooperatives in capitalist countries, despite their genuine socialist aspirations in the past, is eloquent in this sense".[47]

For Mészáros, if the inherited relations of exchange in post-capitalist societies are not radically restructured, then the strategy of subverting the property relations of private capitalism barely scratches the surface, and capital retains full control of the reproduction process, although in a different form. Likewise, nothing can be more absurd than an attempt to institute socialist democracy and the emancipation of labour based on the enslaving fetishism of "market socialism".

For the people of Poland, in the context of the revolutions of the 1980s:

> The self-management proposal meant direct workers' control of production, and therefore, of the economy. It was not merely control over the factories. It was insufficient for workers to elect their leaders at the factory

[44] Mészáros, *Para além do capital*, p. 780.

[45] Idem.

[46] Marx, *Instruções para os Delegados do Conselho Geral Provisório*, p. 655.

[47] Mészáros, *Para além do capital*.

> level. That would represent the risk of creating what the Poles called "group property." It would mean transforming the workers of a given factory, from a given organisation, into its owners, and thus have them defend their private interests against the more general interests of society.[48]

According to Mészáros, institutionally reinforced alienation is merely a material prerequisite of the fragmenting and homogenising capitalist organisation of the labour process and of the complete subjugation of workers to capital. Workers remain at odds or detached, trapped into controlling infinitesimal productive functions, and with no control over the distribution of total social production. In this sense, he believes that the possibility of change—including to the most simple and basic parts of the system of capital—implies the need for constantly renewed "double attacks", both on the "constitutional cells" or "micro-cosmoses"—that is, the way individual workers' workdays are organised in a given productive enterprise—and on the self-regulating "macro-cosmoses" and the self-renewing structural limits of capital as a whole.

For Mészáros, the "workers' councils" in companies have a mediatory and emancipatory potential for rationally solving workers' basic problems, their everyday concerns with housing and work, and major social life issues in line with their basic class needs. At the same time, he warns that workers' councils should not be considered as a panacea for all the revolution's problems. However, without some type of genuine self-administration, the difficulties and contradictions faced by post-revolutionary societies can become chronic and can even create the danger of a retreat to the production practices of the former system, even if those practices are under a different type of personal control.

I should note here that I do not believe it is advisable to salvage any state planning methods, even if we might have to resort to them in some instances. Instead, what we need is the construction of totally new agencies and institutions created by the workers with the goal of attaining "self-government run by associated producers".[49]

[48] L. C. Bresser Pereira, "A revolução autogestionária na Polônia," in R. Venosa, org., *Participação e participações: ensaios sobre autogestão,* São Paulo: Babel Cultural, 1987, p.108.

[49] H. T. Novaes, "Qual autogestão?", in *Revista da Sociedade Brasileira de Economia Política* 22 (June 2008) 7–31.

Moreover, Mészáros reminds us that in the past, when workers' councils have formed spontaneously amid major structural crises, they have tried to assume "precisely the role of self-administrator, in line with their self-imposed responsibility — which is implicit in and practically inseparable from that role — of carrying out the gigantic task of rebuilding the inherited social productive structure in the long term".[50]

In theorising about the dialectic of the parts and the whole, besides showing the need for "double attacks", Mészáros refers to R. Luxemburg's criticism of Bernstein.[51] For her, the problem with cooperatives was not a lack of discipline by workers, contrary to what Bernstein said. The contradiction for cooperatives is that they must govern themselves with the most extreme absolutism, because their workers must assume the role of capitalist business owners, against their own interests. This contradiction explains the failure of production cooperatives that either become mere capitalist initiatives or—if the workers' interests continue to predominate—end up failing economically.

This is a fruitful context for interpreting Mészáros's ideas when he refers to the need for "double attacks". That is, the need for coordinated control of production by means of a substantive producers' democracy, both in the enterprise and in all of society. In the case of recovered factories, that would be overall control over industry by the associated producers, not just over individual factories. Mészáros calls for workers' councils to play the role of effective material mediator between the old order and the long-desired socialist order.

According to Mészáros,[52] because the system of capital is a comprehensive and universal mode of control, it cannot be historically defeated without an equally all-encompassing socio-metabolic alternative. He states that when the vital controlling functions of that socio-metabolism are not effectively occupied and autonomously exercised by the associated producers, and are left to the authority of people in control who are separate from the producers—that is, a new type of personification of capital—labour itself continues reproducing the power of capital against itself, extending the domination of alienated wealth over society. He says that workers' councils and other forms of mediation have a crucial role in

[50] Mészáros, *Para além do capital*, p. 457.

[51] Rosa Luxemburg, *Reforma ou Revolução?* São Paulo: Expressão Popular, 1999.

[52] Idem.

establishing "authentic planning". In this sense, all control mechanisms for socio-metabolism should be progressively appropriated and positively exercised by the associated producers. If not, control over decisions about the production and distribution of social reproduction will remain under the aegis of capital.

Proposals to conciliate socialist principles with "market" mechanisms are not new; they were seen in Proudhon's work. According to Mandel, Proudhon believed that it was a question of emancipating the worker/artisan from the domination of money (capital) without abolishing mercantile production and competition—a typically petty-bourgeois illusion. While Proudhon is sometimes presented as nothing less than the father of the workers' self-management concept, the impasse of "market socialism" seen in Yugoslavia starting in the 1970s was potentially outlined in his ideas.[53]

Lebowitz also criticizes market socialism and the impasse created in Yugoslavia:

> Yugoslavia called its system of worker-management "self-management," and it demonstrated that you don't need capitalists -- that enterprises can be run by workers through workers' councils.... But there was a problem in Yugoslav self-management that is implied in its name -- "Self." True, workers in each firm determined the direction of their enterprises by themselves. But they also looked out primarily for themselves. The focus of workers within each firm was on their own self-interest... What was missing was a sense of solidarity with society... Instead, the emphasis was upon self-orientation, selfishness. In some respects, it was like the worst of capitalist mythology, the concept of "The Invisible Hand": the idea was that if each collective follows its own self-interest, society as a whole will benefit. In fact, the invisible hand in Yugoslavia operated to increase inequality, to break down the solidarity of society -- leading, ultimately, to the breakup of Yugoslavia.[54]

Along the same lines as Proudhon, and perhaps because of the crisis unleashed by the failures of planning under "real socialism", Brazilian

[53] E. Mandel, *O lugar do marxismo na história,* São Paulo: Xamã, 2001, p. 70.

[54] M. Lebowitz, "Constructing Co-Management in Venezuela: Contradictions along the Path," (paper presented at the National Meeting of Workers for the Recovery of Enterprises, Caracas, Venezuela, October 22, 2005), http://mrzine.monthlyreview.org/2005/lebowitz241005.html (Date of access: August 13, 2006).

solidarity economy researchers continue to propose a contradiction: the conciliation between the "self-management" of factories and the competition of the "market"; cooperation and competition, the "efficiency" of the cooperative and the "anarchy" of production.

Final Considerations

Given that we are in a defensive moment, characterised by countless defeats for workers, it would be better to describe the current period as one of subsistence, or resistance, cooperativism. To date, there are few signs of forms of cooperativism and associativism that are capable of overcoming alienated labour with no social meaning and stripped of social content.

This has to do with the historical context, characterised by the advance of social barbarism and, with respect to the Left, the absence of any radical project that goes beyond capital. In my opinion, cooperativism and associativism play a modest role, enabling groups of workers—mainly those in the most precarious situations or the unemployed—to have the right to survival in the context of chronic unemployment and underemployment.

However, according to Mészáros, in an offensive context, cooperativism and associativism can play a role in overcoming alienated labour by expropriating the expropriators—reuniting the snail with its shell—and via overall coordination of production by the associated producers with the goal of producing use values and "developing the rich individuality" of human beings. He criticises commodity-producing societies and foresees the construction of a society based on meeting human needs (use values). In summary, self-management is the positive overcoming of the alienation of labour. That seems to be Mészáros's contribution.

More generally speaking, the process of building a society beyond capital should encompass all aspects of the interrelationship between capital, labour and the State. To conclude, Mészáros uses a fascinating quote from Goethe.

As in the case of Goethe's father (albeit for very different reasons) it is not possible to demolish the existing building and build a completely new building in its place on a totally new foundation. Life must continue in the propped-up building throughout the course of the reconstruction, "pulling out one floor after another, from the ground up, as if the new structure were being grafted, and in that way, even though nothing of the old house is left in the end, the whole new building could be considered merely as a renovation".[55]

In truth, the task is even more difficult. According to Mészáros, "The ruined wooden frame of the building also must be replaced, as humanity is gradually taken out of the dangerous structural framework of the system of capital".[56]

Bibliography

Antunes, R. Adeus ao trabalho? 15. ed. São Paulo: Cortez, 2008.

Bernardo, J. "A autonomia das lutas operárias". In: Bruno, L. e Saccardo, C. (coordenadoras). Organização, trabalho e tecnologia. São Paulo: Atlas, 1986.

Cruz, A. C. M. da. A diferença da igualdade: a dinâmica da Economia solidária em quatro cidades do MERCOSUL. 2006. Tese (Doutorado em Economia) – Instituto de Economia, Universidade Estadual de Campinas, 2006.

Dal Ri, N. M.; Vieitez, C. Educação democrática e trabalho associado no Movimento dos Trabalhadores Rurais Sem Terra e nas fábricas de autogestão. São Paulo: Ícone, Fapesp, 2008.

Faria, José Henrique de. Economia Política do Poder. Curitiba: Juruá, 2004. Volume 2.

Faria, M. "Autogestão, Cooperativa, Economia Solidária: avatares do trabalho e do capital". Tese de doutorado. Florianópolis, UFSC, Sociologia Política, 2005.

Guimarães, V. N. et al. Autogestão como estratégia de sobrevivência das organizações e dos trabalhadores: estudos multisetoriais no Estado de Santa Catarina. Relatório de Pesquisa CNPq. Florianópolis, UFSC, 2004.

Mészáros, I. Para além do capital. São Paulo: Boitempo, 2002.

Mészáros, I. La Rivolta Degli Intellettuali in Ungheria. Turim: Einaudi, 1958.

Nascimento, C. A oposição sindical no exílio: sindicalismo e autonomia. [Mimeo], s/d.

Pinassi, M. O. Da miséria ideológica à crise do capital – uma reconciliação histórica. São Paulo: Boitempo, 2009.

Schimidt, C. Regulação econômica e transformação social: discussão sobre as possibilidades de uma sociedade para além do capital. ORG & DEMO, v. 13, 2008, p. 5–2.

Tiriba, L. Pedagogia(s) da produção associada. Ijuí: Ed. da Unijuí, 2001.

Vieitez, C.; Dal Ri, N. Trabalho associado. Rio de Janeiro: DP&A, 2001.

[55] Mészáros, *La educación más allá del capital*, Buenos Aires: Siglo XXI/Clacso, 2008, p. 804.

[56] Idem.

CHAPTER 3

Brazilian Unions and the Struggle Against the Entrepreneurial-Military Dictatorship (1964–1985)

The entrepreneurial-military dictatorship (1964–1985) had a significant impact on workers' struggles in Brazil. Since President Getúlio Vargas's terms in office (1930–1945 and 1950–1954), an urban working class developed along with urban and rural unions that were coupled to the state. The pre-coup years (1950–1964) were a period of increasing social reforms, including an expansion of Brazil's unions. This chapter analyses workers' struggles against the dictatorship between 1968 and 1985. We aim to show the immensely destructive impact the 1964 coup had on the Brazilian left, especially the Institutional Act No. 5 (1968). The consolidation of the dictatorship led to the dismantling of rural and urban unions, the exile of militants, imprisonments, torture, etc. In the second part of the chapter, we discuss the rise of the Comissões de Fábrica (Factory Committees), the so-called Novo Sindicalismo (New Unionism) and Lula's rise, as well as the limited "re-democratization" process of the 1980s.

The 1964 Coup and Increasing Repression from 1968 Onwards

The USA, the conservative wing of the Catholic Church, the *latifundiários* (large landowners), and the domestic bourgeoisie planned the coup which had profound consequences for workers' struggles

H. Tahan Novaes, *Associated Labor and Production in the Age of Barbarism*, https://doi.org/10.1007/978-3-031-51183-7_3

(Fernandes 1986). The entrepreneurial-military dictatorship (1964–1985) restructured the hegemony of capital in Brazil and inaugurated a counterrevolution (Fernandes 1981).[1] On the other hand, Aarão Reis (1990) observes that the left-wing forces were not sufficiently organized to resist and also disregarded the possibility of a coup in 1964.

The 1964 coup was a clean historical rupture that destroyed the Brazilian left's ongoing process of developing hegemony. For example, on the day of the coup, the headquarters of the União Nacional dos Estudantes (UNE, National Students Union) was destroyed. In 1965, 80% of the professors of the University of Brasília (UNB) were dismissed; many militants were assassinated or forced to leave the country. Glauber Rocha, one of the country's most ingenious film producers, moved to Cuba; Paulo Freire went to Chile; Darcy Ribeiro went to Uruguay; Sérgio Ferro, went into exile in Grenoble (France); Florestan Fernandes went to Canada; Luiz Carlos Prestes, the main representative of the Communist Party, went into exile in Russia.

The coup stopped the historical process of the rise of workers' struggles and the flourishing of intellectual theory and action in Brazil. Francisco de Oliveira describes the repercussions of the coup in Pernambuco, an important state of the Brazilian Northeast:

> The 1964 coup befell Pernambuco with particular fury. It decimated the leftist parties, the workers' movement, the Catholic politico-intellectual movement, and the student movement. It forced a significant fraction of their leaders into exile. The climate of debate and the innovative initiatives vanished, the Popular Culture Movement and Paulo Freire, the reform of

[1] Darcy Ribeiro claimed that Getúlio Vargas' suicide in 1954 deferred the intervention of the military until 1964. In the 1950s, Brazil went through innumerable anti-corruption committees, commonly called the *mar de lama* (sea of mud). They were usually sponsored by big US corporations or by the Brazilian middle class to combat the creation of state or national companies. According to Darcy Ribeiro: "The news of the suicide [of Getúlio Vargas] devastated me like a bomb. Above all, the Carta-Testamento [Testament-Letter], the most elevated document ever produced in Brazil, the most touching, the most significant. Since I read it the political letter has been guiding me. And so it is for the more lucid Brazilians. But the same does not apply to a minority that has made this country unhappy ever since, governing in a corrupt, oppressive and petty way. I perceived instantaneously, after all, like all Brazilians perceived, that the "sea of mud" campaign was a dirty trick of the press supported by the big foreign companies in order to overthrow the president who was creating Petrobras and who announced the creation of Eletrobras opposing very powerful foreign groups connected to the oil and electricity sectors" (Ribeiro 1996). Petrobras and Eletrobras are state companies with a high national profile.

> the Sudene (Superintendência do Desenvolvimento do Nordeste, Superintendency for the Development of the Northeast) were disarticulated or lost their influence because of the coup. The only thing left was Dom Helder Câmara's solitary voice. By the way, he was installed in the archdiocese in the early post-coup days. He gave an inaugural speech, the courage and dignity of which would make it figure in an anthology of the great Brazilian civic-political speeches. The Igreja da Resistência (Resistance Church) came into being there; Dom Helder Câmara and Dom Paulo Evaristo Arns representing its highest and most important expressions. (Oliveira 2008, p. 85)

The Military-Civilian Dictatorship and Union Resistance

The "1968 World Revolution" had some repercussions in Brazil at the end of the 1960s. Certainly the flourishing of struggles at a global level led to a further hardening of the entrepreneurial-military dictatorship in 1968 with the AI-5 (Institutional Act Number 5), the fifth of the seventeen major decrees made by the dictatorship in the years following the 1964 coup. It went into force in December 1968 and produced numerous arbitrary actions with lasting effects. It granted executive power to governors to arbitrarily punish those considered "enemies" of the regime. From 1968 on, torture, assassinations, and prisons became institutionalised and systematic.

The Peasant Leagues (*Ligas Camponesas*), formed by the Communist Party in 1945, raised the flag of "radical land reforms" in the interest of poor peasants. They became a movement of national importance and international impact. By 1963, Brazil had hundreds of these leagues, with more than 500,000 members in 16 states, the largest of which was in the states of Pernambuco and Paraíba. The council of the state of Pernambuco alone coordinated 27 leagues with 120,000 affiliates (Linhart 1980; Novaes 2009).

With the sudden growth of the Peasant Leagues, the conservative wing of the Catholic Church and the Ministry of Labour soon positioned themselves to help create conservative unions that would resist their rise. The coup of 1964, which restored so-called "order", reinvigorated repression against unions and the persecution of the Peasant Leagues. Their leaders were murdered, tortured, exiled or forced to go underground to continue their struggle. An emblematic case is that of Elizabeth Teixeira, the wife of

João Pedro Teixeira, a leader of the Peasant Leagues who was murdered in 1962, two years before the coup. Elizabeth Teixeira, currently 95 years old, fought clandestinely from 1964 to 1979. She moved to São Rafael, in the hinterland of Rio Grande do Norte (a state in the Northeast of Brazil) where she lived in hiding under a false name for 17 years working as a laundress and teacher. Many believed she had died. It was filmmaker Eduardo Coutinho who found her after a long search. In 1979, Elizabeth benefited from the Amnesty Law (Pagenotto 2020).

Urban unions were also hit by harsh repression. Anti-bureaucratic union organisations and strikes were prohibited. Their leaders were tortured and imprisoned or assassinated. The wave of urban repression started with the Cobrasma workers in Osasco, São Paulo state, and the workers at Braseixos in Contagem, in the state of Minas Gerais in 1968. In these factories, committees were deposed and the union bureaucracies took control of the unions.

In this context, workers' reorganisation took place in a molecular way, from their homes and neighbourhoods, eventually leading to the re-articulation of factory groups in the 1970s. They re-grouped until they garnered enough support to agitate again. This happened with the explosion of workers' strikes starting in 1978 in the ABC Paulista,[2] when a series of new factory committees were formed.[3]

With a foundation based on long and patient organisational work carried out by groups influenced by the Church and dissident communists, clandestine groups were formed in various companies. Minor actions and sabotages signalled a possible resumption of workers' strikes and struggles. At the end of the 1970s, from the point of view of the ruling classes, Brazil was already undergoing a "democratic" opening, carried out slowly, gradually, in a controlled manner, and without ruptures (Fernandes 1986).

The organisation of Autonomous workers in the workplace was considered a necessary condition for struggles to be effective and for the development of a new union structure. It was inspired by the experiences of workers at Cobrasma and Braseixos in 1968 and propagated mainly in

[2] T.N.: The ABC Paulista is a group of municipalities on the outskirts of São Paulo: Santo André, São Bernardo and São Caetano.

[3] To find out more about these struggles, see the films *Braços Cruzados, Máquinas Paradas* (Arms Crossed, Machines Stopped) and *ABC da Greve* (ABC of Strike).

the metallurgic and chemical sector by the *Movimento de Oposição Sindical* (Movement of Union Opposition) in São Paulo (Nascimento 2019).

The movement gained ground and in May 1978 it unleashed a cycle of workers' struggles in ABC Paulista which would mark the beginning of a reduction of the tension provoked by the regime towards Brazil's "re-democratisation", through a gradual, slow and safe transition, which was designed by the military so that it would not lose the "reins" of the re-democratisation process. It was in this context that Luis Inácio Lula da Silva, the future president of Brazil, emerged as a leader. The strikes promoted by the unions in the late 1970s and early 1980s were decisive for Brazil's "re-democratisation".

From the late 1970s to the early 1980s, various struggles culminated in the creation of the *Movimento Sem-Terra* (MST, Landless Movement), the *Movimento dos Atingidos por Barragens* (Movement of People Affected by Dams), the *Partido dos Trabalhadores* (Workers' Party), and a series of struggles—e.g. for public housing and public universities, in defence of public schools, in the public health system—emerged. Their common thread was calling for Brazil's re-democratisation.

The first occupation by what would become the MST took place in Rio Grande do Sul (the southernmost state of Brazil), on 7 September 1979, Brazil's Independence Day. The date was chosen because the military would be distracted and busy with parades all over the country, including in Rio Grande do Sul. On 12 May 1978, Scania workers paralysed production and remained in the factory, mainly demanding wage increases. From then on, strikes that stopped production occurred regularly in the industrial region of ABC Paulista, the home of the country's most important automobile assembly plants at the time, and spread from there to other sectors and regions.

Factory committees shaped the dynamic of the strike movement and were a stimulating element: they organised general assemblies within productive units to decide the steps to be taken and involved trade unions in the negotiations (Faria and Novaes 2015). At a certain moment, employers began to focus on disrupting and repressing factory committees, since many committees had achieved a certain institutionalisation as a mediator between workers and management. Even the New Unionism movement, which emerged from ABC Paulista, stopped endorsing the creation of factory committees, arguing that they exposed the rank-and-file leadership to the repression of employers. New Unionism instead supported rank-and-file union committees, which were formed by union leaders active in the workplace and which benefited from the legal stability conferred on members of the union leadership. The committees also faced accusations of "union parallelism".

Tragtenberg's work is essential to understanding the extent of the factory committees' activities, their role in the Brazilian workers' movement, and how they were manifestations of workers' autonomy. Tragtenberg relies on debates started by representatives of heterodox Marxism, such as Anton Pannekoek, Antonio Gramsci and Herman Gorter (Tragtenberg 2008). Opposing the practice of the committees to the practice stemming from corporatist trade union structures, he highlights the deep pedagogical impacts of the factory committees' struggles.

With the experience gained from their participation in factory committees, workers learn that there is a division of labour in the factory, which they must obey, while outside the factory they learn that *politics* must be practised through parties, *economic demands* must be made through trade unions, *knowledge* is confined to schools, and TV and radio define what has or does not have cultural value. Their own life is divided into watertight, sealed fragments. It is the practice of their struggle through the committees which gives them the resources to take a stand at the political, economic and cultural levels. They learn through the "school of struggle". It teaches them that, by struggling for wages (economy), they confront factory hierarchy (power); they have recourse to self-organisation and develop their socio-politico and cultural conscience. They are part of a *whole*. (Tragtenberg 2011, pp. 23–24).

In this process of self-organisation, workers create their own horizontal organisations, forming a "community of struggle" that controls the very process of developing the struggles and their objectives. Thus, they avoid the transferral of the responsibility for dealing with the relationships of domination and oppression experienced outside the workplace to the organisations that supposedly "represent" the workers through vertical processes that reorganise the division between "directors" and "directed".

Through articles in newspapers, books and magazines, Tragtenberg made an enormous effort to propagate the experiences of the factory committees in Brazil. These struggles emerged during the strike cycle which began in 1978 at companies such as Ford, Máquinas Piratininga, Asama, Massey Ferguson, Aliperti, Barbará, etc. Regarding the struggles of the factory committees, Tragtenberg recalls the famous slogan of the International Workers' Association: "workers' liberation must be the work of the workers themselves". Liberation cannot be delegated to the "vanguards" on duty, since it depends on the initiative and participation of everyone involved. We can certainly confirm Tragtenberg's view regarding the factory committee we analysed at Ford. It was a genuine workers' committee, neither tied to the entrepreneurs nor to the trade union. It truly belonged to the workers who toil there. It followed Tragtenberg's principle: "worker, nobody works for you, nobody shall decide for you" (Tragtenberg 2008, p. 25).

Commenting on the experience of the factory committee at Asama (a machine factory in the metallurgical sector), Tragtenberg (2011) points out that it differentiated itself from the others to the extent that its creation aimed to correct the injustices that happened to workers, demanding that employers grant them better work and living conditions. The most important body in the committee was the general assembly, and the union was defined in the committees' statutes as a "consultative body". The mandates of its representatives were revocable at any time.

The importance Tragtenberg attributes to the factory committees and to workers' autonomous struggles is due to his understanding that "the workers' self-organisation in their workplace and the democratisation of work relationships make up the foundation of any democracy modelled on self-managed socialism, because the existence of factory despotism along with formal democracy beyond the factory walls is a profound contradiction" (Tragtenberg 2008, p. 21).

Workplaces remain spaces marked by despotism, currently even more profoundly, since it involves the colonisation of workers' subjectivity by the ideas of capital. If unions have so far been unable to organise the class from the factory floor, the recovered factories in many countries demonstrate that it is possible to go further and establish, at the same time, self-management and collective ownership of the means of production.

Bibliography

Aarão Reis, D. A. A revolução faltou ao encontro: os comunistas no Brasil. São Paulo: Brasiliense, 1990.

Fernandes, F. Poder e contrapoder na América Latina. São Paulo:, Zahar, 1981.

Fernandes, F. Nova república? São Paulo: Zahar, 1986.

Linhart, R. O acúçar e a fome. Rio de Janeiro: Paz e Terra, 1980.

Nascimento, C. Do Beco dos Sapos aos Canaviais de Catende. Marília: Lutas anticapital, 2019.

Novaes, H. T. Peasant Leagues. In: Azzellini, D.; Ness, I. International Encyclopedia of Revolution and Protest - 1500 to the Present, 2009.
Novaes, H. T.; Faria, M. S. . ? Para dónde van las Empresas Recuperadas por los Trabajadores brasileños?. In: Ruggeri, A.; Novaes, H. T.; Faria, M. S.. (Org.). Crisis y autogestión en el siglo XXI - cooperativas y empresas recuperadas en tiempos de neoliberalismo. 1ed.Buenos Aires: Continente, 2015, v. 1, p. 75-91.
Oliveira, F. Noiva da Revolução – Elegia para uma re(li)gião. São Paulo: Boitempo editorial, 2008.
Pagenotto, M. Elizabeth Teixeira uma camponesa marcada pela resistência. Curitiba: Brasil de Fato, 2020.
Ribeiro, D. Confissões. São Paulo: Companhia das Letras, 1996.
Tragtenberg, M. Reflexões sobre Socialismo. São Paulo: Editora da Unesp, 2008.
Tragtenberg, M. Autonomia operária. São Paulo: Unesp, 2011.

CHAPTER 4

Manifestations of Barbarism

The Growth of Child Labour

We saw in the previous section that the "civilising" phase of capitalism ended in the late 1960s. Since then, capital has systematically denied workers the hard-fought achievements of the first half of the twentieth century: limited working hours, right to formal contracts, right to retirement and paid vacations, end of slave and child labour, right to housing, right to a public health system, etc. These and so many other achievements have been partially or completely destroyed in the new phase of capitalism, which some call "flexible accumulation" and others "capitalism under financial hegemony".

Recently I watched a documentary about the growth of child labour in the city of Naples (Italy). The documentary was shown on TV5, and there you can see the "wonders" that financialised, globalised and restructured capitalism has produced. The newspaper *Le Monde Diplomatique* also focused on the growth of child labour in the same city. Naples' deputy mayor said: "Of course, we are the poorest region in Italy, but we had not had such a situation since World War II (...). By age 10, these children are already working 12 hours a day, which clearly infringes on their right to develop". The documentary shows children working in butcher's shops, hairdressers and in drug trafficking (with the criminal group known as Gomorrah). They make $80 a month, a much-needed relief for their families, small as it may be.

H. Tahan Novaes, *Associated Labor and Production in the Age of Barbarism*, https://doi.org/10.1007/978-3-031-51183-7_4

Some 600 million of the world's children live in poverty. 250 million children from the so-called Third World between the ages of 5 and 14 work. 130 million of them do not receive any kind of education. Living the "pedagogy of the street", these children of workers are denied an opportunity to develop.

Those children of workers who do manage to be in schools are functionally illiterate. They leave basic education without knowing elementary math, how to interpret a text, and are geographically and historically illiterate. In Brazil, working children can be found on farms and charcoal factories; they take care of their brothers in the "house" they live in, they work in factories and shops, and they are modern "slaves", working as domestic servants.

In the State of São Paulo, called the "locomotive of the nation" by some, tests place students in 6th place among Brazilian states. Our hypothesis is that the State of São Paulo is implementing a privatist educational policy which continues the destruction of the little that had been achieved with the public school system created in the period between 1930 and 1964, creating the general conditions for the proliferation of commodified, private, profit-oriented education.

The children of the middle strata of society do not live on the streets, but in front of the TV, constantly bombarded by explicit and implicit advertisements. In an interview with TvFiocruz, Becker (2013) warns us that Brazilian children spend only 4 hours in school, but 5 hours in front of the television.

The few children of workers who have access to "quality" school will certainly be fed a steady diet of the new educational mantra, the pedagogy of competences, as we will see in the pages below.

The Return of Work Analogous to Slavery, the Violence of Underemployment and Structural Unemployment and Alienated Labour

From another perspective, from the point of view of the crisis of *real capitalism*, the exhaustion of the "civilising phase of capital" is evident when we observe structural unemployment and underemployment in the current phase of capitalism, which we call "capitalism under financial hegemony". In Spain, unemployment reaches around 40% of young people, who are unlikely to find a decent job in this new century. In

Ireland, Greece and Portugal we see a brutal debt crisis. In France and to a lesser extent in Portugal and Spain, there are strikes against pension reform. In the *Banlieu* of Paris, the children of immigrants from the former French colonies and people from other regions of the country and even Europe fleeing precarious conditions also fail to build a dignified life. Sarkozy, reinforcing the police state, promoted the expulsion of the Roma gipsies from the country. All these manifestations are the result of the partial or complete destruction of the welfare state, the historical moment during which there was the most social control of capital in Europe, based on the struggles of workers and at the same time on the needs of "productive" capital, for full employment, housing, retirement, leisure and dignified pensions that to some extent de-commodify society.

In Spain, unemployment affects 23.6% of people in general and more than 50% of young people under the age of 25. (Dado conflita com o dado acima) In second place comes Greece with 21%. The last on the list are some northern European countries, such as Austria, with around 4%, and Germany, with an official unemployment rate of 5.7%. Portugal now has a generation at risk, the "inflexible precarious" population which has no reasonable future prospects, as portrayed in Giovanni Alves' film, In the US, the group making up 99% of society is trying to find new ways to fight financialised capitalism.

The newest machine for grinding Brazilian people is taking place in the construction of the Santo Antônio and Jirau Dams. Almost 100 years after the internationalisation of the region, when the construction of the "Devil's Railway" took place, the state of Rondônia witnesses a new international construction. The Santo Antônio Hydroelectric Power Plant belongs to the Tractebel group, a Franco-Belgian corporation. The Jirau turbines are being made by a Chinese corporation—which offered the turbines at "very low" prices—and by Voith (a German company). Odebrecht, a well-known "Brazilian" corporation, is in charge of assembly. In Jirau, the construction is the responsibility of Camargo Correa and Enesa is in charge of mechanical assembly. The financing of the dam involves the BNDES, Santander, Caixa, Bradesco, Itaú-Unibanco and Santander.

The construction sites of these dams must be characterised as a rather complex organisation. We get the impression that the construction site is a human meat grinder—the heat is unbearable, there's an utter lack of proper working conditions, overexploitation of workers, mind-blowing work pace, night work, compounded by engineers and foremen pushing for greater productivity. In the concentration camps of Santo Antônio and Jirau, the workers' only right is the right to death by exhaustion.[1]

After many struggles and accusations against the unbearable housing conditions, the workers' living quarters were provided with air conditioning and minimum living conditions. Workers go from the hellish inhospitable heat outdoors to the icy cold of air conditioners inside. They are entitled to a post-lunch break in the non-acclimatised TV spaces around the cafeterias, but soon they are sucked dry by the hard work. Regarding cafeterias, it is curious to note that "engineers and construction workers eat in the same place and the same food", but at different times. There are "leisure" and sport areas to calm the mass of workers.

Workers have difficulty accessing alcoholic beverages, but easy access to brothels. Banks, Hospitals, Worship Rooms, the Internal Committee to Prevent Accidents (CIPA), Dentists. They have easy access to Sedex (the Brazilian Mail Service's express service) and cell phones, but they can't teleport out of hell. An engineer told us that over the weekend at Jirau's construction site, which is "in the middle of nowhere", workers don't kill themselves only because they don't have a gun in their hand. It's the difficult routine of the life of people turned into livestock. The workforce consists of mass migrations from Pará, Maranhão, Rondônia. This is the life of this mass of "projects of the future", who come from so far and give much more than they receive. In the West of Rondônia, many workers leave their families. They are a migrant people within their country, living 2 years constructing Dam X, 3 years at Plant Y. They are exiled within their own country, as Sérgio Buarque de Holanda reminds us, or are workers who only have one small share of land in this latifundium called Brazil, designated for them 7 feet below the ground, as suggested by João Cabral de Melo Neto.

One can notice many women in the construction sites, something that was not so present in other hydroelectric plants. They had to deal with jokes like "you're going to drive the stove", "women don't know how to build anything", "you do not know how to do this".

[1] Any resemblance is purely coincidental. In the film "Conterrâneos Velhos de Guerra", by Vladimir Carvalho, the mistreatment of the candangos (as the masses of migrant workers who came to the rural countryside of central Brazil to build Brasília were called), the spoiled food and the terrible accommodation are evident. Carvalho shows the hidden face of Brasília's construction, based on the overexploitation of work, suicides, diarrhoea, repression of strikes and everything else. The city that was the example of progress did not shelter its worker-builders.

In the construction site we find heavy and expensive machinery and patterns of exploitation of the degrading work of Brazilian construction, compared to the way European machines, equipment and the workforce are used—or at least were until the 1980s. We do not want to ignore the existence of advanced sectors in the Brazilian economy (breweries, the petrochemicals industry, etc.) but to emphasise the coexistence and the umbilical relationship between the modern and backwards sectors of our economy.

The absence of decent working conditions, the struggle for better wages, accommodation, transportation, the struggles for vaccination, "leisure", the right to visit families every three months, among other factors, led to the revolts in the Jirau Plant construction site. After the uprisings of 2012—which led to the murder of the worker Josivan França Sá on 02/12/2012, the concentration camps of Santo Antônio and Jirau have the active presence of the National Security Force—a "novelty" in Hydroelectric Power Plant construction sites. Its strategic function is to prevent the outbreak of new uprisings or to make sure they are run "properly". According to information published in Folha de São Paulo on February 17, 2012:

> Concerned about the violence on hydroelectric construction sites and the growing possibility of collective bargaining, Paulo Godoy, president of Abdib [Brazilian Association of Infrastructure and Base Industry], will take advantage of tomorrow's meeting at the Civil House to ask for police reinforcement. Abdib will defend the need for an action plan by the federal government in the face of repeated cases of violence and fire at hydroelectric construction sites.
>
> The most recent cases of vandalism occurred in the works of Ferreira Gomes (Amapá) and Colíder (Mato Grosso). Jirau, Santo Antônio and Belo Monte also had facilities destroyed. "It is difficult to say that they are coordinated, but the way the events take place is strange and sometimes generated by rumours, as in Colíder," he says. "We also need intelligence work to know if there is a central command or if they are sporadic and regional," he says. "We will ask the federal government to assess whether states are in a position to protect workers and construction sites, which are public goods." For him, some cases require a national security force, at least temporarily. "Now the collective bargaining will start. We observe that rumours are spreading that payments will not be made and of inhumane condition in construction sites. They are the most advanced in the country, unlike other small ones, which can have precarious conditions.

The Situation of the Outsourced Working Class in Brazil

In these construction sites, there is a mass of outsourced workers, very typical of the new pattern of flexible accumulation. They do very similar jobs, but they get paid less.

At the age of 26, Engels wrote the book The Situation of the Working Class in England. Engels analysed all the issues that involve the daily life of work, ranging from working conditions in factories, laws that impose the discipline of work, the problem of housing, transportation, the emergence of philanthropic institutions, the birth of state schools for workers and for the bourgeoisie, the function of prisons, worker nutrition, the struggles to regulate the exploitation of labour, the advancement of machinery, among countless other topics.

In Brazil, since the attempts to cleanse Stalinism and positivist Marxism, countless researchers, with greater and lesser success, have been trying to observe the conditions of existence of our working class. Research on changes in the world of work, on the role of unions in the new morphology of work, the weight of underemployment in our economy, microelectronic relationships, ICTs, work and unemployment, the (re)emergence of the world of associated labour, the "return" of work analogous to slavery, the new demands for worker training, the study on the conditions of reproduction of life (housing, transport, domestic work), the role of the cultural industry and the new sociability engendered by shopping malls, the mass entry of women into the labour market, the sexual division of labour in factories, all themes that have long been considered as residual themes. The factory was everything, and the rest was the rest.

In this wake, it is very rare to see articles and books that address the situation of the working class in Brazil from a totalising perspective. Whether due to academic specialisation or to the difficulties and complexity that this approach involves, these works tend to observe a single dimension of workers' realities, leaving aside aspects vital to understanding the situation of our working class. The positivity of specialisation lies precisely in the possibility of deepening themes that were observed superficially by previous generations, but the negativity also lies in the difficulty that we, researchers who seek a more totalising analysis, face when trying to understand reality without falling into juxtapositions. If reality were a mere sum of its parts, then an unsuspecting reader might think it would be enough to put them all together.

Eraldo Batista's book "Outsourcing in Brazil and its implications for workers" (2013) helps us understand the situation of the outsourced working class in Brazil. Despite its brevity, the book manages to address the main issues involving the living conditions of outsourced workers. The book covers numerous sectors and realities of outsourced workers as it portrays the emergence of outsourcing, its main determinants, the different shapes it takes in factories, in state institutions, in services, the specificities of outsourcing in sectors that employ many women, the emergence of false cooperatives, the modification of laws that favour precarious working condition and worker exploitation. A broader survey should ask the following questions: where do outsourced workers live? What are their homes like? What do they eat? Do they eat in the same places as other workers? Do they frequent the same kind of environment as "formal" workers? What are their day-to-day dilemmas? How are they resisting the new disorders of capital? Will they have the right to retire? We believe that these and other questions should be answered in works that intend to address the outsourced working class in Brazil.

Being proactive, giving it your all, being a team player, being participatory, being a volunteer, becoming a "global player", trimming "fat" and making production lean. These are the catchphrases that have been added to the new dictionary of capital, especially in sectors where flexible accumulation predominates.

However, if Taylorism-Fordism did not die in Brazil, special attention needs to be paid to sectors with taylorist trends to verify the continuity of "primitive" accumulation and absolute surplus value. We agree with Ricardo Antunes when he states that it is possible to verify the coexistence of taylorism and toyotism in contemporary Brazil.

Brazil, perhaps the greatest example of a "platypus country", has undergone a conservative and incomplete bourgeois revolution, which has not even been able to offer adequate conditions for the largest portion of its working class. Alongside formal workers who got a place in the sun in the "advanced" sectors, we have a mass of miserable workers who serve as a marginalised permanent reserve industrial army of the labour market, as suggested by Plinio de Arruda Sampaio Jr. They live in a constant state of entering and leaving extreme poverty, or barely managing to survive in poverty, improvising and hustling to eke out a living in platypus capitalism.

In the new stage of Brazilian capitalism, characterised by financial hegemony and flexible accumulation, a series of phenomena are increasingly important: outsourced workers, the neoliberal city and the new social apartheid, shopping malls, condominiums that integrate work, leisure, residence and school, chaotic traffic in the metropolises, helicopters for business people fly above motorcycles and crowded trains and subway stations in the great metropolises, a scenario portrayed in the song Rodo Cotidiano by O Rappa.

In this context, the workers' villages stimulated during our first phase of industrialisation, the cultural policies that gave rise to institutions such as Sesi (Industry social service) have partially lost their meaning in this new phase of Brazilian capitalism. I say partially because, if our hypothesis that Taylorism has not been replaced by Toyotism, but that they coexist, it will not be difficult to find sectors of the economy that still resort to workers' villages and engineer villages as a factor of "integration", control and inspection of production and reproduction of life. To cite just one example, in numerous PAC construction sites, workers are agglomerated in living quarters that allow greater control of their lives "outside" of work.

On a more general level faced with the ideological decay of our ruling class, it is possible to find work analogous to slavery even in the State of São Paulo. Bolivians working to exhaustion and "living" in their place of work and outsourced workers earning a miserable salary, which does not allow us to say that absolute surplus value has been overcome by relative surplus value. To shed light on the social contradictions that arise from this pattern of destructive accumulation of human beings and nature, we can observe policies of pacification, the creation of the Bolsa Familia, the criminalisation of social movements and other solutions that are within the orbit of capital.

One of the elements not addressed by the researcher Eraldo Batista, but which remains a challenge in the twenty-first century, is precisely the unification of struggles in different sectors of outsourced workers. As far as we know, actions in this field are still small. Dispersed, corporatist and isolated struggles predominate.

The over-extended process of opening up politically from the military dictatorship, described as "slow, gradual and secure", led attempts at democratisation by social movements to the labyrinth of Brazilian totalitarian democracy. We have never really talked about democratisation, as in fact we have had an increase of dictatorship in factories, TVs, schools, commerce and services, which violently attack workers in Brazil outsourced or otherwise. The neoliberal counter-reform knocked out the Brazilian people. The degradation of the Brazilian working class, especially in the case of outsourced workers, has reached appalling and unbearable levels. Even with a slight improvement in the consumption patterns among the elite of the miserable, I do not believe that the outsourced working class, elevated to "class C",[2] is living in paradise. Let us help the workers understand this as quickly as possible. On the contrary, alienation at work and in other dimensions of life will remain a constant.

Returning to the case of the Santo Antônio and Jirau Plants, we note the difficulty—but not impossibility—of organising anti-capitalist struggles in a concentration camp that grinds workers every second, exercising a high level of control of what workers can or could do. Corporations and the National Security Force have almost absolute control over workers' lives—detection and persecution of fugitives, murderers and unionised workers, and spying on consumer habits, hygiene habits, and if workers meet for "subversive" activities, and where. As we know, the Brazilian ruling classes have a habit of reversing crime. Honourable scoundrels are converted into gods and mentors of "progress", of "the development of the country", while workers are converted into murderers.

The engineers told us that, due to the enormous migration of workers to the region and the lack of structure in the state, the corporations themselves built day care centres, schools, renovated hospitals and delivered them to the state. They allege a high probability of deviations and corruption. We are against the control of all spheres of our life by corporations which have started building houses, schools and hospitals, taking the state's role. But we also cannot fail to recognise that the Government of Rondônia has become specialised in the theft and accumulation of capital in the Rondonian Wild West. When walking through the city of Porto Velho, anyone with a tiny amount of curiosity will quickly realise the number of unfinished tunnels and avenues alongside the lack of drinking water and a sewage system, the resources for the construction of which were drained to build the fortunes of regional elites. The regional TV station, controlled by the regional elites, tries to hide and conceal the problems of the Rondonian people daily with content of terrible quality.

[2] Brazilian statistics divide society into 5 socioecomic "classes". Class C sits right in the middle, but would correspond to a lower-middle class.

The "impacts" of these construction works are not limited to the mass displacement of workers to the region, but also: the impacts on fauna and flora; abandoned pregnant women; and the displacement of those affected by dams, ribeirinhos[3] and squatters, who, all rights ignored, start living in places that do not come close to offering the good living conditions they had before. Though built in the name of "progress" in the region, of "giving birth to a new Amazon", of "employment for the development of the region and the country" and of "attracting industries", the Santo Antônio and Jirau Plants actually promote the "self-growth of capital", and an increasingly financialised capital at that, over-exploiting workers and creating new contradictions, preventing workers in the region from integrating into the world by an alternative route to that proposed by big capital.

In Jirau's construction work, the engineers' village is about 20 km away from the site. It is curious that some engineers lived at the site but were removed due to possible kidnappings if there were new revolts. In Santo Antônio's construction sites, the engineers live in luxury houses in the city of Porto Velho, about 15 km from the city centre. We have engineers coming from the Southeast and South—working at a breakneck pace in times of lean production and delivery of the works in the shortest possible amount of time. It is not difficult to notice the intensification of the work of many of these engineers compared to other hydroelectric plants. Glued 24 hours a day to cell phones, holding countless meetings, they bark orders at their underlings to increase production, making them reach the brink of total exhaustion, going crazy, completely stressed out.

The Santo Antônio Plant, which is being built by Odebrecht, one of the last corporations with "national" capital but with its tentacles in many parts of the world, is visited by its main managers from Bahia and Rio de Janeiro, who do not live and would never live in such distant and "inhospitable" places.

In the negotiation for the construction of these complex works, we cannot fail to highlight the revitalisation of a 7 km stretch of the Madeira-Mamoré Railway—the Devil's Railway, a struggle of a small portion of Rondonian society, which had as an ally the IPHAN (Institute of National Historical and Artistic Heritage), the construction of an Indigenous people's museum in the village of Santo Antônio—a very modest one at

[3] Riberinhos are traditional Brazilian population groups whose life is centreed around certain rivers. Ribeirinho literally means riverside-dweller.

that, especially given the importance of the region for indigenous culture. Some researchers at UNIR (Federal University of Rondônia) try to save what they can, but many are intimidated or co-opted by corporations.

In 2006, the Maximum Security Prison of Rondônia was completed, clearly visible by anyone driving down BR 364 highway, about 40 km from Porto Velho. Stretching before and after it by the highway are concentration camps, visible to some, invisible to others, housing the workers from Santo Antônio and Jirau. Our hypothesis is that these works close the fourth long cycle of the people-grinding machine called Rondônia: We have the Devil's Railway, from 1945 to 1960 and the construction of BR 364. May we fight so that there is not a further long cycle of deaths in the concentration camps of Rondônia!

In the same vein, the Port of Suape, the new Grêmio Stadium, the World Cup stadiums and countless other PAC works follow the same pattern of labour force exploitation: they hire labour, grind them down and throw them away as if they were disposable goods, ad infinitum. How to talk about human rights if our "people don't live, they just endure" as Milton Nascimento's song suggested.

The Manifestations of Barbarism in Schools and the Misery of São Paulo's Educational Policy

Brazilian schools are not shielded from the advance of barbarism. Educational workers (teachers) became jailers, opening and closing prison cells (classrooms). Other teachers have become big cat tamers, swerving away from chairs thrown at them. Among other symptoms of barbarism in schools and universities, we have the murder of students, an ingrained competitive logic among teachers, federal and state governments refusing to talk to teachers on strike, textbooks prepared by educational corporations, extension courses made just to raise funds, researchers vomiting articles one after the other, diseases due to overwork, poor quality meals, teachers being beaten by students, teachers beating students and the use of Ritalin left and right to calm the "lions" down.

The "de-civilisation" process led researchers Lima Filho (2017) and Minto (2011) to state that we are living in the era of the "political economy of de-education".

In regard to decadent public schools, a recent film called "Pro dia nascer feliz" (2005), by João Jardim, highlights some of these dramas. To name just one more film, "Entre os muros da escola" attempts to portray the complexity of the modern school and its bankruptcy. Kuenzer (1998) notes that there was a "polarisation of skills" and that schools follow this trend. In a very small pole, schools aimed at preparing the new flexible, participatory worker, who interacts with others, adapted to teamwork and who seeks new solutions, always from the point of view of capital. At the other extreme, schools aimed at young, outsourced workers, who will work with precarious conditions and low wages, jobs like: packagers, telemarketing operators, sugarcane workers, among numerous jobs with Taylorist characteristics. If the reformists of the 1930–1964 period had a republican project, with the polarisation of competences, schools with any quality will be exclusively for the petty bourgeoisie of the miserable.

We can also add that schools that are training young people *to naturalise unemployment*. Research shows that in many regions of Brazil, not to mention other countries, schools are there only to console *unemployable* young people, conveying the message that there is no more employment for all.

We could highlight the pillars of educational counter-reform in the state of São Paulo as follows: (a) the privatisation of educational policy, based on the growth of private universities and schools; (b) the readjustment of the functions of public universities and schools to meet the needs of financialised capitalism; (c) falling wages for public educational workers, (d) the destruction of the working and reproductive conditions of teachers (absence of a dignified career plan, absence of dignified retirement); (e) the enormous mass of temporary and occasional educational workers; (f) the legitimation of the State Council of Education with a majority of posts with life tenure, not elected by the people and representing the interests of educational corporations; (g) the creation of courses for the qualification of teachers, principals, vice principals, supervisors, etc. within the paradigm of managerialism (management shocks, management by results, performance, "efficiency", quantitative evaluations, etc.) and the paradigm of competencies (teamwork, proactive attitude, specific knowledge, etc.); (h) bonuses for results, to make teachers, attracted by this bait, produce more; (i) changes in the curriculum, inserting courses in entrepreneurship, agribusiness, etc.

In the opinion of the political coalition led by the PSDB, public workers are "slackers", "bums" and "lazy". The technique teachers use must come from corporations: "engagement" of workers to increase the productivity of the school-factory. At the same time, schools must seek funds to support themselves. From this perspective, principals should start charging for parking and coffee, something very well addressed in the film "Entre os muros da escola" [Between the school walls], as if in schools we were in a shopping mall, the main goal of which is to be profitable.

As the governments of the coalition led by the PSDB do not, of course, have a solution to the alienation of work, they attack its consequences, and never its causes in education. These and other aspects of education in São Paulo have led us to state that we are witnessing the consolidation of the ideological misery of São Paulo's educational policy (Novaes 2013).

If we compare the early twentieth century attempts to form an educational system with current policies, it is easy to see the programmatic downgrading of the proposals in São Paulo's educational policy. If the ruling class had a reasonably republican project in the first half of the twentieth century, São Paulo's new ruling class has an immensely privatising and destructive project for the remaining public services in the "nation's locomotive".

The Historical Need for an Education Beyond Capital

Numerous Latin American social movements have already shown us that another world is possible and also that another education is possible. Struggles against market-based educational extension projects, struggles for another kind of curriculum, another kind of management and another kind of work-education relationship that escapes the control of the State and its pedagogy of competences have already been carried out in Latin America in the twentieth century, especially in the pre-military coups phase and again starting in the 1990s, especially with the rise of the educational proposal of the Landless Movement.

However, after 20 years of achievements, these experiences—very rich from a qualitative point of view—cannot even dent the armoured behemoth of education dominated by educational corporations and an increasingly less public state education.

For Mészáros, today we live at the crossroads of Socialism or Barbarism. Never before has Rosa Luxemburg's motto been so topical. For us, capital has nothing more to offer than epithelial social policies, which do not touch on the essential problems of workers. Bolsa Família, quota policies without a real transformation of the role of the public university in class society, Minha Casa Minha Vida, Keynesian policies to generate employment and mass consumption, all tend to generate an alienated society and produce more barbarism.

Of the approximately 6.5 billion human beings alive today, about 5 billion live in poverty or misery. They are not part of the "knowledge society", they do not have internet access, decent housing, drinking water, access to non-alienating work and they live amid invisible civil wars. If this trend continues, more and more human beings will be part of what capital considers human waste, the lumpen, because they only cause social problems, pollute cities and reproduce with no restraints.

Looking at the same problem, but from a different angle, the current phase of capitalism has produced a veritable avalanche of educational theories within the orbit of capital, which change everything without changing anything. Swimming against the current, researchers such as Dal Ri and Vieitez (2008), Freitas (2009), Caldart (2004), Tiriba (2001), Iasi (2006), among others, try to rescue and update the thinking of historical and self-managed materialist pedagogues. By connecting theory and practice, courses in this vein can help resolve the contradictions faced by social movements in their anti-capital struggles.

It should be noted that educational theory and practice in social movements are not new. If we take the Paris Commune (1871) as a historical landmark, we will quickly realise that the workers dared and fought for about 70 days to build a new world. In this experience, small in view of the window of time it existed in, but significant in terms of its *impact* on the social movements of the twentieth century, the Communards declared "we are here for humanity", and materialised their proposals to some extent, signalling new paths for humanity, including some educational proposals. All the classic debates about self-management of factories and cities, about the need for a general economic plan, about educational practices beyond capital, about non-bureaucratisation of executive and legislative decisions and about workers' internationalism, among others, appear in the Paris Commune. In late 20th Century Brazil, perhaps the best example we have is the MST and its formal and informal educational proposals.

Last but not least, we know that capital is a totalising social relationship and, in this sense, must be overcome in its entirety. In this sense, anti-capital social movements should incorporate associated labour and an education beyond capital in their proposals. Without these pillars, their struggles will be dissolved within the orbit of capital.

An understanding of history based on thematic complexes/totality can oppose a *society marked by ignorance and* fragmented teaching.[4] The pedagogy of struggle is opposed to the pedagogy of tolerance and entrepreneurship. The study of history from a materialist point of view can overcome the teaching of history as proposed by capital and help us unravel the main causal complexes of capital's socio-metabolism, the particularities of dependent capitalisms, their contradictions and their movements. The study of agroecology will be able to unravel the main causal nexuses of destructive production and of the science of capital, teaching and researching new forms of production of non-poisoned food without exploited labour. The unitary school can overcome the dual school, the pedagogy of skills and the incompetence of pedagogies. If school alone will not solve humanity's problems, it is also not true that it does not have a specific role. For us, the different aspects of an education beyond capital, including an understanding of the main determinants of the socio-metabolism of capital, the history and theory of associated labour, the pedagogy of self-organisation and struggle, the method of thematic complexes and understanding of totality can help us build a society beyond capital.

The need for the revolutionary struggle to overcome the society of capital must combine the articulation of immediate struggles with broader struggles, which attack the nerve centres of capital. From this point of view, the right to an education beyond capital should be connected with struggles for the right to unalienated work,[5] with the right to de-commodified health and substantive equality. The right to water—"water for life and not for death", as the Movement of People Affected by Dams says—and the right to non-poisoned food, without pesticides, are also

[4] For Lukács, totality, as a founding category of reality, means: "firstly, the concrete unity of interacting contradictions; secondly, the systematic relativity of all totality, both upwards and downwards (which means that all totality is constructed by totalities subordinate to it and also that, at the same time, it is overdetermined by totalities of greater complexity…); and, thirdly, the historical relativity of all totality, that is, that the totality-character of all totality is dynamic, changeable, being limited to a concrete, determined historical period" (Lukács 1949 apud Netto 2009).

[5] Cooperatives and associations demonstrate the possibility and need for a more advanced form of work, even though they tend to reproduce all the defects of the capitalist mode of production (Novaes and Christoffoli 2013). It is possible to find in workers' associations the "wealth and misery of labour" associated under the mantle of capital.

very important, as these cause cancer, destroy the immune system of humans and plants. The right to control the city and the country, overcoming the current "democratic" form where financial capital, public debt controlled by rentiers, agribusiness corporations and contractors dominate our lives. The right to build a world self-governed by freely associated labourers, without managers and left- and right-wing technocrats. The right to build a communal system, where producers would plan what to produce, how to produce and why to produce, a planning not permeated by the dictates of the market. Finally, the right to rebellion and the right to civil insubordination. Only in this way will the realisation of human rights, the construction of a society beyond capital and the integral development of human beings be possible.

Bibliography

Batista, E. Terceirização no Brasil e suas implicações para os trabalhadores. Campinas: Pontes, 2013. 2ª edição.

Caldart, R. A pedagogia do Movimento Sem Terra. São Paulo: Expressão Popular, 2004.

Dal Ri, N. M.; Vieitez, C. Educação democrática e trabalho associado no Movimento dos Trabalhadores Rurais Sem Terra e nas fábricas de autogestão. São Paulo: Ícone, Fapesp, 2008.

Entrevista com Daniel Becker. www.canalsaude.fiocruz.com.br. TVNBR, 12/02/2013.

Freitas, L. C. A luta por uma pedagogia do meio: revisitando o conceito. In: Pistrak, M. M. A escola-comuna. São Paulo: Expressão Popular, 2009, pp. 8–100.

Iasi, M. Ensaios sobre consciência e emancipação. São Paulo: Expressão Popular, 2006.

Kuenzer, A. Z. As mudanças no mundo do trabalho e a educação: novos desafios para a gestão. In: Ferreira, N. S. C. Gestão democrática da educação: atuais tendências, novos desafios. São Paulo: Cortez, 1998, pp. 33–58.

Lima Filho, Paulo A. Sobre as revoluções burguesas radicais. In: NOVAES, H. T.; DAL RI, N. (orgs.) Movimentos Sociais e Crises Contemporâneas à luz dos clássicos do materialismo crítico. Uberlândia: Navegando, 2017, volume 2.

Minto. L. W. A educação da "miséria": particularidade capitalista e educação superior no Brasil. Tese de Doutorado, Faculdade de Educação, Unicamp, Campinas, 2011.

Netto, J. P. Introdução. In: Marx, K. Miséria da Filosofia: resposta à Filosofia da Miséria, do sr. Proudhon. São Paulo: Expressão Popular, 2009, pp. 7–16.

Novaes, H. T. A miséria ideológica da política educacional paulista. Marília, mimeo, 2013.
Novaes, H. T.; Christoffoli, P. I. As contradições da auto-educação no trabalho associado: reflexões a partir da experiência das fábricas recuperadas brasileiras. In: Marañon, B. (org.) Economia Solidária. Buenos Aires: Clacso, 2013.
Tiriba, L. Pedagogia(s) da produção associada. Ijuí: Ed. da Unijuí, 2001.

Films

Pro dia nascer feliz. Diretor: João Jardim, 2005.

CHAPTER 5

An Overview of Urban Associated Labour in Brazil: Positive and Negative Aspects of Self-Management in the Productive Microcosm

Introduction: The Structural Crisis of Capital and the Embryos of Anti-Capital Struggles in Latin America

A structural crisis of capital has plagued workers in all parts of the world since the 1970s and brought far-reaching consequences: bankruptcy of the totalitarian democracy of finance capital and the outbreak of innumerable revolts against this "democracy"; precarious processes of urbanisation, including "slummification" and the rise of gated condominiums; concentration of income and land; mass incarceration of miserable workers; increased unemployment; structural precariousness of labour; and the intensification of labour, the return of labour analogous to slavery and the growth of child labour.

This structural crisis of capital, which gains traces of economic, political and social regression, brought with it the resurgence of associated labour in Latin America. More generally, in Latin America as a whole, there was an explosion of struggles mainly to end dictatorships in the region and for classic demands such as land, housing, the right to employment and work, as well as quality public services.

This context saw the emergence of many struggles with great anti-capital potential, although restricted to some regions and economic

H. Tahan Novaes, *Associated Labor and Production in the Age of Barbarism*, https://doi.org/10.1007/978-3-031-51183-7_5

sectors: struggles for land led by peasants and homeless urban workers; resistance of populations affected by dams and large infrastructure works; struggles for self-organisation of labour; and struggles to take down hierarchies of gender, generation, and ethnicity. Struggles against the expropriation of indigenous territory, against the advance of mining and oil companies and against corporations producing GMOs and poisoned foods, among others. Struggles to build forms of collective decision-making that overcome formal democracy and the gulf between representatives and those represented, questioning parliaments dominated by capital caucuses or by representatives coming from the world of workers, but who personify capital. At the same time, we have the emergence of defensive struggles for civil and human rights, against the commodification of public education, against the privatisation of state-owned companies, against governments that plunder their country's wealth, which have led to the fall of presidents in Bolivia, Argentina, and Ecuador.

This chapter aims to recover part of this debate, mainly through an overview of the (re)emergence of urban Associated labour in Brazil. We seek to explore the positive and negative sides of associated labour based on the experiences of companies recovered by workers, joint efforts and associations in civil construction, as well as in garbage collection associations and urban popular cooperatives. We close the chapter with an attempt to sketch out what the pillars of a society beyond capital would look like.

Worker-Recovered Companies (ERTs, from the Acronym in Portuguese)

The Brazilian experiences of Associated labour gained ground from the 1990s, in the midst of a defensive context for Latin American social movements. President Fernando Henrique Cardoso (1995–2002) deepened Brazilian neoliberalism, and the pace of the economy was dictated by capitalist voracity in its neoliberal aspect of financialisation of the economy: open trade and liberalisation of financial capital, low growth, productive restructuring processes (Toyotism[1]), seamless transition with the civil-military dictatorship, state reforms that led to a decrease in certain social functions of the state, attack on social and labour rights, and

[1] T.N. The adoption of industrial practices inspired by the Toyota Production System.

privatisations and denationalizations that significantly increased structural unemployment and subemployment.

In this context, the strategy of factory recovery, represented by a series of isolated experiences in the 1980s, gains momentum at a time when many businesses, especially family-run ones, were in crisis. In the 1990s, there was a significant increase in Brazilian experiences, followed by a stabilisation in the number of cases in the early 2000s. Currently, 67 Recovered Companies are in operation in Brazil, involving just over 10,000 workers. Worker-recovered Companies (ERTs) were the subject of several studies in Brazil. However, most of them were case studies or multi-stage analyses that did not intend to generate data and more comprehensive theories about the universe of experiences. In the 2000s, the study that investigated the largest number of ERTs in Brazil was developed by Tauile et al. (2004), the result of research funded by SENAES/MTE involving 25 Brazilian ERTs. Besides quantifying some aspects, the study established a typology of self-management based on criteria related to management, market, credit, technology, form of ownership and institutional participation. The resulting seven ideal types range from "socially desirable"—companies run by self-managed by workers—to "socially unacceptable"—"fake cooperatives or outsourcers". These types were constructed through the characteristics presented by the ERTs being surveyed to capture trends found in the companies.

In the 2010s, research coordinated by Henriques et al. (2013) identified the existence of 67 ERTs currently operating in Brazil. The study was carried out with the support of the National Council for Scientific and Technological Development (CNPq). It represents the first survey of ERTs in Brazil carried out through a network that covers ten universities in the country.

In Henriques, Faria and Novaes (2012) we found that Brazil and Argentina present most of the existing cases in Latin America. In these two countries, it can be said that existing experiences have similar characteristics, especially regarding the challenges faced to resume production processes and the commercialisation of products and services under self-management. However, these processes develop in different historical and economic situations, resulting in different recovery strategies and different political forms of action in these struggles for the recovery of factories. Fundamentally, it is a matter of realising the variety of relations established by ERTs with other social movements at the territorial and national levels, resulting in variable levels of legitimacy achieved by experiences in the processes of struggle for the maintenance of jobs and self-managed production.

Here, it is necessary to establish the main characteristics of ERTs, largely addressed in Henriques, Faria and Novaes (2012).

a) The regional distribution shows that the vast majority are concentrated in Brazil's South and Southeast regions, representing the most industrialised areas of the country, with special concentrations in urban areas. The main economic sectors are industrial (metallurgy, textiles, footwear, food, among others), as well as mineral extraction and services;
b) Almost all the experiences result from the recovery of family businesses. In many cases, the company's bankruptcy or pre-bankruptcy is the result of an unsuccessful process of succession inside families; it is not uncommon to find factories founded in the early twentieth century, with machinery over fifty years old;
c) These companies commonly had voluminous labour liabilities. Workers often experienced long periods of delayed wages and social and labour rights which were not held up for months and sometimes years;
d) When these businesses are about to shut down, workers mobilise for their labour rights and, at that moment, the prospect of maintaining the factory in operation with the removal of the former owners arises;
e) In many cases, the union takes on the role of active protagonist in worker organisation, in the presentation and discussion of the possibilities for the maintenance of the company in operation, in the negotiation with the former owners and with public and private bodies to seek funding. Sometimes, the union also becomes co-responsible in the management of these companies under workers' control;
f) Sometimes workers give up their labour rights and contractual severance pay in exchange for collective ownership of the companies' means of production;
g) In the vast majority of cases, workers decide to adopt the cooperative model, in the absence of a legal framework that recognises the specificities of this phenomenon in Brazil;
h) The term self-management is often employed, aiming to cover both the changes in the form of ownership of companies, as well

as the democratic characteristics that should govern the organisation of the work process and the cooperative's management style. However, the general trend of the experiences surveyed in Brazil is to maintain the division of previous work, the main changes being related to the division of withdrawals ("wages"), surplus ("leftovers") and the decision-making process in the factory, which, in general, takes place through general meetings. This leads to the maintenance of workers within the places determined by the division of labour at the time when the work restarted, but now adopting framework in which the ownership of the company is collective by all the members of the cooperative;

i) Although we identified changes in the division of withdrawals ("wages"), only one Brazilian experience opted for an egalitarian division. In Brazil, it is also very common to find cases where cooperatives stop associating new workers and all new members are hired;

j) This new situation certainly impacts on the motivation of workers, at least for a certain period, and makes them more inclined to perform productive tasks with greater commitment and zeal;

k) In these experiences, the "competitive strategy" can make use of mechanisms such as the extension of the unpaid workday or even wage flexibility to keep up with market fluctuations. In other words, in the eventual impossibility of redesigning existing technology or of an investment in new technologies, these companies can make use of mechanisms characteristic of absolute surplus value to carry out their economic processes. At the same time, there are many reports among ERT workers that the main change in relation to the old work is the decrease in the pace of work, which in their point of view are responsible for the significant reduction in the number of accidents. According to Henriques et al. (2013), over 70% of experiences report having decreased the accident rate in their dependencies;

l) Since ERTs are immersed in the commodity production system, they are not able to overcome production based on exchange values alone (Novaes 2011; Pateo 2013). The perception of workers on this topic is varied, but it is perhaps possible to state that there is already a wing of Latin American social movements with a reasonable perception of the need to produce to meet human needs (use values);

m) After a company reopens under self-management, one can perceive it gradually distances itself from the experiences of other social struggles and the field of solidarity economy itself, increasingly adopting the discourse that the most important thing is ensuring the viability of the "business". That is, there is a low "politicisation" of experiences, as can be seen by their isolation from other workers' struggles and discussion about the role they can play in the construction of a society "beyond capital" (Mészáros 2002).

In relation to this last item, everything leads us to believe that ERT workers are situated more in the field of "contingent class consciousness" than in the field of "necessary class consciousness" (Mészáros 2006).[2] The distance of Brazilian ERTs from the "Solidarity Economy" movement and a broader movement to build a society beyond capital remains a challenge for this field and should certainly remain on the agenda of new research. The prevailing agenda is to maintain jobs, to receive their money at the end of the month and to resume daily life. This is a similar problem to what the MST faces today, that is, the stagnation of the struggle after being able to get land. Instead of the struggle for land and the recovery of factories being a means towards the combination of internal self-management with the development of other anti-capital struggles and the search for comprehensive solutions in all spheres of work and life, the conquest of land or factory became an end to itself, albeit with some partial victories on the way.

Furthermore, it's important to overcome the tendency of inertial unionism to restrict itself to negotiations for the fulfilment of due labour rights, which inclines them to conservative solutions for these situations, and only rarely attempt the resumption of production from the organisation of workers.

[2] The fundamental difference between contingent class consciousness and necessary class consciousness is that while the former simply perceives some isolated aspects of society's contradictions, the latter understands them in their interrelationships, that is, as necessary features of the global system of capitalism. The former remains entangled in local conflicts, even when the scale of operation is relatively large, while the latter, by focusing its attention on the strategically central theme of social control, is concerned with comprehensive solutions, even when its immediate goals seem limited (e.g., an attempt to keep a factory that is succumbing to capitalist "rationalization" alive under workers' control) (Mészáros 2008: 89).

In general, the experiences that have emerged since the 1980s and, above all, in the 1990s in Brazil were largely motivated by a deep crisis in the labour market and sought to avoid the closure of the companies and subsequent loss of jobs. From the beginning, there was no concern to constitute an alternative model of organisation of the production process that went beyond the generation of work and income which could serve as an example for new types of struggle in other companies.

Another difficulty encountered by recovered companies concerns the organisational "culture" inherited from the factory when under the control of capital. The entire aesthetic conception, panoptic architecture, physical spaces, etc. were designed for the reproduction of social relations of domination and exploitation. When under workers' control, not changing the spatiality of work contributes to the resurgence of social relations based on inequality and fragmentation, such as the complete separation between administration and production. The new social relations that emerged through the struggle should encompass a remodelling of the factory space, bringing workers closer together so that they can dialogue as much as possible about the company's problems, even during the work process.

Nascimento (2023) suggests carrying out "pedagogical strikes" in self-management experiences, that is, some moments of interruption of production during the work week to discuss vital aspects of the production and reproduction of life, "strikes" that help workers to stop so they may reflect on their life, their work and practical ways of transforming it into non-alienated work.

The most important entities representing recovered factories in Brazil, ANTEAG and UNISOL,[3] have their origin in the trade union movement, although this theme also remains somewhat strange and distant from the strategic discussions of the trade union movement. We note that, over the years, these entities that emerged to support the process of recovery of factories started to develop joint efforts with other types of solidarity economic enterprises. At UNISOL, for example, which today has 280 affiliated enterprises, only 25 (10%) are ERTs.

Finally, it is possible to observe Worker-Recovered Companies from different angles. The question of democratic assemblies and the formation of rotating committees for the administration of factory problems creates

[3] There is also the Movement of Occupied Factories, which fights for nationalisation under workers' control and today is represented by the Flaskô factory.

the possibility of building new social relations in the productive microcosm, relations that do not have capitalists, managers and technocrats. As for issues related to ownership of the means of production, they inevitably lead to a debate on the "expropriation of expropriators". Novel forms of labour organisation and of production and distribution of surplus can help us think of forms of production which in some measure surpass alienated labour. The redesign of machines and manufacturing techniques help us theorise about the non-neutrality of Science and Technology and the role of researchers-extensionists leads us to think about the role of intellectuals in class society. Gender relations in ERTs and waste picker associations lead us to think about the intertwined relationship between social class and gender, often despised by twentieth century Marxism (Henriques 2013; Novaes 2012; Wirth 2013).

Cooperative Housing Efforts and Civil Construction Cooperatives: From FUCVAM to the Dom Hélder Câmara Commune

José Baravelli's master's dissertation (2005) reports the influence of Uruguayan cooperativism on social housing in São Paulo in the "democratic transition" period (1980s). It starts with a discussion of the FUCVAM[4] cooperatives and reaches the United Housing Association of Vila Nova Cachoeirinha (São Paulo).

Uruguayan housing cooperatives are still a reference for struggles with self-management characteristics in Latin America, but unfortunately little remembered outside the region because of Eurocentrism. In Uruguay, FUCVAM was a focus of resistance to the military dictatorship, so much so that, not by chance, it was the first place the military invaded at the beginning of the dictatorship. Even after the coup, FUCVAM members persisted in their struggles, creating the "unifying and Uruguayan" front. Meanwhile, in Brazil, the Minister of Agriculture of the military regime was the president of one of the most reactionary Cooperatives in our history, the Cooperativa de Cotia (São Paulo).

Here, you can contrast the two experiences. As far as possible, Uruguayans were able to think and create new spaces for housing and

[4] T.N.: Federación Uruguaya das Cooperativas de Vivienda por Ayuda Mútua, Uruguayan Federation of Mutual Aid Housing Cooperatives.

collective work in the same location. Furthermore, they solved the problem of housing, collective property, leisure, sports, and militancy in the same space, all while creating work with some traces of de-alienation.

The importance of Uruguayan social housing was also portrayed in a work by João Marcos Lopes, one of the founders of the Usina group[5] alongside Cibele Rizek. One of the goals of Lopes and Rizek's (2005) research was to understand how the binomial *mutirão*[6]/self-management had been appropriated by Brazilian social movements. Thus:

> from the indigenous practices of mutual aid for cassava gardens (the "muxirão") or among small farmers who help each other take care of their lands, through the spontaneous urban forms of cooperation for the construction of houses, the *mutirão* will gradually add elements of a rhetoric that extends beyond a simple agreement to organise free labour (Lopez and Rizek 2005, p. 8).

In the words of Lopes and Rizek (2005), public housing provision started in Uruguay in the late 1960s with Law 13.728 (Ley Nacional de Vivienda, or National Housing Law), which, when sanctioned in 1968, implemented the recommendations formulated in the 1962 *National*

[5] According to information obtained on the institution's website, the Usina group was established in 1990 by professionals from various fields of activity as a self-managed architecture collective. In these 20 years, Usina has been working mainly with social movements aiming to build territorial experiences of another order, involving the ability to plan, design and build by the workers themselves, mobilising public funds in a context of social struggle and urban reform. Usina's team intends to overcome the authorial and strictly commercial production of architecture and knowledge, therefore, it seeks to integrate and engender processes that possibly subvert the logic of capital through counter-hegemonic spatial, social, technical, and aesthetic experience. Usina has already participated in the design and construction of over 4300 housing units, community centres, schools and daycare centres in several cities and rural settlements, mainly in the states of São Paulo and Paraná. They also worked in the development of urban plans, favela urbanisation projects and assisted in the formation and organisation of work cooperatives. Usina uses new forms of organisation both in its own team and externally; it seeks to establish new practices with the perspective of overcoming the traditional division of labour and the separation between the moments of conception, production and social appropriation of space.

[6] T.N.: Mutirão, etymologically descended from the Tupi-Guarani *motyrõ,* is used in Brazilian Portuguese to designate any collective unpaid work effort, usually connected to a community priority, including building or renovating houses in the community and public spaces, agricultural work in small properties, cleaning public spaces, providing medical or veterinary services, etc.

Housing Plan. The National Housing Law would end up becoming the main point of reference for the construction of this idea of self-managed housing production. The Uruguayan experience emerged with a much more pronounced political stance, mainly because it was operationally linked to the country's trade union organisations. The resistance that housing cooperatives exerted throughout the dictatorial period in Uruguay is well known.[7]

However, one may warn that this mimetic transplant brought numerous points of difficulty. The procedures for self-managed housing construction were systematically adopted in Brazil without any assessment of local context or adjustments of the means used: when the Uruguayan model was transplanted, it did not fit perfectly:

> there, union organisations; here, popular movements; there, a plan and a law that regulates the self-managed production of housing throughout the country; here, programs that do not even make up a local housing policy; there, cooperatives that legally allow collective mutual, common property and its regulated commercialisation; here, community associations that barely maintain their status as a promoting agent that only acts as a temporary mediator between financial agents and the final borrower (Lopes and Rizek 2005: 13).

Eduardo Ewbank's master's dissertation (2007) shows us the enormous difficulty and complexity in the formation of civil construction cooperatives in Brazil. Often short-lived, Brazilian civil construction cooperatives face numerous difficulties depending on the sector they are inserted in: workers are used to earning based on productivity/goals and on differentiation of pay according to the work performed, holding individualistic capital-based values, etc.... Construction companies also tend to have enormous hiring power. We cannot fail to highlight the attempts to form cooperatives including architects, master builders and masons in which all were at an equal footing in the city of São Paulo.

Despite what the relative failure of these experiences may demonstrate, associated labour in civil construction is a challenging but worthwhile pursuit with the goal of establishing coherent and non-alienating work

[7] For a history of the "entry" of the theme into the popular movements of the 1960s, the influences they received from Uruguay and from popular architects, the case of favelas in Fortaleza (1959), Rio de Janeiro (1965), Belo Horizonte (1979), and São Paulo, see Lopes and Rizek (2005).

processes and the ownership of product of work: houses, day care centres, the university, and the city as use values.

We had the opportunity to observe the formation of the Treme-Treme Cooperative in the Dom Hélder Câmara Commune (CDHC), when we were monitors of the Technological Incubator of Popular Cooperatives at Unicamp (Castro et al. 2015). The CDHC was recently studied by Sandro Oliveira (2010, 2013), one of the members of the Usina collective and a member of the CHDC's Escola de Samba Unidos da Lona Preta. For him, the experience that was born from the need to guarantee the right to housing to dozens of families evicted in 2005 from a favela located on the land of Companhia Paulista de Trens Metropolitanos (CPTM) represents a counter-hegemonic social space in relation to the social determinations of capital.

As a space designed with popular participation and under joint construction among 128 families, the Landless Rural Workers Movement (MST) and the technical assistance of the Usina (which calls itself a work centre for inhabited environments), its process-based existence contrasts with the trends of self-construction, the projects of the Minha Casa Minha Vida Program (MCMV) and gated condominiums by opening precedents to think about a public policy with workers' self-management (Oliveira, 2010, p. 1). Reflecting on civil construction *mutirões* and cooperatives inevitably bring to mind some criticisms made by architects regarding civil construction and the particularities of our brand of capitalism. As we pointed out in Novaes (2011), the criticism weaved by the Usina group is so complete that it is hard to summarise. In a nutshell, we can say that they question: capitalist productive forces; the ownership of the means of production (be it houses, factories, etc.); the city as a source of surplus value and its role in Latin American class society; the loss of control over the labour process and over the product of labour and the territory by both architects and workers; the commodification of life; the fragmentation of the human being; the type of professional that universities train and the role that they play in class society; the myth of progress and the role of contractors; in addition to a broader critique of the capitalist mode of production. Despite being immersed in the commodity production system, these intellectuals try to engage in free intellectual activity with social meaning. Above being architects or social scientists, all members of Usina consider themselves popular educators who are teaching and learning from popular struggles or social movements.

According to Pedro Arantes, "our end is socialism, but what to do before that…?" As far as possible, they are designing the revolution. They are thinking about the complexity of a radical transformation, that is, "that the architected collective is a space of concurrent and non-alienating production, consumption, education, and aesthetics". Evidently, the Usina Group can only create enclaves in the sea of the commodity production system, trying to seek ways for an increasing degree of social control over life in a context of advancing barbarism.

The Collection and Sorting of Recyclable Materials: A Field for Associated Labour?

One of the most nefarious consequences of the structural crisis of capital has been the alarming rise in the numbers of the poor and miserable throughout the globe. With the increase in poverty and misery, added to one of the characteristics of the capitalist mode of production and destruction, that is, production that is intrinsically destructive to human beings and nature, we had the emergence of numerous associations and cooperatives of recyclable waste collectors (Wirth 2013; Fraga 2012).

Brazilian academia is very suspicious of the possibility of Associated labour in this "sector" of the economy. They highlight the inhuman working conditions in dumps and in cooperatives and associations: hot, dirty and foetid sheds where work is very intensive, etc.

Another group of researchers-extensionists, on the other hand, prefer to establish close relations with waste pickers rather than turn a blind eye to this social issue. This is where numerous actions of cooperative incubators arise, with varying degrees of critical and practical radicalism, working with waste pickers. The struggle of waste pickers led to the emergence of numerous "public policies". It is enough to remember that half of the resources of the National Secretariat for Solidarity Economy (SENAES—MTE) in 2012 were allocated to waste pickers.

Marx would possibly call the pickers the lumpenproletariat—lumpen in German means rag. Among the positive aspects of Associated labour in this "sector", we can highlight attempts to organise work under new social relations: the construction of democratic assemblies; attempts to build substantive equality between men and women in production and administration; changes in the ways workers are compensated; the role researchers-extensionists established in the relationship established with the National Waste Pickers Movement; popular education projects in waste pickers' associations, including the construction of libraries and the establishment of literacy programs for many workers who were left behind in the formal educational system. In this wake, some universities are trying to redesign machines, as well as helping to create new, less alienating ways of organising work.[8] Incredibly, it should also be noted that for many of these workers who live on the verge of extreme poverty, the work associated with the collection and sorting of recyclable materials represents a gain in relation to the situation experienced before entering cooperatives and associations (long-term unemployment, begging, social vulnerability, rigidity of the working day, etc.).

Last but not least, in the same way that it is possible for social movements to control housing "public policy" (Arantes 2002; Lopez and Rizek 2005), it is also possible for waste pickers to control urban cleaning "public policy" (Wirth 2013).

Among the negative aspects, we could highlight: the inadequate conditions for non-alienating work; the intense pace of work; market fluctuations; the role of the aluminium industry in controlling the production chain; the role of middlemen in the production chain; and the absence of a minimum income for these disinherited on their own land, disinherited people who are pushed to misery by the structural crisis of the socio-metabolism of capital.

We could also highlight the co-optation of this social movement by "public policies". Just remember the participation of former President Lula in all national gatherings of waste pickers, always at the end of the year. Similarly, we have the assimilation of these struggles by large corporations. For instance, Coca-Cola stamps on its bottles that it "supports" waste pickers' cooperatives and associations.

Recently, a debate has arisen in Brazil between the incineration of garbage, a typical strategy of the petty bourgeoisie, and the strategy linked to the political economy of the workers, that is, attempts to build new social relations and a new conception of recycling in this "sector" of the economy that involves large amounts of resources from city budgets. It is enough to remember that garbage collection is the main "consumer"

[8] In the aesthetic field, we could also highlight the film Extraordinary Garbage. This film follows the Brazilian artist Vick Muniz, who takes photos of the waste pickers and builds backdrops using their work material (recyclable waste). For our purpose the commodification of this art in auctions eager to conform to capital/financialization of capital does not matter so much, rather we care about the meaning that this art has for humanity.

of public resources in many Brazilian municipalities. Garbage collection has killed many mayors in Brazil, enriched many corrupt technocrats and many businessmen who make a living off of garbage.

In the same way as waste pickers' associations, we have other branches of small urban production where work is predominantly female: clothing and textile manufacturing, furniture and wood products manufacturing, etc. (Wirth 2013).[9] In these fields, we have a few advanced associations in political and economic terms. The vast majority of them are improvising solutions to the daily struggle for economic survival/for the maintenance of self-management characteristics, while many others are in the process of degeneration.

The role of women in these urban cooperatives and popular associations should be highlighted. Despite their relative "failure" in economic terms, these cooperatives have played a key role in the political strengthening of women who were previously afraid of their husbands, who had little familial and economic autonomy. In cooperatives and associations, women find the strength of collective struggle. They start to join more dialogues, to socialise their daily dramas and thus find collective answers to their problems. This caveat is necessary, as many economic analyses tend to observe the small income obtained by these cooperatives, disregarding the political victories of these associations. At the same time, we cannot fail to observe the permanence of many of the traits of alienated labour in cooperatives and popular associations.

Some Conclusions: From Embryos of Associated Labour to the Struggle for the Construction of a Society Beyond Capital

The positive aspects of urban Associated Labour outlined on the pages above, along with other research we are carrying out in the field of agroecology and education beyond capital (Novaes 2012; Novaes and Santos 2013) allow us to trace some pillars of a society beyond capital:

[9] See also Singer (2002), Quijano (2002), Schiochet (2012) and the Solidarity Economy Census finally socialised in August 2013. www.senaes.gov.br.

a) Self-management in the productive microcosm: self-management struggles have as their principle the construction of new social relations. They show us that bosses, managers and technocrats are unnecessary. In self-management, we have the hegemony of democratic assemblies: councils are elected by workers and there is rotation and revocability of elected positions. All these measures are anti-bureaucratisation, and they question the loss of control of the work process. Ways of overcoming the wage system are created and funds are usually created for the allocation of surplus;
b) Decommodification: it is impossible to exist a society beyond capital without questioning the production of commodities. From this point of view, self-management advances to the extent that workers gain increasing degrees of control of production with the goal of satisfying human needs, that is, the production of use values without the concomitant production of exchange values. In this wake, there will be the expansion of public spaces and the notion of "public goods", such as water, energy, transport, health, land, telecommunications, education, housing, the city as a use value, etc.
c) Self-management in the social macrocosm: self-management in the broad sense means overcoming the capitalist state, that is, the suppression of the immovable state bureaucracy and the forms of domination typical of formal democracy. In this case, the struggle to end the capitalist state is the struggle for the creation of the general conditions of production and reproduction of the communal economy, and no longer of the general conditions of production and reproduction of capital. For the reproduction of non-alienated social life, workers must necessarily drastically reduce their working hours (in the process of de-alienation), having time to decide the paths to be followed by their neighbourhoods, cities, countries, etc. and for the election of representatives with revocable positions. They will have the time and power to control the fundamental decisions of society. Likewise, they will have time and control over the composition and allocation of public funds (retirement, schools, etc.). Finally, self-management in the social macrocosm is inevitably connected to the debate of the democratic planning of the production and reproduction of human existence, that is, the global coordination of the production and reproduction of life by freely associated producers.

d) Education beyond capital. Here, we can only outline what the foundations of the school of emancipated labour would be: study of history from a materialist point of view and the articulation of particularity/totality, appropriation and redesign of science and technology to satisfy human needs, education for associated/ collective work, education for the struggle /insertion of schools in the struggles of their time, the formation of values of the new human being (Che Guevara). Education for the production of revolutionary art and for understanding art classics, as well as socialist physical education (Novaes 2013);

e) Universalisation of emancipated labour: Labour will be organised through substantive equality, that is, from each according to their possibilities, to each according to their needs. At work, the development of the human being will take place in its entirety. Regarding reproductive work, substantive equality brings with it the overcoming of patriarchy, eliminating the age-old dichotomy wherein women take care of the household and men work to provide for the family.

f) The real ownership of the means of production by the workers: for self-management to advance in society, workers must question the private ownership of the means of production. In Marx's words, we will have the "expropriation of the expropriators" or what we call the "return of the snail to its shell". Reconciliation between workers and the social means of production and material reproduction of social life will take place in different forms of communal economy (Mészáros 2006).

g) Last but not least, there must be the unification of anti-capital struggles to overcome the socio-metabolism of capital, through the political conviction of the workers themselves that another world is possible and necessary.

Acknowledgements We would like to thank my friend Ioli Wirth for her critique.

Bibliography

Arantes, P. F. Arquitetura Nova – Sérgio Ferro, Flávio Império e Rodrigo Lefèvre, de Artigas aos Mutirões. São Paulo: Editora 34, 2002.

Baravelli, J. O cooperativismo uruguaio na habitação social de São Paulo Das cooperativas FUCVAM à Associação de Moradia Unidos de Vila Nova Cachoeirinha. USP, Faculdade de Arquitetura e Urbanismo, Dissertação de Mestrado, 2005.

Castro, Mariana Pereira de. Em busca de uma pedagogia da produção associada. In: Édi A. Benini; Maurício Sardá de Faria; Henrique T. Novaes; Renato Dagnino. (Org.). Gestão pública e sociedades: fundamentos e políticas de economia solidária. 1ed. São Paulo: Outras Expressões, 2015, v. 1, p. 125–166.

Ewbank, E. G. Autogestão: possibilidade de organização da força de trabalho na construção civil e suas implicações. São Paulo, Dissertação de Mestrado, FAU-USP, 2007.

Fraga, L. Extensão e transferência de conhecimento: As Incubadoras Tecnológicas de Cooperativas Populares. Tese de Doutorado, Instituto de Geociências, Unicamp, 2012.

Henriques, F. C. et al. *Empresas recuperadas pelos trabalhadores*. Rio de Janeiro: Multifoco, 2013.

Henriques, F.; Faria, M. S.; Novaes, H. T. "Os distintos caminhos das fábricas recuperadas no Brasil e na Argentina" In: Rodrigues, F. C.; Novaes, H. T.; Batista, E. (orgs.) Movimentos Sociais, Trabalho Associado e Educação para além do capital. São Paulo: Outras Expressões, 2012.

Lopes, J. M.; Rizek, C. O mutirão autogerido como procedimento inovador na produção da moradia para os pobres: uma abordagem crítica. Rio de Janeiro, Revista da Finep, 2005. Obtido em: http://www.habitare.org.br/doc/docs_revista/artigoFinep_usina.pdf. Retirado em 25/07/2009.

Mészáros, I. A teoria da alienação em Marx. São Paulo: Boitempo Editorial, 2006.

Meszáros, I. Filosofia, ideologia e ciência social. São Paulo: Boitempo, 2008.

Mészáros, I. Para além do capital. São Paulo: Boitempo, 2002.

Nascimento, C. Do Beco dos Sapos aos canaviais de Catende. Porto Alegre, 2023.

Novaes, H. T. A Autogestão como Magnífica Escola: notas sobre a educação no trabalho associado. In: Batista, E. L.; Novaes, H. T. (orgs.) Educação e reprodução social: as contradições do capital no século XXI. Bauru: Canal 6/Praxis, 2011.

Novaes, H. T. Reatando um fio interrompido: a relação universidade-movimentos sociais na América Latina. São Paulo: Expressão Popular-Fapesp, 2012.

Novaes, H. T.; Santos, L. *Produção Destrutiva, Agroecologia e Educação Agroecológica do MST-PR*. V Congresso Teoria Política do Socialismo, Marília, agosto de, 2013.

Oliveira, A. U. A questão da aquisição de terras por estrangeiros no Brasil– um retorno aos dossiês. Agrária, São Paulo, No. 12, 2010.

Oliveira, S. B. Repensando a (re)produção social do espaço – um estudo de caso da Comuna Dom Hélder Câmara - MST. Dissertação de Mestrado, UNIFESP, São Paulo, 2013.

Pateo, F. V. Economia solidária: limites e avanços dos trabalhadores sob o controle do processo e do sentido do produto do seu trabalho. In: Rodrigues, F. C.; Novaes, H. T.; Batista, E. (orgs.) Movimentos Sociais, Trabalho Associado e Educação para além do capital. São Paulo: Outras Expressões, 2013, vol. II, no prelo.

Quijano, A. Sistemas alternativos de produção? In: Santos, B.S. (org.) Produzir para viver, os caminhos da produção não capitalista. Rio de Janeiro: Civilização Brasileira, 2002, pp. 300–345.

Schiochet, V. Da democracia à autogestão: Economia Solidária no Brasil. In: Benini, E.; Faria, M. S.; Novaes, H. T.; Dagnino, R. (orgs.) Gestão Pública e Trabalho Associado. São Paulo: Outras Expressões, 2012.

Singer, P. A recente ressurreição da Economia Solidária. In: Santos, B.S. (org.) Produzir para viver, os caminhos da produção não capitalista. Rio de Janeiro: Civilização Brasileira, 2002, pp. 81–129.

Tauile, J. R.; Rodrigues, H. "Economia Solidária e autogestão: a criação e recriação de trabalho e renda". Revista Mercado de Trabalho, Brasília, IPEA, n. 24, agosto de 2004.

Wirth, I. Mulheres na Triagem, Homens na Prensa. Questões de Gênero em Cooperativas de Catadores. São Paulo: Annablume, 2013.

CHAPTER 6

Cooperation and Workers' Cooperatives in São Paulo's MST: An Analysis of the Actions of the Capitalist State that Block the Educational Potential of Associated Labour

Introduction

Since the 1970s, we have been witnessing an offensive by capital. In Novaes et al. (2015), we outlined the main dimensions of this offensive: (a) pressure for the free movement of financial capital, resulting in a restructuring of production in the countryside and cities; (b) technological innovations that intensified the production and diversification of goods; (c) expansion of capital towards sectors and fields not yet subject to full commodification, such as health and education, with a wave of privatisation which took the cycle of commodification to a new level; and (d) the implementation of processes of corporate relocation and outsourcing.

The State of São Paulo is a privileged vantage points to observe this offensive in the Brazilian federation, especially the restructuring of the countryside and the (im)possibility of an agrarian reform that is based on cooperation, work in cooperatives and associations and agroecology in the settlements.

This chapter is divided into two parts. The first part makes a brief historical overview of the political economy of the countryside in the State

H. Tahan Novaes, *Associated Labor and Production in the Age of Barbarism*, https://doi.org/10.1007/978-3-031-51183-7_6

of São Paulo. The second part shows the limits and contradictions of workers' cooperation and cooperatives in the MST settlements in the face of the new agribusiness offensive in the State. We close the chapter with some final considerations. It should be noted that the chapter was written with young people who intend to become Agroecology technicians in mind. We seek to simplify some concepts and analyses without, however, falling into oversimplifications. We would also like to highlight that this is a part of ongoing research that aims to analyse the characteristics, nature, and contradictions of the workers' cooperatives of the MST in São Paulo. The chapter we now present is the partial result of research on the actions of the capitalist state along with cooperatives and associations.

From the Coffee Complex to the Expansion of Agribusiness in the State of São Paulo

The State of São Paulo became prominent in the national scenario in the nineteenth century, with the consolidation of the coffee complex and a nascent industry (Cano 2005). In this process, the importation of Italian and Spanish labour became fundamental (Martins 2013). Not coincidentally, 15 days after the abolition of the transatlantic slave trade, the Brazilian oligarchies proclaimed the land law in 1850.[1,2]

The consolidation of the coffee complex led to the expansion of railway infrastructure in the State of São Paulo, with three main axes of expansion. To illustrate, we could mention the region around the cities of Bauru, Marília, and Presidente Prudente. In the twentieth century, we witnessed the wholesale slaughter of indigenous populations, the clearing of lands, the expulsion of squatters, land grabbing and the installation of enormous properties for the production of coffee and cotton (Monbeig 1984; Pereira 2005). José Teodoro, a miner from Pouso Alegre, bought

[1] Clovis Moura (2014) also observes that in the second half of the nineteenth century struggles against slavery were already at a new level, and this changed the history of black people in the State of São Paulo. In São Paulo, it is worth highlighting the history of the abolitionist Luiz Gama. Born in Bahia, he had been enslaved, then was able to achieve his freedom and was a poet and lawyer. He lived for 42 years in São Paulo and fought for the end of the monarchy and the abolition of slave labour in the State of São Paulo. He died in 1882, 6 years before the abolition of slave labour. See Moura (2014).

[2] T.N.: The Land Law of 1850 highly favoured the concentration of lands in the hands of a few wealthy owners, consolidating Brazil's still prevailing inequality in land distribution.

the lands in the region, leading to urban agglomerations that grew as railroads arrived in the region.

With the stock market crisis of 1929 and the Revolution of 1930, we entered another historical moment. Wilson Cano observed the "roots of industrial concentration" in the State of São Paulo. This is where the country's main banks, commerce, and industries emerged. The emergence of the industry– late as it was–led to the creation of the general conditions for its production and reproduction. It led to the creation of a timid educational system, the creation of Senai/SESI and the Federal Technical Schools, the creation of USP and the Isolated Colleges in the countryside (Saviani 1998). Along with these, a housing policy focused on workers' villages and on controlling rental prices was created (Bonduki 1999). Francisco de Oliveira (2004) also highlights the exchange rate, subsidies, and numerous state policies favourable to industrialisation. With that, the resources coming from coffee production were "drained" for the consolidation of the industrial park. Carone (1981), in turn, emphasises the attachment of trade unions to the State as a way of avoiding and framing the demands of the nascent proletariat within the framework of capital.

From a political point of view, Ianni (2009) notes that the São Paulo elite reacted quickly to the loss of state control to Getúlio Vargas. The Revolution of 1932 was an attempt by certain classes from São Paulo to regain control of the State. Also according to Ianni (2009), from 1930 to 1955 we had a brief moment when autonomous capitalism flourished, but quickly became an associated capitalism, with decision-making centres outside the country. For him, foreign capital began to determine the direction of the nation, something that became clearer from the 1964 coup.

Let us remember that in the period between 1950 and 1964, class struggle intensified throughout the country. Struggles of the nascent proletariat for better wages and living conditions in a country with uncountable scars of slavery, struggles for land in a country dominated by large landowners, urban reform in a country that has replaced slave quarters with favelas, and the creation and reform of universities linked to national development.

Struggles to expand public and secular education, such as those led by Florestan Fernandes and his friends and literacy campaigns, especially those influenced by Paulo Freire. Campaigns such as "The Oil is Ours", struggles for the creation of the Eletrobrás system, among many others. Glauber Rocha became the icon of the "Cinema Novo" (New Film) movement, Sérgio Ferro of the New Architecture, the students of Nelson Werneck Sodré of New History. These struggles were part of the most beautiful and delicate moment in our history.

An alliance between the USA, the industrial bourgeoisie, the Catholic Church, large landowners, and business owners, with prominent participation by the São Paulo elite, led to the overthrow of João Goulart on March 31 to April 1, 1964. Let us remember that in the 1960s, IPES-IBAD [Instituto de Pesquisas e Estudos Sociais—Institute for Research and Social Studies/IBAD Instituto Brasileiro de Ação Democrática—Brazilian Institute of Democratic Action] was already preparing the coup. We also had numerous street demonstrations including the march for "Tradition, Family and Property" and campaigns inciting hatred for "communists", among others (Dreifuss 1981).

Marxist historians are unanimous in observing that the civil-military dictatorship represented a major historical break. Leftist professors and students in USP, UnB and many other federal universities were violently repressed, struggles for land were put to a stop, left-wing parties and unions were made illegal, many influential figures were exiled, critical thinkers were tortured and killed, the leftist part of the Catholic Church was strangled, and the peasant leagues disintegrated. (Fernandes 2006; Novaes, 2012).

The restructuring of São Paulo's countryside, that is, what Florestan Fernandes called its "consented modernisation", led to the installation or expansion of large corporations producing pesticides, synthetic fertilisers, and tractors. For the "modernisation" of the countryside to consolidate, it took a heavy hand from the State to create the general conditions for its expansion: very cheap credit for the purchase of machinery and equipment, technical assistance to implement the "Green Revolution" package, financing exports, repression of the countryside unions, extermination of guerrillas, reform or creation of public universities to adapt the curriculum to the dictates of the "Green Revolution", etc.[3]

Within this history, we could highlight the march of the gauchos[4] towards the west of Santa Catarina, Paraná, Mato Grosso do Sul, Mato Grosso, and Pará. They've even settled in Bolivia. Murders of indigenous

[3] For this debate, see Delgado (1985), Tolentino (2011), Sampaio Jr. (2013) and Novaes (2012).

[4] T.N.: In Brazil, Gaucho is the endonym for those born in the southern state of Rio Grande do Sul.

people and squatters, land grabbing, and control of regional politics by large-scale farmers all reared their ugly head in our history yet again.

Concerning the debate on the restructuring of the countryside, Nelson Werneck Sodré (1995) highlights the contradictions of Proálcool. For him, if on the one hand Proálcool meant the production of national energy, on the other it led to the concentration of rural property and income. At the end of the day, this policy led to the formation of groups of large landowners, with an enormous power to decide the course of Brazilian capitalism.

The explosion of numerous demonstrations and struggles starting in the second half of the 1970s led to the strategy by part of our elites of a gradual, slow, and secure transition out of the dictatorship. This strategy was successful, leading to a transition from dictatorship to "democracy" without major ruptures, a democracy increasingly dominated by financial capital. The control of the strategic positions of the State by capital limited the power of the so-called "new unionism", of the PT and PMDB, Central Worker's Union (CUT), the MST, ANDES, and other institutions that tried to recompose the classic social struggles of a country torn by numerous social contradictions.

When we thought we would win this safe transition, with the 1988 Constitution as our high point, the media conglomerate Globo elected Collor who, together with the increasingly transnational and restructured corporations, knocked the people out once again. Most of the achievements formally inserted in the Constitution were denied to Brazilian workers in practice. To give you an idea, in the 1980s the Pontal do Paranapanema became one of the largest stages of struggle for land in Brazil. On one side we had lands grabbed by large landowners and corporations with the connivance of the State and on the other side the landless movement.

In the 2000s, sugarcane crops, which already occupied 50% of the territory of the State of São Paulo, grew to occupy 80%. The State of São Paulo went from being a large coffee plantation to becoming a large sugarcane plantation. Sugarcane has become a kind of "transparent" gold. Let us remember Lula said in 2005 that sugarcane would be the salvation of the Brazilian countryside. To give you an idea, the profitability of the "transparent gold" led to the installation of over 80 sugar processing plants in São Paulo, Goiás, the Triângulo Mineiro, and Mato Grosso do Sul.

It should also be noted that if until the 1970s the struggle was against "top hat farmers" (as a member of the MST once said), from that point on the struggle is against farmers and transnational corporations that invest mainly in the sugarcane fuel and eucalyptus markets, buying or controlling São Paulo's lands and placing local class struggle on another, much more complex level.

The productive-economic control of agribusiness will manifest itself in the reproduction of the political-ideological apparatus. Regarding the Judiciary Power, there are many studies demonstrating the variety of manoeuvres to delay the creation of landless settlements, question existing settlements and of using every legal means to hinder and block the creation of settlements.

In education, Lamosa (2013) draws attention to Agribusiness Education in the schools of Ribeirão Preto. We believe that currently an education focused on "sustainable development" has gained strength, placing itself next to pedagogies based on "affection", "tolerance" and "entrepreneurship", widely disseminated by the State Department of Education São Paulo, as part of the new dictionary of capital.

In a preliminary analysis of the Brazilian High School Curriculum, conceived by capital's organic intellectuals, one can perceive the absence of a radical criticism of destructive production, that is, an analysis that is not adequate for the perception and fight against transgenics, pesticides, synthetic fertilisers and their fundamental pillars—the control of land by capital. Quite the opposite. The student and teacher textbooks talk about knowledge societies and the evolution of science, propagating an idea of a simple "choice" between organic and transgenic products hovering to young workers in public schools. "You decide", as long as you don't fight the landed corporations and the landowners, let alone the "Green Revolution" package.

One particularity of the State of São Paulo is that the same party—PSDB—has been running the state in coalitions since 1994. The so-called São Paulo Social-Democrats promoted a broad counter-reform of the State, based on privatisations, commodification of education and readjustment of the higher education and research complex, reform of technical schools and an expansion of mass incarceration, public–private partnerships and social organisations (Sanfelice 2010; Novaes 2014).

Molina, Arelaro, and Wolf (2015) also highlight the relentless harassment of rural schools by monoculture companies linked to agribusiness.[5] This situation, which repeats itself throughout the country, can be understood through a text that deals with the situation of rural schools in the municipality of Teodoro Sampaio, in the Pontal do Paranapanema region. In this municipality, a company called "Usina Odebrecht Agroindustrial", using several strategies involving the municipal government, community members, school leaders and agents, has inserted itself into rural schools in the region through the "Social Energy for Local Sustainability Program", disseminating and promoting counter-values among teachers, students, and the community. They extoll the "benefits" of agribusiness for the territory, making it difficult to understand the immense contradictions that are hidden in plain sight in this agricultural model. One of the most perverse has been trying to convince the youth of the agrarian reform settlements to give up the greatest victory achieved with the struggle for land, that is, allowing for this means of production to proliferate, convincing the youth to sell their workforce to these monoculture companies. They can even convince many families to lease their lots to these companies.

At the same time, social movements are criminalised. Let us just remember the State's reaction to the Cutrale-MST case in Iaras,[6] the Pinheirinho tragedy,[7] the repression of the Free Pass demonstrations in 2013[8] and numerous aggressive responses to social demands in recent years. The phrase of a former Brazilian president who came from São

[5] For this debate, see Cerioli (1997), Menezes Neto (2001), Leandro (2003), Dalmagro (2003), Caldart (2004), Dal Ri and Vieitez (2008) and Vendramini and Machado (2013).

[6] In 2013, around 300 people occupied Fazenda Santo Henrique, in the municipality of Iaras/Borebi and Lençóis Paulista-SP. The Landless people denounce the land grabbing of 2600 hectares by the company Cutrale. In 2005, the National Institute of Colonization and Agrarian Reform (Incra) notified the company to vacate the area, as the land had been recognised as public. Cutrale, however, ignored the notification.

[7] The Pinheirinho Massacre took place during a repossession operation carried out in January 2012. With an estimated population of 9 thousand inhabitants, Pinheirinho was an immense occupation located in São José dos Campos, São Paulo. The land, which was abandoned, belonged to the bankrupt estate of speculator Naji Nahas and his company, Selecta.

[8] Movimento Passe Livre (MPL) is a Brazilian social movement that defends the adoption of zero fares for public transport. The movement was founded in a plenary session at the World Social Forum in 2005, in Porto Alegre, and gained prominence when it participated in the organisation, in 2013, of the first protests in São Paulo due to the

Paulo, Washington Luis, becomes current once again: "social issues are a matter for the police". To illustrate this, let us remember it was a *paulista*[9]—Domingos Jorge Velho—who was in charge of the destruction of the Quilombo dos Palmares.

On the other side of the battlefield, we have teachers asking for "less bullets and more chalk", homeless people fighting for "more rights and less right-wing", and people affected by dams saying "water for life and not for death". As the fractions of capital that command the State of São Paulo no longer have republican solutions on their horizon, the recurring solution is police aggression (Novaes 2014).

In our view, it is within this context that the scarcity of policies for land redistribution and settlements, in contrast to plentiful policies for financialised corporations, must be analysed—that is, as a project to create *obstacles* for agrarian reform and the annihilate anti-capital social movements. For hard-won agrarian reform settlements, we have sparse, slow, inadequate, disconnected state policies, the diffusion of an utilitarian vision of cooperatives and associations by the Federal and State Government, and an exotic view of agroecology, in which it isn't the fundamental pillar of agrarian policy.

For the corporations, we have "innovation" policies, policies for the expansion and installation of sugar and alcohol plants, industrial parks and hubs, real estate speculation in strategic regions for financial capital, such as Campinas, Greater São Paulo, Ribeirão Preto, Araçatuba, and the Paraiba Valley. Given this scenario of aggressive capital, it is unlikely that workers' cooperatives and agroecology can flourish, as we will see in the section below.

Conceiving Cooperation in the MST

The struggles and resistance to slave labour and against the ills of land monopoly are part of our history (Moura 2014). Several experiences of resistance such as Quilombo dos Palmares (destroyed in 1695), Canudos (1887), the Cabanagem (1840), Contestado (1916) and the Peasant

increase in bus fares, which culminated in protests throughout country after increased police repression against protesters and journalists.

[9] T.N.: The endonym for people from the state of São Paulo.

Leagues (1947 to 1964) were harshly repressed by the Brazilian State representing a pact of elites and landowners with foreign capital.

In the region of Ribeirão Preto, for instance, the Peasant League of Dumont was created with the help of the Brazilian Communist Party (PCB). It was led by João Guerreiro Filho, Pedro Salla, Miguel Bernard and Vitório Negre, militants defending the interests of the peasants. In 1947, after the PCB became illegal, the home of the Guerreiro Family was invaded and searched by state forces (Welch 2010, p. 131–32). Welch (2010) notes that the PCB's rise in popularity between 1945 and 1947 and its electoral success led the government to make the party clandestine in May 1947; the peasant leagues were gradually repressed. Welch continues:

On May 9, the police raided the party at the UGT(General Workers' Union) headquarters and confiscated a long list of political apparatuses and organisational material, including six red invitations for the "Rural Workers of Barrinha", a statute for "Agricultural Salaried Workers" and two monthly receipts for members of the Peasant League of Dumont. Within a day, the police raided Guerreiro's parents' home and took away the league materials he had left there. Six police officers ransacked the house of peasant Pedro Salla, but no documents were found [...] (Welch 2010, p. 145).[10]

The emergence of the MST and other social movements that contributed to the process of "re-democratisation" of the country in the 1980s, through the direct action of workers (with the tactic of occupying unproductive land in large estates) shows the struggle for land was still latent in the scenario of the Brazilian State, which despite harshly repressing these struggles, failed to contain the reorganisation of the working class in the countryside.[11]

This strong stance of struggle and land occupation by organised workers, particularly in the MST, forged the creation of several agrarian reform settlements. The territories, acquired under the organisational

[10] "In September 1949, in the municipality of Tupã, a meeting of militants from the Brazilian Communist Party (PCB) that was holding a Congress of rural workers in Alta Paulista was violently repressed by the police. Three communists and a policeman died in the clash. Despite the great national repercussion at the time, the episode was relegated to oblivion in the history of the city" (Lima 2009).

[11] See Martins (2004), Stédile (1999) and Rodrigues (2013).

influence of the MST, fought to maintain and progress in a more or less independent way, not subordinated to agribusiness and big capital.

Considering that settlements are immersed within a broader space of capitalist nature, the settled territories were not and are not immune to capital's offensive and a possible reconcentration of the settlements if no alternative socio-productive organisation action was taken (Christoffolli, 2012).

After the first settlements were established, it became increasingly clear to the militancy of the MST that the struggle for land could not be limited only to establishing settlements, as capital would not give up its lands without resistance, without trying to convert them to its operating logic, when not directly reclaiming that lost territory. We highlight the process of commodification of the countryside, encouraged via the Green Revolution and all its stages during the military dictatorship, which had a great impact on the productive organisation of Brazil. Landless workers were not immune to this process of dependent industrialisation and commodification of the Brazilian countryside.

Within this context, the Movement saw that besides the occupation and conquest of territories, there was a need to organise and enhance production in established settlement areas. The stance taken was to "develop cooperation as a type of strategic action in view of the advance of capital over redistributed areas, but also as a test run for the future organisation of agriculture in a socialist society" (Christoffoli 2012, p. 171).

It is noteworthy that at first—between 1979 and 1983—the organisation of the struggle for land was greatly influenced by the Catholic Church. In this dynamic, a logic that we can call "Land of God, land of brothers" was disseminated. Productive organisation was thought of less in the perspective of economic results, but more in a perspective of divinity linked to the logic of the church (Mateus 2015).[12]

Organised in family units with small productive scale, low intensity of capital use, labour-intensive technologies, "low" development of the productive forces and almost no insertion in the markets, it was a subsistence economy complemented by the insertion in the market through scarce lines of credit (Christoffolli 2012, p. 172).[13]

[12] See also Stédile and Fernandes (1999).

[13] See also Cerioli and Martins (1999) and Martins (2004).

The concept was that everyone should work together, sharing what they have, and to have subsistence as a goal. In this dynamic, small associations were created, not with an economic objective, but with the aim of building Catholic peasant communities. However, the 1980s saw a growing mass movement in the countryside happening alongside an opening process in the tail end of the Military Dictatorship, bringing the MST to political involvement, with struggles, occupations and achievements that transcended the concepts of the church, leading the MST to discuss its own concept of cooperation (Matthew 2015).

Christoffolli (2012) points out that the first experiences of associated labour, despite being vital for the survival of workers, failed to reach high levels of coverage. Many initiatives were made unfeasible by the difficulties imposed by the state bureaucracy and mainly by the logic of capitalist production (access to capital, technologies, and management).

The difficulties faced in this first moment of the associative and/or cooperative workers' organisations, whether due to the limits of the workers' own concepts or because of the land regularisation process carried out by the State without considering the economic viability and support of the families, led to the constitution of impoverished settlements, causing many workers to seek external employment to supplement their income.

Considering the experiences of this first moment, which was based on collective and semi-collective groups, and later on studies of the experiences of socialist countries (Cuba, China, East Germany, Bulgaria), a reference of cooperative organisation with a "socialist" nature was gradually developed in the MST. Based on the collective use of the means of production and labour, it begins through small collective groups that later become large fully collective cooperatives. A higher level of organisation of cooperatives encompassing entire settlements is called Agricultural Production Cooperatives (CPA).

João Bernardo (2012) describes that, faced with a scenario where rural policies penalised small farmers, the MST focused its efforts on building cooperatives. It was necessary to find means and conditions that would allow workers to have access to financial and technical resources and favourable conditions for production and distribution.

The leap in quality in the Movement's concept would be to socialise everything, all the "factors of production": land, capital, and work. In this scenario, the MST enters a new phase, based on the Cuban experience: the Movement developed its debates and actions, thinking about the concept of a cooperative system for Brazil, a national system with the function of meeting the demands of settlers in different realities throughout the country.

The organisation of cooperatives associated with the consolidation of agro-industries had the objective of inserting agrarian reform products in the market. It was believed that through these actions there would be a qualification of production and consequently social and economic development for settled families.

It is noteworthy that, at that time, the MST was fighting for a classical type of agrarian reform. For Toná (2011), the Movement believed that there was an interest of the ruling class in playing along, and consequently the possibility of inserting peasants in capitalist production, with complementary interests between these and the industry.

In the early 1980s, the number of agricultural cooperatives in the Movement's settlements had increased considerably. In the late 1980s, the MST created the Cooperative System for Settlers (SCA). This process led to the formation of the National Confederation of Agrarian Reform Cooperatives in Brazil (Concrab) in 1992, from approximately 55 production and marketing cooperatives and 7 state cooperative centres. Alongside this, over 40 CPAs were organised, "many entirely collectivist, true socialist islands not only in terms of the organisation of work, but also in terms of certain aspects of domestic life, such as the use of cafeterias and day-care centres" (Bernardo, 2012).

The production cooperatives founded by the MST had legal registrations so that they could enter the market. Their organisation seeks the autonomy of the settlements in addition to production planning and the creation of direct commercialisation routes, eliminating traditional middlemen. In other words, the idea was to have control over the entire production chain (Bernardo 2012).

Despite the euphoria, the challenges and contradictions imposed by the capitalist logic were huge:

> [...] the lack of knowledge and peasant distrust of these collective forms resulted in a partial reversal of experiences, initially breaking up into semi-collective groups and finally in the complete dismantling of several complex cooperation initiatives. The gap between the proposal conceived by the movement, of total self-managed collectives, with the lack of state support, insufficient technical preparation and the contradictions derived from the artisanal organisational consciousness of the peasants were fatal for many

of these experiences and forced a tactical retreat from the movement. (Christoffolli 2012, p. 175)

It cannot be ignored that, at this juncture, state action itself posed several obstacles and difficulties to materialise the Movement's proposals. The lack of understanding and use of institutional legal apparatus to enable self-management and the collectivisation of the means of production and work acted as strong inhibitory agents and using them ran against the MST proposal.[14]

In view of this, mainly through Concrab, which started to focus on actions related to cooperation from 1994 onwards, efforts began to be directed towards creating regional cooperatives for the provision of services and no longer on self-managed collectives. This model allowed greater flexibility for the organisation and agglutination of settled families who produce individually on their lots.

In the midst of this context, the concept of cooperation in the MST seeks to transcend the simple issue of production or even bureaucratic legal organisation. It must also explore the potential of an ideological/political formation necessary for the settlers to participate in struggles and solidarity claims to other categories beyond field workers.

For Christoffoli (2012, p. 55), the MST's current concept of cooperation has a perspective that joins economic and social development by developing humanist and socialist values. He believes that it should not be restricted only to organisational, political, and economic objectives: it should also be understood as a tool of struggle built collectively so that it should contribute to the organisation of workers settled in grassroots nuclei, as well as the practical training of militants (workers) for the political, economic, and cultural struggle.

[14] The Collor government, for example, restricted credit and technical assistance for small-scale agriculture, extinguished the Ministry of Agrarian Reform and Development, emptied the National Institute of Colonization and Agrarian Reform, Incra, and used the Federal Police to repress the MST, ordering state secretariats to be invaded, seizing documents and arresting and instituting legal proceedings against its leaders. This period of repression caused a drop of almost 50% in the total number of land occupations, which dropped from 80 in 1989 to 49 in 1990, and practically half the number of mobilised families, which dropped from 16,030 to 8234 in the same period. In this difficult context, having to survive defensively and relying mainly on its own resources, the MST focused on the development of production cooperatives (Bernardo 2012).

Cooperation in the São Paulo MST in Face of the Capitalist State

As highlighted in the previous topic, during the 1980s land occupations grew as a tactic to force the agrarian reform process. In the State of São Paulo—during the Montoro government (1983–1987)—there were 3 occupations, in the regions of Itapeva and Campinas/Sumaré and in Pontal do Paranapanema. At the time, the Institute of Land Actions (IAF) was created, a state agency that established dialogue with the MST and other social movements in the countryside. Today the MST has around 150 settlements in the State of São Paulo.

In parallel with the transformations in the MST as a whole, the internal discussion of the Movement was already seeking to overcome those first associative and/or cooperative concepts and organisation models founded on the perspective of the church. Their goal was creating cooperatives or associations to improve production and market access with the goal of improving the income of settled families.

Besides creating the IAF, other instruments that no longer exist were also created during the Montoro government, such as credit lines and technical assistance teams for the settlements. The perspective was to move forward with the agrarian reform in the state of São Paulo and, to do so, machines were financed through Caixa Econômica Estadual[15] to enable the creation of associations of machines and services.

The experience of a settlement in the city of Pirituba can be used as a reference. Unlike the currently adopted process, the settlement was not divided into individual lots, but organised into collective plots made up between 10 and 15 families that received support and assistance from the machines and services association. In this sense, the Movement's own concept of cooperation was already under development, aiming to create a cooperative system in Brazil, a national system that sought a certain autonomy of the Movement alongside control and qualification of the production chain.

With the change from the Montoro government to the Quércia government, problems arose for the advancement of agrarian reform in the state, directly affecting the discontinuity of the new cooperative

[15] The Caixa Econômica do Estado de São Paulo was a bank run by the State of São Paulo from 1916 to 2009, when it was incorporated to the federally managed Bank of Brasil (BB).

system. It's not that problems were exclusively due to the change in the state government. Rather, we're pointing out that it had an important influence on the process. With the new administration, a movement against the dialogue of the government with working-class social organisations took hold, causing the replacement of the entire staff of the agency in charge with a new team that was opposed to the MST in the State of São Paulo, indirectly fighting the Movement's experience which excelled in self-management and collective organisation of settlements.

Both in the state and in the federal scenario, with the start of the Collor de Melo government and the adoption of neoliberal policies, alongside the Movement's limits in internal capacity building, the CPAs fell into disarray, many of them succumbing definitively. Of the few remaining in the state of São Paulo, Coopava in Itapeva stands out (Santos 2015). In this context, at the national level the MST resorted to a posture aiming to avoid being completely overwhelmed by the crisis. To this end, regional cooperatives were created to provide services and commercialisation, to meet the demands and strengthen the organisation of settlers regionally.

If we look at the MST's advances and setbacks, it is possible to see that there is an oscillation directly linked to the way governments repress, react and anticipate the actions of anti-capital social movements. At times when the agrarian reform debate advanced and the government, to some extent, gave in, that is, when they created some mechanisms to actually advance agrarian reform, the experiences advanced. In periods when the government reversed course, however, the experiments went into crisis.

As an example, we highlight the federal government under Fernando Henrique Cardoso, which sought to conduct the economic aspects of agrarian reform, in order to isolate the MST politically and dismantle its social base. To this end, in 1998 it created the Banco da Terra, with the aim of replacing occupations with access to land through market mechanisms.

João Bernardo (2012) points out that the most striking strategy taken by Fernando Henrique Cardoso in his confrontation with the MST consisted of supporting family farming and promoting the direct relationship of peasant families with the market, to the detriment of the collective relationship carried out through settler cooperatives.

This action resulted in the blocking of the Special Credit Program for Agrarian Reform, Procera, which was extinguished in 1999, but which was replaced in 1995 by the National Program for the Strengthening of Family Agriculture, Pronaf, whose name is illustrative. "The following year, Pronaf ceased to be just a credit line and became a government program. It was about dismantling production cooperatives, diverting credit to family farming" (Bernardo 2012).

The replacement of Procera by Pronaf put the CPAs in huge financial trouble and forced the MST to stop privileging the formation of cooperatives with a more complex scope, instead presenting cooperation proposals linked to conventional forms of commercialisation that do not guide work processes. Since then, the MST management has given priority to service provision cooperatives.

By initiating this new line of promotion of family farming through Pronaf credits, Fernando Henrique Cardoso achieved a notable strategic triumph, in a presidency that was otherwise not marked by great successes. As in so many other aspects, the Lula government extended the guidelines of the previous government. Pronaf funds quadrupled between the 2002–2003 and 2006–2007 harvests (Bernardo, 2012).

Cooperation and Cooperativism in the MST of São Paulo

We could illustrate our arguments with the experience of the Reunidas Settlement (Promissão—São Paulo State), of COCAMP in Pontal do Paranapanema and of the Sepé Tiarajú Settlement (Serra Azul—São Paulo State).

According to Santos (2007), Fazenda Reunidas was the centre of the social dispute over land in the region. In 1983, the possibility of expropriating the farm for Agrarian Reform began to be considered, which eventually materialised with the First National Plan for Agrarian Reform. The Reunidas Settlement is located in the municipality of Promissão, in the countryside of the state of São Paulo, 450 km from the capital. It appeared in the mid-1980s, contemporary with the reformulations of the National Plan for Agrarian Reform (PNRA). Local discussions on agrarian reform and democracy resulted in the formulation of a concrete demand: the expropriation of Fazenda Reunidas. In June 1985, Fazenda Reunidas appears in the list of properties that could be considered a priority for Agrarian Reform in Brazil.

Also according to Santos (2007), on June 30, 1986, President Sarney signed Decree-Law No. 92,876 expropriating Fazenda Reunidas. In 1987, a Declaration of Possession was made by the Union and the registration and accommodation of families began. At first, 800 were selected, alongside a group from Campinas, which had camped with 350 families, and a Group of 44 families who had been camping there for over a year. Soon after, the Group of 44 received authorisation to use the farm's land for their specific purposes.

The workers who occupied Fazenda Reunidas came from several cities, such as: Lins, Getulina, Promissão, Ubarana, José Bonifácio, Sabino, Birigui, Penápolis, and Campinas and its surrounding regions. These workers lived different histories, marked by the experience of salaried work, sometimes temporary and sometimes permanent, or even by the experience of being sharecroppers, tenants and partners (Santos 2007).

In June 1988, some families began to be settled, grouped by their municipalities of origin. In this phase, most of the newly settled families built their canvas or mud shacks divided into "agro-villages" (from the Portuguese *agrovila*), a way found to organise the settlement socially. These agrovillages were organised by the workers' region of origin, thus, the distribution of families was as follows: 101 families belonging to the Agrovila dos 44; 78 families to Agrovila Birigui; 98 to Agrovila Lins or Central; 12 families belonging to the Grupo dos Doze; 80 families to Agrovila José Bonifácio; 74 to Agrovila de Campinas; 83 to Agrovila Penápolis; 31 families in the Agrovila do Cintra; 30 to Agrovila São João; and finally 42 families belonging to Agrovila São Pedro. A total of 629 families distributed in 8 agrovillages were settled in 19.36 hectares each, except for Agrovila de Campinas, where, due specificities in the land occupation process, each family was entitled to 17 hectares of land on average.

Santos (2007) divides the constitution of the Reunidas settlement into three moments. The first results from the organised action of workers near Promissão in 1986 with guidance from the Pastoral Land Committee—CPT, when 44 families camped on the edge of Fazenda Reunidas, aiming to pressure the government to expropriate the land. In the following moment, in 1987, after the farm was taken over by the Union (October 29, 1987), three hundred and fifty families from the region of Campinas/SP arrived at Fazenda Reunidas, on the edge of BR 153, and formed another camp, called Padre Josimo Moraes de Tavares. These families were organised by the Landless Rural Workers Movement—MST and by a group of the Ecclesiastical Base Communities (CEBs) of the region since 1985. And the last moment, in July 1988, in which the families selected by the selection committee are settled by the Federal Government, organised according to their cities of origin.

The foundation of the settlement's social organisation was the agrovillages, which can be compared to neighbourhoods in urban areas, and are divided according to each family's city of origin. The agrovillages have an area set aside for houses, schools, a health centre, a community centre, and leisure areas (Santos 2007).

As for the process of the Reunidas Settlement's formation, there was no discussion or creation of a Program, project, or Settlement Development Plan with the settled families, nor was a diagnosis of the area of the Settlement Project prepared to come to proposals that contemplated a vision of the settlement's future with production programs, considering a production system to be implemented and economic feasibility analysis and observation of social aspects. Given the delay in the project's implementation, the lack of infrastructure and the lack of definition in the division of the lots, the first families called by the selection committee came to the site with the single aim of occupying the area. In the early 1990s, the vast majority of these settlers moved to the settlement without their families. The peasants built their shacks and made small gardens that were tended only by them, with occasional help from family members.

Santos (2007) observes that there was still no financing for investment, nor were there resources to invest in any productive activity. The choice of productive activities was much more linked to the credit lines that were available than to the aptitude or economic viability of these activities.

Regarding the internal organisation of settlers, the "tractor groups" stand out among the first organising experience the settlers had. This initial organisation resulted from the release of investment credit in the late 1980s, in which over 400 families had access to this financing for the purchase of tractors and implements that were distributed among groups of 10 families throughout the settlement. Hence the name: tractor groups. This experience of group work lasted for two harvests—after that, the groups were disarticulated, and since then, there has been a strong predominance of family work (Santos 2007). For him, "what we see is that there is a cultural problem in relation to these organisation practices. There is a predominance of individual property and a culture of the settler being his own boss, so settlers see the formation of an organisation as a loss of freedom to produce and grow with their family" (Santos 2007).

Also according to the author, the experience of the Padre Josimo Tavares Agricultural Production Cooperative—COPAJOTA was the one that most contributed to the development of workers' organisations in the Reunidas Settlement. Since then, four more organisations have emerged.[16]

In 1995, COPAJOTA had 15 greenhouses growing lettuce, tomatoes, bell peppers, cucumbers and green beans, with a weekly production of over 150 boxes; in dairy farming, there were 90 heads of cattle with a daily production of 400 litres of milk. The advance of surplus gains happened monthly and the value per family was around two minimum wages (R$ 200.00, at the time), not counting production for self-consumption. The only source of funding for new investments was funding from PROCERA and FEAP. This was reflected in 1998, when a high degree of indebtedness could be observed. The cooperative could no longer continue its productive activities, and backlogged payments for financing, loans and debts started to accumulate. In 1999, the cooperative stopped all its activities. It was only in 2004 that the process of individualisation and renegotiation of PROCERA, FEAP and Finsocial debts was resumed in order to regularise the financial situation of its members. This experience of organisation has an extremely important contribution, both in discussions about the different forms of worker organisation, production models, planning and management models, types of distribution of profits, as well as in relation to their role in the development of the settlement (Santos 2007).[17]

Ribas (2004) analysed the case of COCAMP in Pontal do Paranapanema. It was founded on December 28, 1994, by 291 partners at the headquarters of Fazenda São Bento, in Mirante do Paranapanema. Between the end of 1994 and throughout 1995, the cooperative focused exclusively on activities related to the organisation of its documentation. Starting in April 1996, the cooperative started to have physical structures based on its agricultural and agro-industrial projects.

[16] According to Santos (2007), "COPAJOTA represented several advances for its period, 1992 to 1998, but it was also rife with serious internal organisation, management, and political problems. The internal organisation model was based on the experiences from the South of the country, mainly Rio Grande do Sul. The distribution of surplus was through hours worked and not through capital contributions, that is, work prevailed over capital. In 1994, this form was strongly questioned by the associates, as they wanted the distribution of leftovers to be based on ownership of the lot, that is, divided in equal parts by family and not by the hours worked by the partners, resulting in the departure of 17 families and over 30 members, the first 'split' in the cooperative's history".

[17] To learn more about the Reunidas settlement, see also Leandro (2003).

Ribas (2004) states that the genesis of COCAMP is linked to the territorialisation process of the MST in Pontal do Paranapanema. Since the settlements' founding, the movement began to connect the struggle for land with the need for political and territorial management of the settlements (organisation of production, distribution, construction of houses, basic sanitation, etc.).

Ribas (2004), as well as almost all the other researchers mentioned here, observes that the first experiences on cooperative organisation developed by the MST consisted of collective groups, mutual aid groups, based on the practices of the Catholic Church. Subsequently, they encouraged other experiments with machine groups and associations. In the late 1980s, the MST began its experiments with small cooperatives, the Agricultural Production Cooperatives (CPA's), characterised by an entirely collective management of lots and production.

In this author's point of view, the MST leadership learned from these attempts that there was a growing need to enhance mass cooperation. This redefinition resulted in the creation of the Service Provision Cooperatives (CPS's) and from these new experiences discussions about regional cooperatives began. In 1993, COANOL, in Laranjeiras, in the state of Paraná, and COAGRI, in Sarandi, Rio Grande do Sul, were born. In 1994, in Pontal do Paranapanema, COCAMP was created, resulting from a series of discussions to assist groups of families from existing settlements (Gleba XV de Novembro, Água Sumida, Santa Rita, Che Guevara, São Bento and Rosana). COCAMP currently has 2220 members distributed across 12 municipalities in the Pontal do Paranapanema region (Ribas, 2004).

The Sepé Tiarajú Settlement is in the State of São Paulo between the municipalities of Serra Azul and Serrana, near Ribeirão Preto. In April 2000, 100 families occupied an area of approximately 790 hectares of the former Usina Nova União, on land taken by the São Paulo State government from the mill owners, as payment of debts and social taxes.[18]

[18] Scopinho (2006) also observes that the changes resulting from the internationalisation of the economy accelerated the reconfiguration of the productive base, causing a strong impact on the supply of jobs in the state of São Paulo. In regions with an agro-industrial economy such as Ribeirão Preto, the intensification of agricultural mechanisation through the use of mechanical harvesters caused structural unemployment in agriculture, especially in sugarcane-producing regions. Unemployment, both urban and rural, combined with the absence of alternatives for income generation and the State's omission regarding the situation of the unemployed, forced this population to survive

In August 2003, INCRA bought the area, and on September 20th, 2004, the process of settling 80 families distributed in four agrovillages began as a PDS—Sustainable Development Project (Scopinho 2006).

The presence of the MST in the area put organisational models for rural settlements into question. For the movement, a settlement becomes a space for the construction of new social relations insofar as it is structured from an organisational process that considers both the economic dimension and the survival strategies of families and dimensions related to social interaction and political and community participation. This is important in order not to reproduce the social relations prevailing in the Brazilian rural world which, according to movement leaders, occur because the worker, by force of circumstances, organises his time and his life around the family's immediate survival strategies, limiting their political participation in demanding wages and/or better prices for their products. From the MST's point of view, organised settlements can become spaces of economic and political resistance for rural workers (Scopinho 2006).

At Sepé Tiarajú, the main challenge of the organisational process was how to converge sociocultural diversity in the sense of carrying out a settlement project, collectively built on the basis of cooperation and agroecology, with socioeconomic and environmental viability, without denying the traditions, customs, needs and interests of the settlers. For Scopinho (2006), coexistence and dialogue were important strategies to understand the characteristics, thinking and daily work and life of families.

In the settlement, since the camp days, production has always been "agroecological". Due to a lack of resources to buy inputs, seeds and large machines and under the guidance of the MST, the settlers had to rescue old techniques or invent ways of producing that did not require "advanced" technology. The biodiversity of plants and animals in the orchards and improvised gardens around the shacks has always attracted the attention of visitors, which gradually brought back some species of birds and small animals to Fazenda Santa Clara (Scopinho 2006).

precariously from informal work on the outskirts of the so-called "dormitory cities" as freelance rural workers (known as *boias-frias*) or to migrate seasonally to monoculture regions. The desire for social and political participation revealed the most unequivocal evidence of the possibility of creating roots, because it concerned the desire to actively participate not only in that collective, but also to help in the construction of others (Scopinho 2006).

Among the main advantages pointed out about cooperation, Scopinho (2006) highlighted those related to improvements in the organisation, in the planning system and in production management. The settlers saw the social advantages of cooperation, in the sense of facilitating social, political and cultural relations and improving living conditions. They also understood that the rational use of scarce resources reduces production costs, because together they can buy inputs and provide the necessary logistics to produce. Both idealised and abstract meanings were revealed, ranging from increasing the settlers' self-esteem to minimising isolation (Scopinho 2006).

Scopinho (2006) points out that for those who had no experience with rural work, cooperation also meant a space for coexistence that favoured training for work through learning cooperative and agroecological ways of working the land, creating the possibility of getting to know the people who live in the community, of discussing common problems and planning production and life with a smaller margin of error, for improvement of living conditions, for more dignity and social protection from the insertion and coexistence in an organised group, enabling discussions on political and social issues of interest to the settlers, such as the national political situation and the directions of agrarian reform, the causes of rural exodus and the absence or inadequacy of public policies for rural populations.

Scopinho (2006) believes this learning would increase the chances of participation and interference in political decisions at the local, regional and national levels and would help in the creation and maintenance of organisational structures to enable cooperation and training. In short, for the settlers, cooperation could be a new path to new roots, contributing to create conditions for the economic, social and political survival of their communities.

Also according to this author, the contradictory meanings of cooperation were present in individual values and in the way the settlers saw their own condition in the relationships they established with each other in daily life at the settlement. In Sepé Tiarajú, many settlers saw cooperation as an imposition of the MST and INCRA and their responses were controlled by the fear of losing the opportunity to be settled. For this reason, we sought to learn what meanings were attributed by settlers to cooperation in terms of perceived advantages and disadvantages when experiencing it in the daily life of the settlement, mainly from the experience of working collectively.

In the settlement, some challenges arising from individual differences were mentioned, including the belief that cooperative work could be similar, in a hierarchical character, to the wage labour. The perception of these individual differences leads to a crucial issue in the cooperation ideology, which is the notion of justice in the distribution of work and its results. Two important issues are involved. The first concerns the idea of a lack of standardisation tasks and worker behaviour, which is a characteristic requirement of heteromanagement to guarantee the reduction of production costs, the increase of work productivity and quality assurance of the product.

For this researcher, the principle of equality inherent to the cooperative ideology would have the disadvantage of not standardising and not homogenising. Consequently, the second issue refers to a perception that there was a lack of mechanisms for equitable distribution of the results of the work that, according to the settlers, would be related to a lack of rules non-compliance to them. At the same time that they felt autonomous and felt like the owners of their own mechanisms to eliminate social inequalities, they saw themselves as salaried workers and did not see differences between the working dynamics of the collective work in the settlement and the work they did for larger landowners when they were "boias-frias" (seasonal rural workers) (Scopinho 2006).

In summary:

Although the settlers were generally against the idea of forming a cooperative, cooperation was as a social action was very present in the daily lives of families and in small work groups that were formed as needed and just as easily dismantled. We can say that in the Sepé Tiarajú spontaneous cooperation prevailed, organically arising according to the settlers' needs. More than the ownership of a piece of land and income, the settlers hoped to obtain housing, work and physical and psychological security in Sepé Tiarajú, as well as the possibility of social and political participation (Scopinho 2006).

We believe that the Lula and Dilma governments at the federal level, as well as the PSDB government in São Paulo, blocked land reform in its broadest sense. However, some symbolic policies were created by the Federal Government, among which we could highlight the National Policy on Agroecology and Organic Production (PNAPO) and the "Terra Forte" ("Strong Land") Program.

These policies were formally created, but there was and is no political will for the dissemination of agroecology and cooperative experiences, as we have seen in the previous pages. For this to happen, there must be the unification of anti-capital struggles in Latin America and the overcoming of the capitalist state that sustains agribusiness.

Let's look at a news article published by the MST website: "Settlers achieve the creation of the 1st agro-industry of the Terra Forte program in Andradina—São Paulo".

The families settled near Andradina (SP) will be pioneers with the first agro-industry project financed by the Terra Forte Program in the state of São Paulo. Coapar will receive approximately R$ 12.8 million to invest in the agroindustry's construction. For Lourival Plácido de Paula, president of COAPAR, the signing of the agreement means recognition of the work carried out for years in the settlements. The Andradina region was based on beef cattle, but as the settlers and their production developed, rural workers migrated to dairy production. "Industrialization is a necessary element to add value to the raw material produced by the settlements. We hope to contribute more and more to cooperatives and to the development of Agrarian Reform", said the Minister of Agrarian Development of São Paulo, Laudemir Muller.

The Terra Forte Program, launched in 2013 by President Dilma Rousseff, aims to support agro-industrialization projects in Agrarian Reform settlements.

According to Delveck Matheus, from the MST's national leadership, the program results from years of struggle by rural social movements, and was consolidated through a joint action between the movements, the General Secretariat of the Presidency of the Republic, the Ministry of Agrarian Development, the National Supply Company (Conab) and the National Institute for Colonization and Agrarian Reform (Incra). The signing of this agreement is important to enable some old requests made by settled families.

The national president of INCRA, Carlos Guedes, recognised that "this is a project for each and every settler. Each settler who fights daily for their rights and for the recognition of their land. It is a step, not the end of the journey. Our role is to invest and support actions that prioritize the sustainable growth of the settlements. This is a sign that rural workers are on the right path."

With 46 settlements and over 4,500 families, Andradina is the only city in the country to have a Special Secretary for Agrarian Reform. For the city's mayor, Jamil Akio Ono, the investment made in the region through cooperation will benefit the entire city.

The agro-industry will be built in the industrial district of Andradina. With the effective release of the funds, the mayor expects construction to begin in early 2015. The cooperation agreement is the first of a total of 33 projects appreciated by the federal government. Of these, 23 were approved and are awaiting the release of funds. The plan, which has a duration of five years, does not provide a deadline for the transfer of funds" (MST 2015).

This blocking of agrarian reform neutralised the creation of more advanced actions for productive and distributive organisation models in the settlements. While it is true that the PAA and PNAE contributed to improving the income of the settlements, it is also true that these programs gave a utilitarian and economistic character to the workers' cooperatives and associations.

To make matters worse, in the absence of the creation of general conditions of production based on associated labour and agroecology, it is natural that in the few settlements created in the State of São Paulo, things operate in a logic of "every man for himself". Each family tries to produce on their piece of land in an attempt to extract the means for their immediate survival from the land. Resources for infrastructure and housing are promised but not delivered, and with that, the experience of collective life and collective work lived in the camps or in previous experiences tend to fall apart.

It is also worth noting that in the last 10 years MST-São Paulo has had enormous difficulty in mobilising the masses to fight for land, for new ways to organise work and life. These changes stem largely from the attenuation of unemployment in the Lula-Dilma governments, the Bolsa Família Program and other social policies that have changed the scenario over the last 10 years.

Final Considerations: Islands/Settlements Surrounded by a Green Sea of Sugarcane and Eucalyptus

Florestan Fernandes, in his classic book "The closed circuit", sought to show in the late 1960s that the Latin American bourgeoisie had clear responses to popular struggles. Instead of incorporating and absorbing the classic demands for land, better wages and living conditions, access to public education, etc., they responded by "closing the circuit" of demands and worse than that, strangling social struggles, including by the use of torture, murder, other types of extreme violence.

In the current historical moment, the reaction of the capital installed in the State of São Paulo is clear: blocking Agrarian Reform and autocratic/violent repression of popular demonstrations, leading to a kind of "closed circuit" in short circuit, as more and more latent demands appear in society.

This way, one can observe that the few settlements that manage to pierce the blockade of this closed circuit (now in short circuit) become islands surrounded by a green sea of sugarcane and eucalyptus. A good example of the negligent arrangement of the elites that command the State of São Paulo and the Federal Government is the case of the Maracy settlement. Located in the Cabrália Paulista-Agudos region, in the centre west of São Paulo, it reflects what our ruling class wants for the Brazilian people. "Do you want land? There you have it, a settlement full of stumps!"

Bibliography

Bernardo, J. MST e agroecologia: uma mutação decisiva. Passa Palavra, 2012. Disponível em: http://passapalavra.info/2012/03/97517.

Bonduki, N. Origens da habitação social no Brasil. 2 ed. São Paulo: Estação Liberdade, 1999.

Caldart, R. A pedagogia do Movimento Sem Terra. São Paulo: Expressão Popular, 2004.

Cano, W. As raízes da concentração industrial do Estado de São Paulo. São Paulo: Unesp, 2005.

Carone, E. Movimento Operário no Brasil. São Paulo: Difel, 1981.

Cerioli, P. Educação para a cooperação: experiência do curso técnico em Administração de cooperativas do MST. São Leopoldo, UNISINOS-RS, 1997 (Especialização).

Cerioli, P.; Martins, A. Caderno de Cooperação Agrícola - Sistema Cooperativista dos Assentados. n. 5. São Paulo: MST, n. 5, 1999.

Christofolli, P. I. A cooperação agrícola nos assentamentos do MST: desafios e potencialidades. In: Rodrigues, F. C.; Novaes, H. T.; Batista, E. L. (orgs.) *Movimentos sociais, trabalho associado e educação para além do capital*. São Paulo: Outras Expressões, 2012.

Dal Ri, N. M.; Vieitez, C. Educação democrática e trabalho associado no Movimento dos Trabalhadores Rurais Sem Terra e nas fábricas de autogestão. São Paulo: Ícone, Fapesp, 2008.

Dalmagro, S. 25 de maio: vida e luta de uma escola do campo. In: Alternativas de escolarização dos assentamentos e acampamentos do MST. Veranópolis, 2003.

Delgado, G. C. Capital financeiro e agricultura no Brasil. São Paulo/Campinas: Ed. Ícone/ Ed. da Unicamp, 1985.

Dreifuss, R. 1964: A Conquista do Estado – ação política, poder e golpe de classe. Petrópolis: Vozes, 1981.

Ianni, O. Estado e Planejamento econômico no Brasil. Rio de Janeiro: Ed. da UFRJ, 2009.

Lamosa, R.; Loureiro, C. Agronegócio e educação ambiental: uma análise crítica. [Obtido na Internet] 2013.

Leandro, J. B. Curso técnico em administração de cooperativas do MST: a concepção de educação e a influência no assentamento Fazenda Reunidas de Promissão-SP. Dissertação de Mestrado, Faculdade de Educação, Unicamp, 2003.

Lima, A. S. A Militância Comunista e as Lutas Camponesas no Interior Paulista (1945–1958). Dissertação de mestrado. UNESP, Marília, 2009.

Martins, A. Potencialidades transformadoras dos movimentos camponeses no Brasil contemporâneo: as comunidades de resistência e superação no MST. Dissertação de Mestrado, PUC-SP, São Paulo, 2004.

Martins, J. S. O cativeiro da Terra. 9 ed. 1 reimpressão. São Paulo: Contexto, 2013.

Mateus, D. Entrevista a Henrique Novaes, João Henrique Pires e Douglas Silva. Agudos, maio de 2015.

Menezes Neto, A. J. Além da terra: a dimensão sociopolítica do projeto educativo do MST. Tese de Doutorado. Faculdade de Educação, USP, 2001.

Molina, M.; Arelaro, L.; Wolf, S. Resumo do 2° Encontro do Residência Agrária, Brasília, agosto de 2015.

Monbeig, P. Pioneiros e fazendeiros de São Paulo. São Paulo: Hucitec, 1984.

Moura, C. As rebeliões no Estado de São Paulo. In: Moura, C. Rebeliões da Senzala. São Paulo: Anita Garibaldi, 2014.

MST. Assentados conquistam 1° agroindústria do Terra Forte em SP. http://www.mst.org.br/2014/09/25/assentados-conquistam-1-agroindustria-do-terra-forte-em-sp.html, Obtido em 20/01/2015.

Novaes, H. T. A decadência ideológica da política educacional do Estado de São Paulo – notas sobre a precarização estrutural do trabalho docente. Marília – XIV Jornada Pedagógica, 2014.

Novaes, H. T. Reatando um fio interrompido: a relação universidade-movimentos sociais na América Latina. São Paulo: Expressão Popular-Fapesp, 2012.

Novaes, H.; Mazin, D.; Santos, L. (Orgs.) Questão Agrária, Cooperação e Agroecologia. São Paulo: Outras Expressões, 2015.

Oliveira, F. Noiva da revolução. São Paulo: Boitempo, 2004.

Pereira, V. A. Terra e poder – formação histórica de Marília. Marília: Unesp, 2005.

Ribas, A. D. MST, Cooperativismo e território: dinâmica e contradições. In: Thomaz JR., A. (Org.). Geografia e Trabalho no Século XXI. Presidente Prudente: Centelha, 2004, v. 1, pp. 8–40.

Rodrigues, F. C. Educação política dos trabalhadores: a centralidade da exploração do trabalho na análise da questão agrária no Brasil - a contribuição de Octávio Ianni. In: Rodrigues, F. C.; Novaes, H. T.; Batista, E. (orgs.) Movimentos Sociais, Trabalho Associado e Educação para além do capital. São Paulo: Outras Expressões, 2013, vol. II.

Sampaio JR, P. A. Notas críticas sobre a atualidade e os desafios da questão agrária. In: Stedile, J. P. (Org.) A questão agrária no Brasil: debate sobre a situação e perspectiva da reforma agrária na década de 2000. 1 ed. São Paulo: Expressão Popular, 2013.

Sanfelice, J. L. A política educacional do Estado de São Paulo: apontamentos. Nuances (UNESP Presidente Prudente), v. 18, pp. 145–160, 2010.

Santos, S. Aparecida dos. A trajetória do Assentamento Reunidas: o que mudou? 133f. (Dissertação de Mestrado). Instituto de Economia, Unicamp, 2007.

Santos, S. História da Coopava. In: Novaes, H. T.; Santos, J.; Pires, J. H. (Orgs.) Questão agrária, cooperação e agroecologia, vol II. São Paulo: Outras Expressões, 2015, no prelo.

Saviani, D. Escola e Democracia. (Edição Comemorativa). Campinas: Autores Associados, 1998.

Scopinho, R. Controle do trabalho e condições de vida em assentamentos rurais: possibilidades e limites da cooperação autogestionária. Controle do Trabalho e Condições de Vida em Assentamentos Rurais: Possibilidades e Limites da Cooperação Autogestioária. In: VII Congreso Latino Americano de Sociología Rural, 2006, Quito-Equador. VII Congreso Latino Americano de Sociología Rural. Quito-Equador: ALASRU, 2006.

Sodré, N. A farsa do neoliberalismo. Rio de Janeiro: Graphia, 1995.

Stédile, J. P. A questão agrária no Brasil. São Paulo: Atual (Espaço e debate), 1999.

Stédile, J. P.; Fernandes, B. M. Brava Gente: a trajetória do MST e a luta pela reforma agrária no Brasil. São Paulo: Perseu Abramo, 1999.

Tolentino, C. O farmer contra o Jeca - O projeto de revisão agrária do Governo Carvalho Pinto. Marília: Oficina Universitária, 2011.

Toná, N. Elementos de Balanço do Processo de construção da Agroecologia no MST – PR. In: Queiroz, J. G; Toná, N. Nossa História: Agroecologia e as Escolas de Formação do Paraná. Curitiba: Acap., 2011.

Vendramini, C. R.; Machado, I. F. (Orgs.). Escola e movimento social: experiências em curso no campo brasileiro - reimpressão. 2. ed. São Paulo: Expressão Popular, 2013.

Welch, C. A. A semente foi plantada – as raízes paulistas do movimento sindical camponês no Brasil, 1924–1964. São Paulo: Expressão Popular, 2010.

CHAPTER 7

Associated Labour as an Educational Principle: Notes from Worker-Recovered Factories in Brazil and Argentina

Introduction: The Advance of Barbarism in the Late Twentieth and Early Twenty-First Centuries

This chapter aims to address school and non-school education in Latin American Recovered Factories (RF), especially in Brazil and Argentina.

To achieve our goal, we made a brief assessment of the current historical moment and then tried to differentiate anti-capital struggles from localised struggles. In the third section, we made a brief retrospective of the first phase of the struggles of the Recovered Factories (hereinafter RFs) characterised by extreme creativity, embryos of de-alienation of work and adoption of self-management principles. The fourth section deals with how the factories fell back into the order of capital, State co-optation or degeneration into the capitalist market. The professional education projects in the RFs, the demands of content and school forms signalled by the RFs were exposed in the fifth section.

In this introduction, we would like to begin the chapter with the following question: why is it necessary and urgent to fight for the construction of a society based on the free association of producers?

We believe that in the twenty-first century, the world under capital will only produce barbarism if workers don't fight to reverse these barbarous trends. The partial or complete destruction of the welfare state in Europe

H. Tahan Novaes, *Associated Labor and Production in the Age of Barbarism*, https://doi.org/10.1007/978-3-031-51183-7_7

and the continuation of the "hellfare" state in the rest of the world are consequences of an irrational society. To give some examples, the Pope—who resigned—did not look like a pope, Berlusconi held Bunga-Bunga parties and had an explicit relationship with the mafia, Sarkozy expelled gipsies and promoted pension reforms despite demonstrations by thousands of workers.

We've seen before that young Europeans are unemployed. In England, in 2011, young people protested the irrationality of capital and were pedagogically punished. The capital media and the English Government insist on classifying them as "vandals without a cause", obviously disregarding the social roots of the revolt. Stratospheric public debt, neo-fascism, unemployment, underemployment and the return of hunger and misery to Europe are recurring phenomena in a region that has managed to create a somewhat reined-in capitalism that, despite partial decommodification, still orbits around the capital. We are talking about the period from 1945 to 1973.

Capitalism under financial hegemony, turbo-commodification and the return of "primitive" accumulation led Otávio Ianni (2000) to say that we are living in a world of counterrevolution. This offensive of capital can only survive through increased repression, "preventive" wars, the criminalisation of social movements and the assassinations of leaders, such as those that have occurred recently in the Amazon.

At one end, the State punishes social movements and relegates them to social and economic ghettoes; at the other, it promotes an immense drain of public funds to rescue financial institutions during world crises. To cite a Latin American example, Argentinian society reacted to the process of financialisation of its economy in 2001, which had gained strength starting with the coup of 1976, which subdued Argentinian popular forces. In 2001, they fought and said, "Enough! Everyone out!" It was a sign of weariness of neoliberal reforms and the neo-colonisation of Argentinian society. However, the popular and middle-class uprising in 2001 quickly turned into a neo-developmentalist proposal under the hand of the Kirchner family. Today we have an Argentina dominated by multinational corporations, public debt creditors, pension funds, banks and the meat and leather export sector, all of them directly or indirectly promoting the overexploitation of labour, either with a signed portfolio or through underemployment. The country still grows, but the gap between the ruling classes on the one hand and the middle strata of society and the workers on the other has widened.

In Brazil, the integration of parts of the working class into the society of disposable good consumption and precarious employment has only deepened the alienation of workers. If Fernando Henrique Cardoso was a bird of prey that liquidated public assets and destroyed the nation, the pact *of* domination espoused by the Lula-Dilma duo is more sophisticated, as it generates employment and neutralises the struggles of social movements. FHC represented the short-term interests of a voracious capital, while Lula and Dilma represent the capital that learned from the mistakes of the 1990s and resumes strategies of long-term domination, giving a minimum share of the income to the miserable, creating what Paulo Lima Filho and Macedo (2011) had called the "petty bourgeoisie of the miserable".

In the 1990s, in exchange for international "support" for carrying out neoliberal policies and monetary stabilisation, Latin America will receive large flows of short-term financial capital (Dos Santos, 2000). The "response" given to the investment crisis from the 1970s onwards was devised by social scientists belonging to the neoliberal model. One solution proposed by neoliberalism to the crisis of capital accumulation was the gradual reduction of the State's actions in certain roles which carried some "public" interest. Among other phenomena, it was during this time that defenders of this maxim called any state-produced goods and services "inefficient". This pressure led to numerous privatisations. Some Latin American authors summarised the issue with the following expression: Minimum State for workers and for national sovereignty, Maximum State for capital, especially finance capital. Non-market pores or gaps were closed through direct and indirect privatisations of public universities and state-owned enterprises (iron ore, oil, gas, telecommunications, etc.).

The adoption of structural adjustment policies in Latin America in the 1990s deepened deindustrialisation, destroyed state-owned companies, dismantled the wage and labour structure and led to the loss of hard-won social rights and protection (Svampa and Pereyra 2003), leading to increased unemployment, underemployment, social poverty and technological dependence (Dos Santos, 2000). It is noteworthy that this reorganisation of world capitalism was one of the main factors that led to the bankruptcy of many Brazilian companies and the emergence of RFs.

Analysing the impacts of transformations of the 1990s, Azpiazu and Basualdo (2001) note that processes of concentration and centralisation of capital in Argentina were deepened, which resulted in the reconfiguration of economic power in the country. Most of the 200 largest companies are in the hands of foreign capital either through the acquisition of public companies or through association with small "national" groups. For these authors, these privatisation processes have allowed local and foreign conglomerates to consolidate themselves as the hegemonic nucleus of economic power in Argentina, adapting the State to their needs.

In her doctoral thesis, Isabella Jinkings Mello (2008) informs us that the recent transformations of world capitalism point to simultaneous movements of privatisation and deregulation of social and economic life, attack on democratic rights and strengthening of the State's coercive apparatuses, characterising an increasingly penal State. The adoption of "zero tolerance" security policies in the USA is an expression of these pillars of globalised capital under the hegemony of neoliberalism, which disinherits broad social segments from the basic conditions for survival.

Increasingly distanced from social policies and committed to transnational capital, hiring, in the words of Aécio Neves, NGOs to "develop diagnoses" and carry out "professional training workshops [...], working alongside private companies to offer [alienated] job vacancies for prisoners and former detainees", the neoliberal state is increasingly strengthened in its repressive mechanisms, a phenomenon that some authors have dubbed the "emergence of the Criminal State", replacing the so-called European welfare state and the state with mild public characteristics in Latin America (Novaes 2012).

In this sense, the State fulfils a fundamental function by "forcing" the privatisation of public policies that were once under its command. This seems to be the proposal of Governor Aécio Neves, Mayor Kassab and the Governors of São Paulo, when placing Minas Gerais' prisons and São Paulo's schools under the sphere of capital profit, disguised under the guise of Public–Private Partnerships and NGOs. Certainly, this trend is found in other governments in Brazil, including those headed by the Worker's Party (PT).

At the same time, the State maintains its function of creating vocational courses for prisoners to return to work "normally", selling their labour force, obviously without disobeying the established "order" again. In the same vein, it encourages entrepreneurship courses—a very fashionable theme in the 1990s, which blames individuals for unemployment and propagates the pedagogy of total quality.

During the Lula government, curiously, sugarcane, a major user of slave labour in the sixteenth and seventeenth centuries Brazil, became the new "saviour crop". At the same time, it resumes the construction of large hydroelectric plants, plants where the construction site brings unbearable working and living conditions. One must only look at the accusations made by workers in the construction sites of Santo Antônio and Jirau (Rondônia).

But the salvation of the Brazilian "entrepreneur-cracy" was also achieved through a very sophisticated countercyclical policy, the *Minha Casa Minha Vida Program*, which meets the needs of medium-sized "Brazilian" companies, but also international investors eager to reproduce financial capital. Construction companies and large developers, allied with landowners close to cities that want to transform acres into square metres and urban planners who occupy key positions in the state all work to build the space of Brazilian *apartheid* in the twenty-first century in the name of the expanded reproduction of capital. Finally, it should be noted that in 2010, 44% of the Federal Government's budget was committed to public debt, the most important predatory capital in Brazil (Novaes; Benini, 2012). Francisco de Oliveira called this weird animal that is Brazil a platypus. I prefer to say that we are now a great platypus powerhouse.

Still in the words of the aforementioned author, we are living hegemony in reverse, because "The dominated or their representatives can assume moral command of the country as long as they do not touch the economic bases of domination" (Oliveira 2003, p. 7). This is the scenario of twenty-first century Brazil that anti-capital social movements must confront, and this will be the theme of our next section.

Some Differences Between Anti-Capital Struggles and Localised Struggles

Before characterising Recovered Factories, we intend to differentiate the specific struggles that occur here and there from the anti-capital struggles promoted by class social movements or anti-systemic struggles. Darcy Ribeiro (1996) once stated that Brazil is a country in permanent civil war. Since its "birth", every day sees the outburst of specific struggles that we do not even know are happening (for water, housing, daycare, public transport, employment, land, etc.), often silenced by capitalist media. For us, these struggles stem from our platypus characteristic, from a capitalism that can only reproduce itself in a barbaric way.

One-off struggles can be accommodated within the order and so-called "rights of citizenship". They can be sheltered in the form of concessions by the capitalist state and tend to restrict their demands to specific/corporate issues (salary, neighbourhood demands, etc.). Anti-systemic struggles, unlike specific struggles, contest the pillars of capital and to some extent experience, albeit in an embryonic way, what would be a society beyond capital. They give rise to new social relations in the social microcosm in question.

In the lines below, we will give some examples of anti-capital struggles. The struggles of Peasant Women in Rio Grande do Sul take place in the field of substantive equality. They dispute the family hierarchy to the extent that women "don't want to wash their husbands' underwear" and actively oppose the re-establishment of patriarchy in the settlements. At the same time, and in an umbilical relationship to gender issues, labour issues, private property, GMOs and pesticides, direct attacks on transnational corporations appear.

The struggles of the Zanón Bossless Factory are creating new social relations in the factory microcosm. The workers defend a revolution, they have taken back the ceramic workers' union, long dominated by sold-out unions, and they are trying to expand class struggles in the ravaged landscape of Argentina. Zanón functions with a number of anti-capital principles: rotation and revocability of positions, unification and internationalisation of workers' struggles, modification of gender relations in the factory, a new relationship with intellectuals and teachers, attempts to de-commodify production and overcoming the Taylorist-Toyotist organisation of work. Ultimately, it represents an attack against alienated labour, even if confined to the narrow limits of the current context of advancing barbarism and despite its many contradictions (Novaes 2010).

Going into tougher terrain, some social movements timidly contest other dimensions of the commodity-producing system and create solutions for decommodification. This can be seen in the attempts to produce use values with increasing degrees of social control, such as in some movements for housing in Uruguay that approach construction differently and create jobs and income in target neighbourhoods.

The Itinerant Schools, the most advanced Agroecology Centres, the Josué de Castro School and the Florestan Fernandes National School analyse history from a critical point of view and seek to understand the particularities of our "platypus capitalism". They practice pedagogies that insert schools and universities in workers' struggles, that prepare students for collective work, for carrying out socially useful work and democratic management, that theorise and help solve problems concerning the production of healthy and de-commodified foods, in addition to inducing self-managing habits and the understanding of social reality in its totality. Ultimately, they seek to overcome the alienated work for teachers and workers.

The struggles of the CEMOP (Centro de Memória Operária e Popular, Popular Worker's Memory Centre), Flaskô (a de-commodified culture factory), the struggles for free babaçu groves, the struggles of some Recovered Factories in Latin America for control of the work process and adoption of factory floor assemblies, alongside challenges to the ownership of the means of production and attempts to create new social relations in MST settlements are all phenomena which touch on issues vital to the anti-capital social movements of the twenty-first century.

On this last issue, Iasi (2011) recently stated in a lecture at the 5th EBEM [Brazilian Meeting on Education and Marxism] that capitalists should "give the means of production back to workers so that their lives are spared". The "expropriation of the expropriators" (Marx) or "Giving the snail back its shell" (Novaes 2011) is an urgent task, but beware: it can leave the alienation of labour intact (Mészáros 2002). However, the failure of "real socialism" showed us that despite numerous early advances, the experience degenerated. For Mészáros (2007), the USSR created a "post-capitalist society that was not post-capital". The workers contested the means of production, but a distinct body of workers—the party bureaucracy—controlled the strategic decisions of society: how to produce, what to produce and for whom to produce, thus reproducing capital under a new guise. In this experience, the social meaning of work was not changed. To put it another way, commodity production remained intact (Lima Filho and Macedo 2011).

Associated Labour as an Educational Principle in Recovered Factories: Some Positive Aspects

In capitalist corporations, there is a sharp division of labour between those who think and those who execute, between those who work and those who control the means of production. Even within the limits of a labour process that involves countless production chains and countless factories, recovered factories try to overcome the "structural hierarchy of capital" within their microcosm (Mészáros 2002, p. 22); in short, they try to reunify *homo faber* and *homo sapiens*. Decisions are taken in democratic assemblies, workers rotate in strategic posts and positions are revocable. From this point of view, there is a process of partial de-alienation, in the sense of "devolution" of power to workers, at least in the productive microcosm.

The partial devolution of power to the workers in the factories, that is, self-management in the productive microcosm, is quite possibly one of the most important anti-capital struggles in the twenty-first century.

It is worth remembering that, in the late 1920s, Gramsci witnessed the struggles for the formation of workers' councils in Turin, leading him to theorise about the pedagogical role of workers' councils for anti-capital struggles. For him, factory councils were a "wonderful school". The title of this section stems precisely from this: we believe that associated labour is extremely pedagogical, but obviously, it does not single-handedly exhaust the possibilities of education in a possible and necessary transition beyond the capital, as we will see in the section on professional education.

Actions were carried out in the Recovered Factories (RFs) to increase knowledge of the work processes in the factories. This is a partial overcoming of the alienation of labour coexisting alongside elements that preserve the alienation of labour. From this, we can infer that the exercise of self-management in the productive microcosm carries with it the need for non-bureaucratisation of unions and involvement in broader struggles.

Some RFs overcame a part of the divisions of capitalist labour to the extent that knowledge, which was retained in the hands of a few, began to be socialised. The dependence on the "foreman engineers" and the complex work done by them has been modified to some extent. Here it is also important to remember that in the Carnation Revolution (Portugal) if most engineers fled with their bosses, a few, influenced by their beliefs, helped to overcome the Taylorist organisation of work. If they fought solely for wages, they would certainly not stay in factories taken over by workers.

In the most advanced cases, they start developing the outline of a method to overcome the wage system based on the principle of: "from each according to his ability, to each according to his need". In other cases, there is a closer approximation of withdrawals (equivalent to wages) and the creation of funds, either to support the struggles of other workers, to allow some workers to access higher education or to improve year-end earnings, etc.

It is important to highlight the case of an RF in Argentina where they created a fund to improve the "wages" of workers who had higher spending on children. This reminds us of the principle of "substantive equality" developed by Mészáros based on the writings of Babeuf and Marx. To articulate his argument, Mészáros resorted to the following paragraph by the French socialist Babeuf:

> Equality must be measured by the ability of the worker and the needs of the consumer, not by the intensity of work or the quantity of things consumed. A man endowed with a certain strength, when he lifts a weight of ten pounds, works as much as another man with five times his strength who lifts fifty pounds. He who, to quench a burning thirst, drinks a large mug of water, enjoys no more than his comrade who, less thirsty, drinks only one glass. The goal of the communism under discussion is equality of jobs and pleasures, not of consumable things and workers' tasks. (Babeuf, *apud* Mészáros 2007, p. 42)

Certainly, this principle does not exhaust the problems experienced by anti-capital social movements, but we believe that it also helps to guide the struggles of more advanced "feminist" movements and other social movements connected to generational and ethnical causes that try to implement the principle of substantive equality. In this regard, we should remind the reader of a case reported by our friends at the Usina Collective (a group of architects and social scientists who provide advice to social movements). They said that, at a joint effort, at first they thought of dividing the work "equally" among all members. Soon, they realised that there were elderly people, people who had been stroke victims and workers with other problems who could not perform heavy work "equally".

Even in the most advanced cases of RF, associated labourers do everything to avoid having a differentiated status in relation to outsourced workers, that is, they fight for everyone to be cooperated. It is important to highlight this fact because we will see below that a reasonable share of RFs is hiring outsourced workers. In our point of view, this represents a symptom of their degeneration.

Last but not least, it should be remembered that FaSinPat Zanón and, to some extent, Flaskô—occupied factories—are bringing together "class-aware" workers, which can be interpreted as an attempt to unify portions of the Argentine working class that have goals laying beyond the capital.

We can already say that FaSinPat Zanón is one of the few RFs that has not succumbed to accommodation and degeneration under pressure from the capitalist market. It remains alive and well and its struggle is renewed every day. All these principles exercised daily in the RFs are pedagogical—which allows us to state that associated labour is an educational principle. They also allow us to state that these struggles will be fundamental for the disalienation of work, and they acquire some characteristics of anti-capital struggles.

In Brazil, we have about 68 RFs in the metallurgical, textile, footwear, etc. sectors, mainly in the states of Rio Grande do Sul and São Paulo (Henriques et al. 2013). In Argentina, we have 200 RFs, smaller than their Brazilian counterparts, but with a greater degree of radicalism in their struggles. It is evident that RFs play a more qualitative than quantitative role, as Professor Dermeval Saviani (2012) pointed out. Contrary to what many expected, we didn't have a huge expansion of experiences.

The Tendency to Accommodate the Recovered Factories Within the Order of Capital: Some Negative Aspects

In the research we carried out in the RFs, even with all the positive aspects regarding the productive microcosm, we were unable to find a document that points to a horizon beyond capital, that is, a theory and a consistent practice that points to a society beyond capital.

The vast majority of RFs entered a "well-behaved" cycle, where workers seem to be "happy" with the improvement in revenue, production and wages, characteristics seen as "petty-bourgeois" or reformist in the history of the cooperative movement.

In other words, everything suggests that most RFs are "content" with what they have already achieved. As an aside, this same trend reproduced in a more or less similar way among the share of Brazilian workers who were "integrated" into the mass consumption market. Alienation is perpetuated from the perspective of the work performed—work without social meaning—but it also materialises in fetishising consumption.

This does not mean, however, that the learning generated by workers' struggles in the late twentieth and early twenty-first centuries can be neglected. In the 1990s, in the face of the crisis of unemployment and underemployment in Latin America, the increase in misery and hunger, the RFs played a very important role. They were configured not only as forms of resistance but also to build "alternatives" in the face of fleeing bosses and bankruptcy of factories. At a time when it was said that there were no alternatives, that only productive restructuring, neoliberal counter-reforms and the advance of turbo-commodification were possible, these struggles were fundamental.

Let us also remember that for Pinassi (2009, p. 34), the working classes were, and continue to be, so deeply struck and jettisoned from an authentic perception of the dominated class that, especially in situations of deeper crisis, their ideological horizon manifests itself much more as a function of historical contingency than of their more than necessary revolutionary potentiality.

Social movements such as that of the *piqueteros* in Argentina, the Landless Movement (MST) in Brazil, Union of Housing Movements (UMM), among others, have found it difficult to carry out anti-systemic struggles that are autonomous in relation to the State, the market and corporations. In our point of view, the difficulty of independence from the State is not exclusive to the RFs. We repeat, it is something difficult, but not impossible to exercise in this twenty-first century. The current context of capital's offensive creates difficulties but does not preclude the existence of anti-capital practice.

For Antunes (2010), even noting a huge downturn for social movements, there are "potentially revolutionary social forces". According to the author, the experiences of the twentieth century were not able to defeat the socio-metabolism of capital. They were unable to break with the logic of capital. For him, the struggles may even begin in the national space, but they have to expand. Still for this author, if even one of the tripod's feet—fetishised work, state and capital—remains, the system recovers. He notes that there in Latin America we see a return of socialism to the public debate. The theme is at least present, and he reminds us that 10 years before, those who proposed it were considered laughing stock.

On the other hand, this difficulty also stems from a deep theoretical crisis, which even shook Marxism. In this sense, a good theoretical arsenal that needs to be analysed more calmly in this twenty-first century is the one offered by István Mészáros, one of the few Marxist intellectuals who followed the trails left by K. Marx. Alongside Mészáros, other older social thinkers who did not succumb to Stalinist thought could be mentioned: R. Luxemburg, G. Lukács, A. Gramsci, J. Mariátegui, Caio Prado Jr. and Florestan Fernandes. In the field of self-management, K. Korsch, M.

Adler, M. Tragtenberg, João Bernardo and Claudio Nascimento also gave us fundamental contributions.

Without the advance of this theory beyond capital in Latin America, anti-capital social movements will have a hard time advancing practices beyond capital.

At the same time, if workers do not advance in anti-capital practices, intellectuals remain "lost" in the sea of formulas to change the postmodern world.

In recent books and articles, we have tried to show that RFs have enormous difficulty in circumventing monopolies and oligopolies. If at the beginning of the twentieth century, cooperatives and associations faced an enormous difficulty of survival in monopolistic and oligopolistic markets, let us imagine the problem in the current context, in a society totally subject to financial capital.

In a nutshell, because they are umbilically linked to production chains dominated by monopolies and "financialized" oligopolies, RFs tend to reproduce the production parameters "given" by the market. As José Ricardo Tauile (2002, p. 109) reminds us, "the market is ruthless". Direct contact with the market creates a trend of overexploitation of labour, return of wage differentiation, outsourcing processes and therefore the imposition of differences between cooperative members and non-member workers. This is not a law set in stone, but it is a reasonably powerful force that RFs alone have not been able to overcome.

Finally, FRs tend to degenerate into capitalism and this can be seen from the emergence of (a) new bosses, managers or technocrats in cooperatives and associations, that is, the formation of a new technocracy that recomposes the overexploitation of work and bureaucratises decisions; (b) increases in the wage gap in different functions; (c) decrease or absence of ties with other RFs or social movements; (d) the search for public funds without questioning the role of the capitalist state in the reproduction of class society; (e) the search for public funds to increase the qualification and attitudes of workers necessary for survival in the market, with a view solely and exclusively to improving the productivity of the cooperative or association, just like any other company.

Qualification Projects for Recovered Factories

In this section, we would like to highlight the systematic education processes adopted by the RFs. With this, we will try to show the contradictions in the qualification demands of RF workers. The first qualification demands arise due to the pressure of ANTEAG (National Association of Workers in Self-Management Companies), an entity that unfortunately ceased to exist under the Fernando Henrique Cardoso government. Its actions were articulated with the activities developed within PLANFOR, one of the neoliberal government's qualification policies from the perspective of "each to his own". In the Lula government, the policies of qualification and schooling of the RFs and other experiences of cooperativism and associativism took place within the actions of the PNQ/Proesq[1] and also through the creation of the Training Centres in the Solidarity Economy (Alaniz 2012).

In general, we had short courses aimed at RF leads to socialise the survival strategies of the "companies" in the capitalist market. To a lesser extent, there were courses for factory floor workers.

These capacity-building projects were demanded directly by entities representing the factories and mediated by public managers working in the National Secretariat of the Solidarity Economy (Ministry of Labor and Employment), at first by ANTEAG, and later also by Unisol-CUT, another entity that brings together RFs.

In a country that has undergone an incomplete and conservative bourgeois revolution, a country that has never built a school system to ensure the masses are literate, it goes without saying that RF workers have a low level of education, and at most a Taylorist training.

The vast majority of them graduated and qualified at their jobs, in the processes of struggle and cooperation between capital and labour in the daily life of the factory, something quite typical of a Taylorist pattern, in which the factory is a powerful "educational agency", which at the same time educates and de-educates workers (Silva 2005, p. 2). Others were trained in courses that socialise technical knowledge and internalise the values of the hegemonic Taylorist standard in the 1980s marked by hierarchy, respect, subordination, cooperation and consent with the bosses, technical knowledge for work in metallurgy, in the textile, footwear, or other industries.

[1] National Qualification Plan—Special Qualification Projects.

We have a few researchers in Brazil who have focused on school and non-school debates in the RFs, in addition to the training debate. We must rescue the research of Erika Alaniz (2007) carried out in the master's degree that resulted in the book *Professional Qualification: a study of educational practices in a self-managed company*, as well as in her doctoral thesis, defended in 2012, which reflects on the educational projects prepared by the National Secretariat of the Solidarity Economy (SENAES-MTE), especially the Training Centres in the Solidarity Economy.

Furthermore, the works of Candido Vieitez and Neusa Dal Ri (2001) on the educational project of Anteag and Dal Ri and Vieitez (2008) deserve to be highlighted, which sought to observe the pedagogical project of ANTEAG and the MST. Tiriba and Fischer (2009) focused on the knowledge of associated labour.

In ANTEAG courses, the first thing that caught our attention was the name given to the courses: "MBA in Self-Management", which is a contradiction in terms. The question remains: why did they give the course this name? Was there no other word to symbolise what they intended or is the name consistent with the purposes of the project? Did the entity want to make ex-workers from the factory floor and administrative sectors become "executives" and managers?

ANTEAG also created some booklets, more focused on factory floor workers. This material reached our hands at the time of the creation of the "booklets" of the Technological Incubator of Popular Cooperatives at Unicamp, at the time we were doing the Incubator's training course. Marilena Nakano was one of the educators hired in 1998 by ANTEAG to prepare the material used.

In Argentina, we should highlight the "popular bachilleratos" that use RF spaces to teach Youth and Adult Education classes for workers of all ages in the neighbourhoods around the RF. These courses have great autonomy in relation to the State and are given by militant intellectuals from various Argentine associations (Elisalde and Ampudia 2011).

Unisol (Central de Cooperativas e Empreendimentos Solidários), connected to the CUT, hired cooperative workers to transfer their specific knowledge to other cooperatives, Senai technicians to solve specific problems, lawyers with experience in the area of cooperativism, associativism to teach courses on fiscal council, etc.

According to Alaniz (2007), in associated labour organisations there is a "new configuration of power", which we could call self-management power. For her, the degree of democratisation of the relations of a given organisation conditions the expansion or not of the education of its workers, although there is not always the effective appropriation of decision-making spaces by the collective.

The expansion of professional training occurs as new intellectual, behavioural and affective attributes become part of the profile of workers' collectives, resulting from the still embryonic social relations that begin to be established from the moment they act on the management of the organisation in its foundations (Alaniz 2012). According to this author, by expanding the training of the worker collectives, there is also a greater possibility to deepen direct democracy in view of self-organisation in labour relations, because as workers appropriate knowledge about management, they will have greater conditions to interfere in decision-making processes:

> In self-managed companies, training transcends technical issues and it is evident that qualification refers to the way social relationships are established in the factory. Training is central for self-managed companies, since collective management requires everyone to participate in the decision-making process, with the training of all cooperative members to choose the best strategies, visualize the possibilities of future investments, enabling cooperative development and survival in the market. (Alaniz 2007, pp. 274–275)

For this researcher, the concept of professional training is closely intertwined with the dynamics of new forms of power relations that point as a possibility in associated labour organisations. She concludes that the capitalist training model is not suited to the needs of the associated labour. We could also add that existing institutions have not provided sufficient responses to the challenges they face.

For Alaniz (2007), education is also a fundamental issue, and it is necessary that it allows workers to create forms of organisation and technologies appropriate to the nature of collectivised work. Therefore, the formal education system, either because of the contents it teaches, the fragmentation of knowledge regarding the world of labour or even due to the hierarchy of the organisation of pedagogical work, tends not to meet the needs of self-managed production.

Dal Ri and Vieitez (2008) also highlight another dimension: political training or training for self-management. Although this dimension is crucial for the survival of organisations under the assumptions of associated labour and democracy, little has been observed in terms of educational "investment" for this purpose.

These researchers found that there are few resources for the systematisation of educational practices that arise in the associated labour process. Alaniz (2007) observed that despite ANTEAG having carried out this type of training with the factories it advised, at Cooperjeans—the company she studied—the courses were located more in the administrative and fiscal councils and rarely addressed the collective of workers, which seems to be a problem or a serious limit.

For her, learning self-organisation already begins when workers collectively take over their organisation. However, the presence of elements inherited from the "culture" of previous labour relations is supported on the objective bases by reinforcing these elements due to the contingency of being inserted in a commodity-producing system, a factor that functions as a centrifugal force that departs from the objective of self-government.

Alaniz (2012) also reminds us, from the reading of Dal Ri and Vieitez (2008), that it is essential that associated labour organisations break with the immediacy of only generating "work and income" and seek to be linked to the broader struggle of class-based social movements, otherwise there will be a tendency for a downturn of these self-organisation initiatives. In this sense, according to the aforementioned authors,

> [...] political education, based on the criticism of capitalism and the proposal to overcome it through socialism or real democracy, constitutes one of the forces capable of inducing OTAs [Associated Labor Organisations] to participate in workers' social movements.
>
> Paradoxically, in the OTAs we examined, either directly *in loco* or indirectly through the examination of the literature, we could not point out a single example in which the action of formal political education as a catalyst for the participation of OTAs in the general workers' movement is sufficiently clear. In OTAs, it is common to find some kind of more or less formalized educational activity, such as literacy courses, elementary school, short technical courses and several others. Courses aimed at the study and dissemination of democratic self-management are practically absent in OTAs. This type of educational activity was developed, for example, by the National Association of Workers in Self-Managed Companies (ANTEAG). However, the courses aimed at clarifying what self-management and cooperatives are, when they do take place, are centreed on associated labour and

its economic development. The necessary connection between the OTAs and workers' more general struggles is often missing. (Dal Ri and Vieitez 2008, p. 25)

In the OTAs under study, we did not find noteworthy political education courses that focused on a broad-spectrum view of capitalism or the current or historical struggles of the working class. (Dal Ri and Vieitez 2008, p. 31)

"Senai Does Not Serve Us": Notes of an Education and "Training" Beyond Capital

In the research we carried out, which focused on the observation of the preservation and overcoming of alienation in RFs, we could indirectly observe two trends of workers' demands in relation to training and education.

A first trend—the most conservative of all—calls for a greater participation of agencies such as SEBRAE [Brazilian Support Service for Micro and Small Businesses] in the RFs to promote "technical" assistance and worker training. This trend, although a minority, gained strength with UNISOL—which does not share exactly the same principles as SEBRAE, but advocates for the survival of RFs in the capitalist market and, therefore, demands a type of "technical" assistance very close to that of conventional factories. Ultimately, proposals such as these fall into the fetish of the State and technical assistance within the parameters of capital, precisely because they believe that state agencies of technical assistance, training and education serve the interests of workers. We do not deny the inherent contradictions of these institutions and the existence of some well-intentioned technicians. However, it is unlikely that they contain the educational content and form necessary for education beyond capital.

A second trend states that "Senai does not help us",[2] even without knowing how to develop the complexity of this problem in theoretical terms and without being able to forward "solutions" in daily practice. These workers tend to deny capitalist education and training, but they do not yet have the necessary elements for the theoretical and practical overcoming of this problem. We have here a beautiful field of research and

[2] SENAI: National Industrial Apprenticeship Service.

theoretical development for the coming years that we can only outline in the pages below.

It is very likely that if these workers fight for substantive educational changes, they will create professional education experiences that combine non-alienating work and qualification for the production and reproduction of life on a self-managed basis. Research can play an essential role in the emancipation of workers, so we believe that studies already carried out in Latin America and others that may arise should rescue and update the debate on education beyond capital, interrupted at some moments in the history of the twentieth century, and which has been rescued by some schools of Marxism. These lines of research should also be resumed to put into historical perspective the indispensable need to build a society beyond capital in this twenty-first century.

In this sense, the anti-Marxist Stalinist aberration caused serious damage to the advancement of educational theory and practice beyond capital. At the same time, the advance of fascism in Europe also had similar consequences. Recent research shows that Stalin's rise to power led to the assassinations, poisonings, or exile of countless intellectuals committed to human emancipation. To name a few, M. Pistrak, V. Shulgin, Krupskaya, Lunacharski, etc. (Freitas, 2009).

The civil-military coup of 1964 in Brazil and other military coups that swept Latin America interrupted a cycle of rising workers' struggles. From this point of view, in the twenty-first century, there is an urgent need to resume the contribution of socialist pedagogy and its role in a radical transformation that transcends alienated work. In the same vein, it is vitally important to rescue the theory of the Brazilian revolution and to update it based on the changes that have occurred in Brazilian capitalism in the last 40 years (Rodrigues 2013).

If the denial of capitalist education—"Senai does not serve us"—was identified by some workers and, from another perspective, by Latin American intellectuals, the same can no longer be said about what to put in the place of state schools, vocational schools and state universities. This leads us to the following questions: to what extent can the state school be reconfigured in a context of "political economy of miseducation"? (Lima Filho et al. 2012; Minto 2011), that is, the qualitative worsening of state schools and universities destroyed or commodified? To what extent should autonomous social movement schools be developed? Can social movements "pull" the state school in their direction, towards their purposes and needs, in the absence of a revolution?

To some extent, Iasi (2011) gave an answer to this problem in a lecture at the 5th EBEM. Faced with the current challenges:

> either you give up and become postmodern or you go to the class to seek the political, educational and organisational mediations necessary to build the overcoming movement. In this work, formal and non-formal education is essential. I believe, like Paulo Tumolo, that formal education is necessary, but insufficient. It is essential that the class create its own educational spaces, because it is not true that knowledge, considered neutral in this stance, helps us in our tasks simply because it is accumulated human knowledge, simply by socializing it. Knowledge is coated with ideology, directed to a functionality of reproduction and guarantee of order. In the Gramscian point of view, workers must make their inventory, rescue the most developed universal knowledge, forming bases for the constitution of their class autonomy, unveiling the political foundations and class interests that permeate knowledge and educational forms. This is a task that involves the socialization of knowledge in formal spaces, but also requires that we know how to build our own formative spaces, since certain themes and educational forms require their own independent spaces. (pp. 129–130)

Ever since he conceived a Popular University (PUP) project for the Vale do Ribeira (SP) in 1999, a project we took part in, Lima Filho (1999, 2008) has been theorising and trying to put into practice a university created entirely for the emancipation of workers. To do so, he believes that one should start with the ends, the objectives of a Popular University and the choice of its staff. Such a Popular University would operate a "regional revolution" with a view to conscious and planned action on social reproduction in order to achieve increasing degrees of self-determination.

Even permeated by struggles that shape Brazilian state schools, we must recognise that capitalism under financial hegemony destroyed the state school. There are many studies that show the increase in functional illiteracy, even in Europe. If in the period of 1945–1973, the pressure of workers and the needs of capital led to processes of universalisation of education with a reasonable quality, in the recent period educational and training projects are increasingly permeated by the needs of a "pedagogy of total quality" for a small group of workers and a pedagogy of illiteracy, of pedagogy for precarious work or the pedagogy of unemployment for a good portion of humanity.

A good way to see this civilizational crisis is through the world of labour, where we have a mass of unemployed, outsourced and underemployed people, and a smaller share that has formal contracts, labour rights, better training, but still does not escape overexploitation of labour. This is one of the faces of capitalism under financial hegemony, called by Mészáros as "structural crisis of capital", a crisis that cannot be confused with catastrophe.

Based on what was exposed in the previous lines, at least in the short term and in a defensive context, we believe that the educational centres of class-based social movements should rescue some pillars of pre-Stalin Soviet schools, adapting and enriching them from the contributions of historical materialism in the last 70 years. They must rescue the theoretical accumulation of Latin American Marxism, whether in the educational field or in the field of critical thinking, in addition to the international Marxism heir to Marx's thought, to develop a theory and practice beyond capital.

In an offensive context, in view of a revolutionary leap permeated by actions contesting private property and advocating for the control of the means of production by freely associated producers and decommodification, the educational field—school and non-school—should adopt the pillars below. These principle are based on the pedagogy of self-organisation/creation of new social relations in the school; the performance of Socially Useful Work in schools; preparation for the struggle; use of the method of thematic complexes/study from the totality with a view to understand the socio-metabolism of capital within a totalising, dynamic and contradictory perspective, which combines totality and particularity; topicality: insertion of the school in the contemporary struggles of society; aesthetic education: preparation for the understanding and construction of non-market culture; physical education for the development of the human body; study of history from a materialist point of view and rescue of the Theory of the Brazilian Revolution; exercise of unalienated work, closely linked with self-management and the non-separation between conception and execution, that is, the school must prepare for collective and unalienated work; socialisation of historically accumulated knowledge and at the same time the realisation of a balance of the science of capital, that is, how science and technology are not neutral, carrying out an *inventory* and *filter* of the productive and destructive forces created by capital and the development of technoscience for human emancipation, with a view to the complete decommodification of society and self-government by freely associated producers.

Final Remarks

Capital's irrational responses to the contemporary world crisis—which cannot be confused with catastrophe—once again pose the challenge of building a communist society in the twenty-first century.

History has already shown us that self-management is possible. Marx showed us in several of his writings that it is possible to build a society without social classes, without bosses, that overcomes the wage system and the state. He also said that cooperatives and associations outline what would be a higher form of production, even if they reproduce all the defects of the capital mode of production.

Work activity can make social sense, it can become associated labour, there can be increasing degrees of control of the production and reproduction of material life and a total decommodification of life. Likewise, the overcoming of hierarchy in factories and the urgent need for global coordination of production by freely associated producers within a revolutionary project are challenging themes for this new millennium.

We believe that self-management is possible and necessary as a totalising proposal. For us, the problem of Latin American workers is not limited to work in the *strict* sense. The fragmented, segmented, dispersed and diffuse departmentalised "solutions" implemented by one-off struggles will no longer do in the twenty-first century. But we must not forget that capital tries to directly or indirectly co-opt any form of emancipation, bringing it into the fold. In this sense, it only takes one step for workers' resistance strategies to be transformed into entrepreneurship, social responsibility, etc.

On the other hand, the structural crisis of capital, its uncontrollability and destructive advance, tend to create new struggles that oscillate between the search for specific rights and the conformation of anti-capital struggles that call into question the main determinants of the sociometabolism of capital (Mészáros 2002). In this regard, associated labour is a fundamental educational principle, insofar as it surpasses—embryonically—alienated work. At the same time, we already have numerous more autonomous education strategies in Latin America that to some extent escape the control of the State and the "social responsibility" of corporations that can be inserted in the field of anti-capital struggles. We could highlight the Itinerant Schools of the MST, the Zapatista schools, the most advanced Agroecology Centres of the MST and the creation of the Florestan Fernandes National School. All these schools have played a fundamental, albeit insufficient, role.

We have seen in this chapter that this insufficiency is the result of historical contingencies and the absence of an educational theory beyond capital in unions, parties and social movements that theorise the role of school and non-school education within a project of overcoming class society.

In relation to the upper end of our precarious educational system—the public university—in our doctoral thesis, we seek to observe that there are a few "niches" of critical thinking (Leher 2008), but they survive as hostages in the enemy citadel: they can even survive and create some deeper relationship with social movements, but they do not have the power to help workers in a possible and necessary transition beyond capital (Novaes 2012).

The educational struggles of the twenty-first century must necessarily create parallel systems that are independent of the state and, at the same time, revolutionise the state educational system. However, here we will have a huge problem to be solved, since the state system consists mainly of educational workers coming from private universities, temporary and occasional school workers working in two or three schools, teachers without working and retirement conditions, who tend to reproduce the dominant ideology.

Bibliography

Alaniz, E. P. A política pública de formação para economia solidária no Brasil (2003–2011): análise de um projeto PROESQ/PNQ executado pela Rede Abelha/RN e do CFES nacional. 2012. 371 f. Tese (Doutorado em Educação) – Faculdade de Educação, Universidade de São Paulo, São Paulo, 2012.

Alaniz, E. P. *Qualificação Profissional: um estudo das práticas educacionais em uma empresa de autogestão*. São Paulo: Editora da Unesp, 2007.

Antunes, R. *Palestra*. VI Colóquio Internacional Marx e Engels. Unicamp, IFCH, outubro de, 2010.

Azpiazu, D.; Basualdo, E. *Concentración económica y regulación de los servicios públicos*. Obtido em: www.wilsoncenter.org/topics/docs/concentración%20economica.doc. Retirado em junho de 2007, 2001.

Dal Ri, N. M.; Vieitez, C. Educação democrática e trabalho associado no Movimento dos Trabalhadores Rurais Sem Terra e nas fábricas de autogestão. São Paulo: Ícone, Fapesp, 2008.

Dos Santos, T. Teoria da dependência: balanço e perspectivas. Rio de Janeiro: Civilização Brasileira, 2000.

ELISALDE, R.; AMPUDIA, M. "Movimientos sociales y escuelas populares de jóvenes y adultos. Notas sobre la construcción de un proyecto de educación popular". Marília, Mimeo (impresso), 2011.

Freitas, L. C. A luta por uma pedagogia do meio: revisitando o conceito. In: Pistrak, M. M. A escola-comuna. São Paulo: Expressão Popular, 2009, pp. 8–100.

Henriques, F. C. et al. *Empresas recuperadas pelos trabalhadores*. Rio de Janeiro: Multifoco, 2013.

Ianni. O. O declínio do Brasil-nação. Estudos Avançados, 2000.

Iasi, M. Educação, consciência de classe e estratégia revolucionária. Revista Universidade e Sociedade, Distrito Federal, n. 48: 122–130. July 2011. (Transcrita a partir da palestra no 5° EBEM – Encontro Brasileiro de Educação e marxismo – Florianópolis, abril de 2011).

Leher, R. Reforma Universitária de Córdoba, noventa anos. Um Acontecimento Fundacional para a Universidade Latino-americanista. In: Sader, E.; Gentili, P.; Aboites, H. (compiladores). La reforma universitaria: desafíos y perspectivas noventa años después. - 1a ed. - Buenos Aires: CLACSO, 2008.

Lima Filho, P. A. Carta sobre a Universidade Federal da Grande Fronteira Sul. Campinas, Impresso, outubro de 2008.

Lima Filho, P. A. O Projeto Universidade Popular. São Paulo, impresso (mimeo), 1999.

Lima Filho, P. A.; Macedo, R. A poeira dos mitos: Revolução e contrarrevolução nos capitalismos da miséria. In: Benini, É.; Sardá De Faria, M. S.; Novaes, H. T.; Dagnino, R. Gestão pública e sociedade: fundamentos e políticas públicas de economia solidária. São Paulo: Outras Expressões, 2011. pp. 150–182.

Lima, A. Guhur, D. Toná, N.; Noma, A. *Reflexões sobre a educação profissional em agroecologia no MST*: desafios dos cursos técnicos do Paraná. In: Rodrigues, F. C.; Novaes, H. T.; Batista, E. L. (orgs.) Movimentos Sociais, Trabalho Associado e Educação para além do capital. São Paulo: Outras Expressões, 2012.

Mello, I. J. Sob o domínio do medo: controle social e criminalização da miséria no neoliberalismo. Tese de doutorado, Unicamp, 2008.

Mészáros, I. O desafio e o fardo do tempo histórico. São Paulo: Boitempo, 2007.

Mészáros, I. Para além do capital. São Paulo: Boitempo, 2002.

Minto. L. W. A educação da "miséria": particularidade capitalista e educação superior no Brasil. Tese de Doutorado, Faculdade de Educação, Unicamp, Campinas, 2011.

Novaes, H. T. A Autogestão como Magnífica Escola: notas sobre a educação no trabalho associado. In: Batista, E. L.; Novaes, H. T. (orgs.) Educação e reprodução social: as contradições do capital no século XXI. Bauru: Canal 6/ Praxis, 2011.

Novaes, H. T. Reatando um fio interrompido: a relação universidade-movimentos sociais na América Latina. São Paulo: Expressão Popular-Fapesp, 2012.

Novaes, H. T.; Benini, É. Quem controla o Estado Brasileiro: o capital rentista e a dívida pública. In: Benini, E. A.; Faria, M. S.; Novaes, H. T.; Dagnino, R. (orgs.) *Gestão Pública e Sociedade: fundamentos e políticas públicas de Economia Solidária*. São Paulo: Outras Expressões, 2012.

Oliveira, F. Crítica à razão dualista - O ornitorrinco. São Paulo: Boitempo Editorial, 2003.

Pinassi, M. O. Da miséria ideológica à crise do capital – uma reconciliação histórica. São Paulo: Boitempo, 2009.

Ribeiro, D. Confissões. São Paulo: Cia das Letras, 1996.

Rodrigues, F. C. Educação política dos trabalhadores: a centralidade da exploração do trabalho na análise da questão agrária no Brasil - a contribuição de Octávio Ianni. In: Rodrigues, F. C.; Novaes, H. T.; Batista, E. (orgs.) Movimentos Sociais, Trabalho Associado e Educação para além do capital. São Paulo: Outras Expressões, 2013, vol. II.

Saviani, D. Pedagogia histórico-crítica: primeiras aproximações. Campinas, SP: Autores Associados, 2012.

Silva, F. A Fábrica como Agência Educativa. Araraquara: Editora Cultura Acadêmica-Unesp, 2005.

Svampa, M., Pereyra, S. Entre la ruta y el barrio: la experiência de lãs organizaciones piqueteras. 1° ed. Buenos Aires: Biblos, 2003.

Tauile, J. R. Do socialismo de mercado à economia solidária. Revista Economia Contemporânea, Rio de Janeiro, 2002, p. 107–122.

Tiriba, L; Fischer, M.C.B. Saberes do trabalho associado. In: Cattani, A. D.; Laville, J. L.; Gaiger, L. I.; HESPANHA, P. Dicionário Internacional da Outra Economia. São Paulo/Coimbra, Almedina Brasil Ltda/Edições Almedina S.A., 2009, pp. 293–298.

Vicitez, C.; Dal Ri, N. Trabalho associado. Rio de Janeiro: DP&A, 2001.

CHAPTER 8

The National Training Centre in the Solidarity Economy: The Contradictions of Self-Management Education of the Solidarity Economy Movement

Introduction

This chapter aims to reflect on the contradictions of the Solidarity Economy Movement's self-managed education. To do so, we rely on the experience of the National Centre for Training in Solidarity Economy (CFES—Nacional).

In recent years, numerous social movements have created their formal and non-formal education strategies. We could highlight the May 13 Centre for Popular Education, the CUT Trade Union Schools and several MST initiatives: the Josué de Castro Institute, numerous travelling and Basic Education schools, the MST Agroecology Schools and the Florestan Fernandes National School. In Argentina, there are the *bachilleratos* in the Recovered Factories and the Latin American Political Training School "José Carlos Mariátegui"; in Mexico, the Zapatista schools; in Ecuador, the Intercultural University of Nationalities and Indigenous Peoples, among others.

The National Centre for Training in Solidarity Economy is part of this trend but has some specificities that we intend to outline. In the

H. Tahan Novaes, *Associated Labor and Production in the Age of Barbarism*, https://doi.org/10.1007/978-3-031-51183-7_8

first part of the chapter, I briefly analyse the Solidarity Economy Movement and the experiences of Associated Labour, as the National CFES was created to produce/reproduce the values and qualifications necessary for the flourishing of the Solidarity Economy. I think it's worth it to share that I have misgivings in relation to both the term and the political-educational project that represent the main currents of the Solidarity Economy Movement.

In the second part, we will focus on some dimensions of the Solidarity Economy courses in the National CFES to point out some of its contradictions. The purpose of this approach is to glimpse at the potential, but mainly to observe the limits, of this formative proposal towards confronting the capital system.

In the third part of the chapter, I continue the debate on the positivity of associated labour, affirming my belief in it as an educational principle. Next, in this same section, there are a few lines about the historical necessity of education beyond capital and an outline of some of its pillars.

The Solidarity Economy Movement and Associated Labour

Faced with the offensive of capital against labour, leading to reduction of the bargaining power of the traditional left organised in unions and parties, contradictorily, new forms of social struggle emerge amid workers and those *excluded* from the formal market challenging the mechanisms of oppression underlying the processes of capital expansion.

Contrary to "rock bottom" theories, which state that there is no alternative to capitalism (Silva 2005), the new waves of contestation and social movements are represented, on the one hand, by the diversity of anti-globalisation movements that propose to attack the global constituents of capital, including Seattle in 1999 and the World Social Forum, and on the other, by movements that are based on the self-organisation of the means of production and workers' struggles. Although we cannot directly link the latter to the autonomist struggles that occurred at different historical moments, due to their specificity and diversity, we can say that they constitute a form of resistance to capital that has the self-organisation of workers as its foundation.

Since the mid-1980s, Brazil has witnessed the emergence of new forms of workers' association based on the collective organisation of the means of production through what they call self-management. These experiences emerge both with the recovery of bankrupt factories by workers, as well as other community social processes that are based on the cooperative form of production and commercialisation. In the latter case, one of the pioneering experiences was the Community Alternative Projects (PACs), many of them advised by Caritas Brazil.[1] From the experiences of the PACs came the term Popular Solidarity Economy, an expression used by this institution.

The emergence of the Solidarity Economy in Brazil represents one of these experiences of associated labour constituted of marginalised sectors of the population which are subject to the precariousness of the labour market. Cruz (2006) pointed out that Solidarity Economy initiatives are similar in four cities of the southern cone—Buenos Aires, Montevideo, São Paulo and Porto Alegre—and they follow the steps of *new* social movements. Their history of struggle begins with opposition to the military coups in their respective countries and is linked to populations *excluded from* the traditional working class.

Arantes (2002) and the Usina collective (2012) observed the emergence of collective projects from the 1980s that share the following principles: self-organisation of work; the attempt to mitigate the exploitation of work; the construction of houses based on their use values and not exchange values; the role of architects as intellectuals who do not separate conception from execution and are at the service of social movements. It should also be noted that civil construction cooperatives in Brazil are very rare, that is, we have few experiences of associated labour in the field of civil construction (Ewbank, 2007).

[1] Caritas was created in Brazil in 1956, by the action of Dom Helder Câmara during the 3rd Assembly of the National Brazilian Bishops' Council (CNBB). Its actions are strongly influenced by the changes with the Second Vatican Council, initiated in 1962, which ruled on conceptual and practical changes to make the church more attuned to the misery of the world (Borghetti 2007). At that time, Caritas' actions were focused on social assistance work for the miserable funded with donations. Since the 1960s, Caritas member entities have approached liberation theology and Freirean liberating pedagogy through actions aimed at raising awareness of the miserable in the Community Ecclesial Communities (CEBs). In the 1980s,Caritas was an important articulator and promoter of subsistence experiences aimed at the poor population in PACs (Alternative Community Projects), which were replaced, between the 1980s and 1990s, by the Popular Solidarity Economy. Bertucci and Silva (2003, p. 15) say that the stiffening of international cooperation funding entities led Caritas to seek new forms of financing through agreements with the government and depend more on funding campaigns.

Observing these "*mutirões*"[2] in the city of São Paulo, Arantes (2002) points out that self-managed *mutirões* are not only an alternative for the homeless but a space for experimenting with what may become an emancipated design of homes and cities. As Sérgio Ferro (2006) points out, the fact that construction is a simpler process than making an industry makes it a laboratory for workers to exercise control of production and prepare for emancipatory transformations. The contradiction of the self-managed *mutirões* is that they build a use-value, that is, houses that manage to escape the space of production and consumption of commodities. However, they have not yet managed to devise ways of emancipating themselves from wage work, either because these men and women work in factories, where they sell their labour power, or because they work in the informal market, or because they are unemployed.

Although they reach a higher degree control over their own labour, it remains a challenge for these social movements and for the intellectuals who advise them to push towards unalienated construction work on a broader scale.

In the 1980s, numerous rubber tapper associations emerged in the Amazon Rainforest, mainly in the state of Acre. Rubber tapper associations try to use forest resources appropriately, adopting methods to distinguish themselves from destructive production. The rubber tappers' associations try hard to survive in this unfair market and to some extent have a different political project from large-scale loggers, since they try to build new social relations and do not live on the theft of wood from public lands or the inappropriate exploitation of nature's resources for profit.

In the states of Maranhão and Tocantins, there were various struggles to Free the Babaçu Groves. Babaçu is a plant in the palm family (Arecaceae), endowed with drupaceous fruits with edible oilseeds and from which an oil is extracted which can be used in food, medications and cosmetics, in addition to being the subject of advanced research for the manufacture of biofuels. When big landowners in the region tried to prevent the access of workers and peasants to babaçu groves, one of the most beautiful social struggles in Brazil emerged, driven mainly by women. There are already some cooperatives and associations that are

[2] See footnote about Mutirão in Chapter 5.

industrialising babaçu products, like soaps, in small association-owned factories.[3]

Wirth (2013) and Fraga (2012) highlight the emergence of waste picker recycling cooperatives and associations as one of the most important phenomena springing from neoliberalism and, we would add, from the structural crisis of capital and the subsequent social regression. In a country that does not generate many jobs with formal contracts, leading to concentrations in income, which in its own turn generates an immense amount of recyclable material, it has become more or less natural for countless workers to find a way to survive dealing in recyclable materials.

Regarding associated labour in rural areas, Christoffoli (2000, 2012) and Dal Ri and Vieitez (2008) also highlight the emergence of the Landless Movement (MST) in 1984 as one of the main social movements that brought the debate and practice of associated labour to the forefront. The MST has a reasonable variety of forms of organisation of property and decision-making, but it is possible to identify at least three trends within the movement: (a) production divided into individual/family units, with some degree of collective decision-making in each settlement; (b) mixed formation, which combines collective property and individual property, but with numerous moments of collective decision-making; (c) the formation of cooperatives where ownership, work and decision-making are totally collective.[4] It should be noted that the MST has found it difficult to induce the emergence of fully collectivised cooperatives.

It should also be noted that, since 2001, the MST has elected agroecology as one of its fundamental pillars. However, a good part of the settlements still use "green revolution" techniques or are barely surviving the daily struggle to pluck their livelihood from the earth. At the other end of the spectrum, we have Bionatur and some more advanced experiments that combine associated labour and agroecology.[5]

[3] To learn more about the cooperatives and associations that emerged around the struggle for free babaçu groves, see Tavares (2008).

[4] To learn more about the different forms of production organisation in the MST, see Christoffoli (2000, 2012).

[5] Bionatur should be understood as a practice that has characteristics of decommercialization or *fair trade* of native seeds. According to information obtained on the MST website, Bionatur is an agroecological seed production cooperative. Bionatur's experience, "which began in the MST settlements in Candiota and Hulha Negra, in the south of Rio Grande do Sul, represented the end of dependence on companies and the adoption of an agroecological production system. In the beginning, before the founding

After this brief retrospective of the resurgence of associated labour, it should be noted that the inclusion of the social movements mentioned above in the field of associated labour or the Solidarity Economy varies according to the political-ideological view of the researchers. Paul Singer (2002), for example, would include all the social movements mentioned above within the field of the Solidarity Economy. Dal Ri and Vieitez (2008), in turn, adopt a stricter criterion, bringing the concept of associated labour to the forefront of the debate. For them, there is a need to criticise the term Solidarity Economy, including its limit precisely regarding the absence of a vision and a programme of radical modification of society and not only of modification of productive units.

Currently, the concept of Solidarity Economy is quite comprehensive and not very precise in relation to the experiences that integrate it, as indicated by Cruz (2006). In general, it refers to the experiences of worker self-organisation in various sectors of production and presents a varied potential of opposition to capital. Artisans, small entrepreneurs, cooperatives and urban and rural associations all participate in the Solidarity Economy Forums, carrying with them varying degrees of criticism of the socio-metabolism of capital.

From 2003 on, in the context of the Lula government, some of the organisations of the Solidarity Economy became *protagonists* of public policies, with the creation of the National Secretariat of Solidarity Economy (SENAES) in the Ministry of Labor and Employment (MTE). This power group in civil society started to pressure the State to create the general conditions of production and reproduction of the Solidarity Economy without, however, ensuring proper autonomy from the capitalist State. It is the result of the demand of several fronts of the Solidarity Economy social movements in the space of the World Social

of Bionatur, settled families sold their vegetable seed production to companies in the region. Since they were often unable to sell to businesses, farmers began passing the seeds on to other farmers. Bionatur is an instrument to show society that Agrarian Reform works. In addition, for settled farmers, Bionatur is "the gateway" to the agroecological model. Bionatur has at least 230 families producing pesticide-free seeds in 20 municipalities in southern Brazil and Minas Gerais. The network has already developed techniques to produce 117 varieties of vegetables, 15 green manure products and 10 crops essential for the self-sustainability of families. The seeds have agroecological production certification from the Ministry of Agriculture and are marketed in virtually all Brazilian states. Bionatur is now coordinated by the Cooperativa Agroecológica Terra e Vida (Conaterra), since June 2005 (MST 2010).

Forum (WSF), but also as a strategy of the Lula and Dilma governments to increase governability over social movements.

When entering the field of public policies, specifically in relation to professional education policies, the Solidarity Economy was included among the priority groups in the National Quality-Building Plan (PNQ) and the National Secretariat of the Solidarity Economy (SENAES), as it understands that training is a fundamental activity for this social movement, which dedicates most of its actions to it, as well as forging its own training project through the creation of six Training Centres in the Solidarity Economy.[6]

The National Training Centre for Solidarity Economy (CFES Nacional)

We will now recall some aspects of the analysis carried out by Alaniz (2012) on the training policy of the National CFES, in order to think about the elements existing in this experience that allow us to glimpse the contradictions of a training process that, still at an embryonic stage, proposes to be an alternative to the proposal of official professional training, which has as reference the labour market and capitalist production.

According to the Thematic Conference on Training and Technical Advisory (2010, p.9), CFES is specifically intended for the training of trainers, educators, public managers in the Solidarity Economy, members of public employment policy councils, sustainable territorial development of the Solidarity Economy and related areas, besides the development, systematisation and socialisation of methodologies and didactic-pedagogical materials.

CFES was introduced by SENAES as a political strategy to strengthen the Solidarity Economy movement, according to the managers of the secretariat and members of the Brazilian Solidarity Economy Forum

[6] The CFES are distributed in the five regions of the country: North—coordinated by the Federal University of Pará, Northeast—coordinated by the Federal Rural University of Pernambuco; South—coordinated by the University of Vale dos Sinos (UNISINOS); Southeast—coordinated by the Marista Institute of Solidarity; Midwest—coordinated by the Central-West CUT Training School (ECO/CUT), and a national headquarters in Brasilia—coordinated by Caritas Brasil, responsible for national actions and the articulation of regional CFES.

(FBES) (Alaniz 2012). The national CFES is coordinated by Caritas Brasileira, which has a significant impact on the definition and implementation of the policies introduced by SENAES.[7]

The influence of Caritas in this secretariat can be seen in the strategic role that the entity occupies in the national and executive coordination of FBES, including their presence in the National Council of Solidarity Economy (CONAES) and in the coordination of three expressive SENAES projects, namely: Local Brazil, considered the project that absorbs the largest percentage of the secretariat's resources, the Solidarity Fund and the CFES. It should also be noted that a member of Caritas occupies a strategic secretariat within the framework of SENAES managers.

However, the performance of the national-level CFES has frustrated the expectations created with its implementation. According to the data presented by Alaniz (2012), it was expected that CFES Nacional would become a reference centre for discussions on the Solidarity Economy, with theoretical potential and deepening of experiences focused on training and dissemination of methodologies specific to this social movement. This dimension projected for CFES Nacional with its creation is explained in the account below:

> [...] I think that CFES Nacional should not be responsible for giving courses, but we kept on doing these activities because we were starting out, but Nacional should to be a space to deepen the organisation of the system and not to take courses. However, in the project it said that we had to give training sessions, so the CFES methodological committee discussed these things [...] The role of CFES Nacional had to be assuring quality in the pedagogical discussion, and to have an appropriate team to do so. It seems to me that the team was not thought of in this sense [...].[8]

[7] It is never too much to remember that the influence of the Catholic Church in the State, in Brazilian public policies and especially in education, is not new. Paiva (1980) highlights Paulo Freire's proposals within the conciliatory and national-developmentalist project of the 1950s–1960s. In addition, it should also be noted that Caritas represents a reformist wing of the Catholic Church, very distinct, for example, from the so-called *red priests* who are in the Pastoral da Terra and who helped build the Landless Movement.

[8] Information provided by the former member of SENAES, from the Department of Studies and Dissemination, in an interview granted on September 10, 2011.

The importance of deepening workers' theoretical knowledge in self-organisation was the subject of academic discussions in theories that considered the role of the vanguard of the party and factory committees, as in Mandel (1974), as well as by theorists who discussed autonomist experiences, which, in their process of self-management of production and struggle, are equipped with theoretical and practical foundations to advance autonomy and expand social movements' subversive potential.

Despite the difficulty CFES Nacional had to become a reference centre in theoretical deepening and systematisation of methodologies specific to the Solidarity Economy, we note that this dimension was deemed important by some members of SENAES when designing this centre. In this sense, the understanding that the self-organisation of the struggle and the work process is not done without the necessary theoretical deepening of the historical experiences of the workers and without reflection on and systematisation of the practices that the movement develops is an important aspect to be considered in the performance and evaluation of CFES Nacional.

Although there has been a political discussion focused on forms of production and commercialisation, CFES Nacional did not advance—or had no political interest in advancing—in this discussion in the sense of understanding the Solidarity Economy/associated labour movement, its potential for action before the mechanisms of capital, in its strategies of struggle and discussion of the development of appropriate technologies for associated labour, even considering the incipient stage of these discussions. The account below expresses this dimension:

> [there is a lack of] tools that we can develop with the community [...] but we understand that it comes from accumulation, we already had a reference from the discussions with the Solidarity Economy forums and until last year we did not have this perspective on how to develop methodological processes regarding broader issues. [...] I believe that we need to have an understanding of what the capitalist system is and not everyone knows this history, especially the entrepreneurs. This is necessary so that they can understand themselves as true agents of creation of a society with another economic system. Of course, in everyday life this does not interfere much in production, but in the construction of a political point of view, in their roles as social agents, it is important to see themselves inserted in an economically and socially transformative process [...] (CFES Nacional Participant, 2011 *apud* Alaniz 2012, p. 228)

We can see that some of the associated labourers who participate in CFES activities see a need for political training aimed at understanding their struggle, its practices and the capital system.[9] Furthermore, associated labourers speak of the need to offer these instruments to members of the movement as a condition for establishing their strategies of struggle.

The fact that the training process is organised in courses and workshops and not as a permanent process, in which they continuously resort to organisations and permanent education of teachers in the Solidarity Economy movement, is also one of the factors that hinder theoretical deepening. In this case, permanent training (Mészáros 2005), necessary for the processes of coping with the social order and the construction of self-management practices, is not yet a reality and there is no glimpse of its future adoption.

The CFES organisation stems from the fact that the training program is conditioned to the SENAES public policy in the context of the policies in force in the Lula and Dilma governments.

Although these governments contemplated the Solidarity Economy as a target of public policies in different programs, they had a political project that can be characterised as a project of political concession, since its central axis is the reproduction of financial capital. Thus, the public training policy is presented through pulverised, specific and non-permanent actions, in accordance with the logic of public notices organised in predetermined periods.

The impossibility of significantly expanding training actions for the Solidarity Economy is made evident when we consider the mismatch between the budget of SENAES and the significant demand for training actions. Resources are also very scarce in other programs, such as the National Training Plan (PNQ), when compared to private institutions that offer professional training, such as the S system, for example, as shown by Alaniz (2012).

We understand that access to knowledge regarding the structures of capital and the struggles waged by the labour movement throughout history, alongside with organising work based on workers' power, are fundamental prerequisites to advance strategies to confront capitalist social relations, to organise associated labour and to work on integrating struggles while using a broad conception of social life. Bernardo (2009)

[9] For the debate on political formation in social movements, see Rodrigues (2013).

observes that this knowledge is dear to capitalists, as acquiring it is contingent on your rank in social hierarchy, as the very reproduction of this class is based on this knowledge.

Another dimension of political formation is the construction of mechanisms aimed at the integration of workers' struggles. In Alaniz (2012), we pointed out the importance of the experience at the Florestan Fernandes National School of the Landless Rural Workers Movement (MST) for political formation. However, some members of the CFES Nacional lacked knowledge regarding the MST and its organisation and saw its instruments of struggle in a strange light, which helps us to explain, once again, that Caritas represents a wing of the Catholic Church that does not want class struggle. Rather, their goal is social change through the *humanisation* of human beings through dialogue.

While some parts of the movement keep a certain distance from the MST, it is mentioned as part of the Solidarity Economy movement, according to the members of SENAES, FBES and CFES.

There was a noted difficulty in unifying the struggles through educational processes, mainly because it does not figure among the objectives and goals in the main official reference documents for the Solidarity Economy. In the 2nd module of the CFES Nacional's opening seminar (Centro de Formação em Economia Solidária 2010), two of the four training centres, CFES Centro-Oeste and CFES Sul, indicated that there is no close relationship between the movements, although they are part of the CFES training activities. However, at times, this issue appears in the national CFES seminar and is perceived as a difficulty that restricts the movement's action towards a more combative stance (Alaniz 2012).

Unifying struggles is important to expand the combative power and proliferation of workers' organisations, since the fight against the organic and expansionist system of capital cannot be carried out without a corresponding expansion of workers' movements structured in comprehensive, autonomous and horizontalised social practices. Bernardo (2009) observes that by developing radical forms of struggle in collective and egalitarian relations and by the generic social interrelationship that represents the connection between struggles, the working class can present an alternative social model to capitalism. The author mentions that the struggle allows workers to come into contact with the bases of capitalism—when held under the yoke of factory discipline, losing control of their time to work, workers cannot globally challenge capital and do not have a generic understanding of economic mechanisms. Only in this way can they build new social relationships.

Although the theme of integration of struggles appears unsystematically here and there in the training process, there has been no systematic reflection to further deepen this discussion. This indicates little potential to advance understanding of the processes of resistance and unification of struggles based on workers' historical experiences of self-organisation. This dimension is a central condition to propose an education beyond capital.

However, discussions related to the strengthening of Solidarity Economy enterprises have not aimed at problematising and deepening the actions of the movement itself in capitalist society. Quite the opposite, a perspective of ecological discussion focused on sustainable development has been established as the field of action for the Solidarity Economy movement. This aspect can be seen in reference documents for SENAES and CFES Nacional (I and II CONAES 2006 and 2010; I and II Workshop 2006 and 2007; IV FBES Plenary 2008).

By adopting a reformist discourse proposing *another model of development* based on ecological sustainability as their educational basis, they neglect the issues of destructive production and alienated labour. By not scrutinising the political proposal of development, typically created by capital to mislead and mitigate class struggle, they do not question the fundamentals of the exploitation-alienation of labour.

By converting *sustained development* into a goal and excluding the confrontation with the international logic of capital from the horizon of workers' movements in training, it contributes to the dissemination of a discourse focused on improving living conditions from within the system, removing the radicalness of the struggle and the organisations created and nurtured within it. In this sense, although the Solidarity Economy training uses terms such as social transformation, autonomy and self-management, it aims to insert itself in capitalism with some adaptations to make it less *exclusive*, or even to preserve elements of capitalism that are essential such as competition and technology while transposing them to another, more sustainable, society. In other words, socialist thought based on radical critiques of capital cannot have *sustainability* from within the capital system as its goal. Quite the opposite: this line of thinking understands that any humanising or preservationist project is incompatible with any perspective based on exploitation-alienation and profit (Alaniz 2012).

Another concept often used alongside *sustainable development* is *empowerment*, a widely used term in SENAES and FBES training documents. The term is linked to the ability of workers to focus on public policy in favour of training and promotion actions for Solidarity Economy enterprises. The use of this term in SENAES documents shows us that CFES training is permeated by the idea of fighting for public policies.

The struggle for public policies, which is an integral part of CFES Nacional training, is related to its own constitution as a space designed to operationalise and improve this training policy. Furthermore, it reflects the position taken by a significant part of the subjects, enterprises and advisory institutions that develop SENAES policy.

The proposed formation of FBES, in line with SENAES guidelines, also emphasises that fighting for public policies is an important objective. Some of its educational proposals highlight this idea: public funding for research and technologies to improve production and other economic aspects; creation and maintenance of Public Centres to support the Solidarity Economy; inclusion of the Solidarity Economy in formal education; public campaigns and programs for the dissemination of the Solidarity Economy; and national technical assistance programs for the Solidarity Economy (Brazilian Forum of Solidarity Economy 2008, pp. 24–29).

The question is, what does it mean for the Solidarity Economy to have the adoption of public policies as the ultimate goal of its struggles? It is enough to remember that historical experiences of autonomous struggles, such as the Paris Commune (1871), the Russian Revolution (1917), the Ukrainian Revolution (1917), the German Revolution (1919), the Hungarian Revolutions (1919 and 1956) and the Carnation Revolution (1974), developed independently of the State, with the establishment of factory councils and neighbourhood committees (Tragtenberg 1986). As a matter of fact, many even opposed the State as a form of organisation and any interference by it in workers' organisations. For Tragtenberg (1986), the degeneration of the Soviet system occurred through a conservation of state capitalism, which kept state centralisation under the control of the party and unions. This recreated a hierarchy in state administration and led to factories with Taylorism and salaries. In this understanding, Yugoslav self-management, which was characterised by the formalism of companies, was limited because it maintained a political apparatus and state power.

We can say that if the workers' struggle focuses on the self-management of isolated collective properties and seeks to participate in the development of public policies within the scope of the State, there is a strong propensity to cool its combative potential and reproduce capitalist social relations. We do not deny the need to access public funds, but we must emphasise that historical trends from the twentieth century have shown us that social movements tend to degenerate or be co-opted as they enter the state structure. One of the greatest challenges of the twenty-first century is how social movements can have access to and control of public funds while maintaining proper autonomy.

On this topic, Pinassi (2011) highlighted two trends in contemporary social movements. The first trend has the following characteristics: it is generally assimilated by the State or capitalist corporations; it tends to restrict its struggle to specific/corporatist issues, generating accommodation/integration of the social movement within the order of capital. If this happens, it is quite likely that we will have a reformist social movement and we are in the field of contingent class consciousness. At the same time, it can result in a stronger ruling class with the capacity to absorb and incorporate social conflicts to maintain its hegemony. The second group, consisting of class-based social movements, tries to continue anti-capital struggles and see reality from the point of view of class consciousness. Within these movements, creativity does not die, the pillars of anti-capital struggles—breaking the structural hierarchy of capital, fighting for substantive equality, expansion and internationalisation of the struggle, overcoming the capitalist state, joining specific struggles with labour-based issues, etc.—are exercised and it is very hard for them to be co-opted by the state, even when the movement aims to access public funds.

Some considerations about the nature and organisation of the modern state help us to understand the contradictions posed by the Solidarity Economy movement when it chooses public policy as a central objective to be pursued within a perspective of *sustainable development*. When discussing the Jewish Question, Marx (1993) says that it is not enough for politics to free itself from religion if the same role of conducting social life is transferred to the state. Thus, politics, as the foundation of social organisation and the expression of the set of rules created by human beings to conduct collective life, is alienated from those who begin to establish strange relations with themselves and with others to find their place within the state. For this reason, Marx states that there is no human emancipation within the modern state.

In alignment with Rosa Luxemburg (2005) regarding the class character of the state, Mészáros (2002) considers that the state is the only structure compatible with the structure of capital because it is constituted in a similar way with regard to its basic command structures: hierarchy and bureaucratic power, in addition its function as the regulator of the social reproduction system. In this perspective, the state takes on central roles to perpetuate the functioning of the capital system in its process of expansion through increased productivity, because the state is a totalising structure of political command of capital intended to complement the elements of material reproduction. The effects of this complementary character of the state are actions like consenting to mergers, granting tax exemptions and even stimulating an education to turn individuals into consumers, including through various social policies aimed at regulating the imbalance generated between production and consumption.

In view of the issues pointed out above, the objective pursued by the Solidarity Economy, which permeated discussions in the development of CFES Nacional, becomes quite contradictory. In the absence of significant changes, the pedagogical political project of CFES Nacional is likely to have a corrosive effect capable of undermining the potential of the movement in proposing emancipatory education and actions.

An expression of the contradiction that permeates CFES Nacional as a public policy in the Lula-Dilma governments is the definition of the objectives of training at the Centre. For this public policy, the goal of training is *social inclusion*, in alignment with other policies of these administrations, but for CFES members and Solidarity Economy activists, it is about social transformation, that is, a more radical dimension and contrary to the idea of inclusion into capitalist society.

> [...] If we take what the project says, it talks about social inclusion, but in my point of view we act in the scope of social transformation. That is the concept we followed, our debates have to do with countering the hegemonic structure, thinking about a new logic of education, of finance, so it is a project of social transformation far beyond creating a space for inclusion in this society that exploits everyone.[10]

[10] A member of the executive coordination of Caritas Brasileira in an interview granted on August 30, 2011.

This fact highlights the different logics in dispute in the Solidarity Economy's relation to public policy. In this case, the pedagogical project ended up being aligned with the broader guidelines of the current State policy. If the Solidarity Economy movement envisions that the training process should support it in confronting the logic of capital and deepening the experience of self-organisation, the Lula-Dilma Government, in contrast, envisions the insertion of these workers into the economy with some kind of work capable of generating income and consumption, in a *country for everyone*.

This perspective of the State is consistent with the economic policy aimed at minimising poverty to insert the impoverished portion of the population in some sphere of consumption, as well as enabling the expansion of capital in this new stage of globalisation of production relations through the combination of complex labour with simple labour. In this sense, the State does not aim at a rupture in the social order, as it is contrary to its nature, but to integrate marginalised populations into the circuit of capital. Faced with the subordination of social policies to the expansionist process of capital, it is not only a conceptual problem but an objective issue, as it modifies the goal of training, adapting it to the adversities of the expansionist movement.

Thus, the CFES Nacional educational program presents certain contradictions that can evolve into an education capable of building mechanisms aimed at contesting and tensioning the capital system towards the construction of socialism, as well as adapting to society aiming at social inclusion—a more likely hypothesis.

In view of the announced intention to strengthen the Solidarity Economy movement through the improvement of self-organisation processes and the projection of the Solidarity Economy on the national scene as a democratic form of workers' organisation, the training experience of the CFES Nacional proposes to link work and education.

Although permeated by contradictions, the existence of CFES Nacional presupposes deepening and continuing the educational process initiated in production when workers collectively took on the management of the cooperative or association, positioning themselves as subjects and challenging the division of labour, which is one of the central pillars of capitalist organisations, as we will address in this text.

In general, the link between education and production is a characteristic trait of education within social movements that collectively organise productive activities, since the material survival of workers and the very survival of the movement drive the search for technical-political improvement with a view to building democratic production relations. Thus, a workers' movement needs an educational process with emancipatory objectives as a mechanism to reinvigorate the movement and radicalise the struggle.

Although the link between education and production is a fundamental part of the educational process, the analysis of the training of trainers at CFES Nacional demonstrated that one of the hardest aspects of the training process is deepening the link between production and training in the courses. This is made evident by the fact that some members and participants of the course (Alaniz 2012) highlight a difficulty to assimilate the demands of the participating projects and that, in most cases, the training did not reach the movements' bases. This means participatory management, which is adopted in the documents, is experienced in the pedagogical process, but without a deep link with the associative experiences of the participants.

Regarding the Self-Management of Pedagogy developed in the training courses of the National CFES, we observed that there is a tendency to highlight full participation during pedagogical activities. This is because the activities in CFES courses are organised jointly with the participants, based on an initial proposal from the course coordinating team. Throughout the course, all activities tend to be divided into teams, which are responsible for part of the course.

However, the Self-Management of Pedagogy cannot be limited to pedagogical activities, but must presuppose links to all social decision-making processes involved in the training activity, so that the content of the training expresses the demands of productive organisations in the deepening of democratic practices and other technological issues of associated labour, as well as participation in the definition of public policies. In this case, participation in budgetary decisions and in defining training content is beyond the power of the collective. The contents suggested in the CFES Term of Implementation, although relevant, are not based on demands made by the participating social movements.

The theoretical-epistemological assumptions that make up the pedagogical discourse of CFES are marked by a certain pedagogical eclecticism. This is especially clear in the documents from the first and second workshops, in which the inclusion of different pedagogical approaches is emphasised, including Paulo Freire's pedagogy, the pedagogy of alternation, the neoliberal ideology of "learning to learn" and the Pedagogy of self-management. Furthermore, there is an omission of the main references of traditional socialist education embraced by leftist workers' movements, whose experiences refer to the educators of the Soviet revolution, among them Pistrak, Krupskaya and Makarenko.

The choice to adopt a variety of pedagogical approaches was made to contemplate the diversity of the Solidarity Economy movement. However, using some notions linked to hegemonic thinking in education, like the motto "learning to learn", which Duarte (2004) described as being focused on social adaptation, is contradictory to the purpose of an education focused on emancipation, which envisions and moves towards a rupture in the current social order. Thus, we do not believe that it is not enough to mention popular education among the methodological guidelines used in the project, as it either does not develop towards opposition to the social order or it is distorted to fit the dominant discourse and appears as multiculturalism and respect for differences.

From this perspective, we believe that the Pedagogy of Self-Management tends to find little room to develop as a pedagogical proposal committed to the emancipation of workers as a result of its conflicting approaches and the absence of theoretical guidance that considers socialist educational experiences.

With these notes, we do not want to disregard the innovative character of this pedagogy. The root of the problem seems to lie in the lack of linking productive enterprises with the training processes in CFES Nacional, which, besides making it difficult to capture educational demands from social movements, assigns a task to their pedagogical process that it cannot fulfil. The II Thematic Conference on Education announces that the role of methodology in training is to unite theory and practice, which seems quite contradictory if we consider that the object which should guide training in Solidarity Economy is the workplace of those in training. This discussion around methodology is very present in schools, which is understandable because they are separated from the *locus* of production in capitalist society. But it shouldn't be a problem for associated labour organisations. In this case, there is a pedagogical discussion to be overcome in the CFES training proposal.

Another aspect that deserves to be highlighted, based on the data collected by Alaniz (2012), refers to the difficulty in contemplating discussions on social technologies, although they are provided for in the Implementation Term of the Centre for Training in Solidarity Economy (2007).

To meet the needs of associated labour, technologies must be redesigned, since they are not neutral (Novaes 2007). Thus, every training process must be developed with the goal of improving the organisation of work, which leads to a rethinking of organisational models and of the techniques to be employed, reflecting on the power structure to constantly review it and improve participatory and decision-making processes, interpersonal relationships, the values of producers and *consumers*, the questioning of specialties and the division of alienating labour that is based on the division of knowledge and is reproduced by differences in pay. All this while seeking an increase in the useful life of machines, equipment and products. To leverage this debate, it is essential to examine the experiences that have brought associated labourers closer to science and technology research developed in universities and other research institutions.

Alaniz (2012) notes that the difficulty in adopting an approach based on Sociotechnical Adequacy in CFES Nacional is directly related to the budgetary difficulty of SENAES and the provisional nature of this training space. The exercise of thinking about social technologies and deepening the discussion requires continuous, organic processes and integration with other similar experiences.

This array of aspects indicates that it is premature at this moment to declare that "educational processes inspired by the Solidarity Economy announce a new sociability, a new society, a new way of producing life", as defended at the I National Workshop of Education/Training in the Solidarity Economy (2006, p. 15).

The same goes for the predominant discourse in the Solidarity Economy, which includes that of SENAES Secretary Paul Singer. An example is his statement that these concrete experiences indicate an alternative that is already creating a new model of society, opposed to the hierarchical logic and exploitation of labour, arguing that "[…] in a way, we are carrying out the social revolution in the country […]" (Alaniz 2012).

We understand that it is more fruitful, in this historical moment, marked by an offensive capital, to explain the contradictions of the CFES Nacional training processes so that we can contribute to an understanding of the scope of this experience and submit it to radical criticism, seeking to advance the discussion of an education that proposes to go beyond capital.

Associated Labour as an Educational Principle and the Historical Need for an Education Beyond Capital

After analysing the contradictions of CFES Nacional, we will now hark back to our research in the world of associated labour, as these have shown that in these experiences there are embryos of de-alienating work. We could mention the case of the Recovered Factories (RFs), where one can observe attempts to overcome the capitalist division of labour between those who think and those who carry out the work, between those who work and those who control the means of production. Even within the limits of a labour process that involves countless production chains and countless factories, recovered factories try to overcome the "structural hierarchy of capital" within their microcosm (Mészáros 2002); in short, they try to reunify *homo faber* and *homo sapiens*. Decisions are made in democratic assemblies, workers rotate in strategic posts and positions are revocable.

Actions are carried out to achieve an increased knowledge of work processes in the factory, allowing us to state that they partially overcome the alienation of work, while still preserving some of its elements.

The pages above presented the many limits alongside some positive elements of the thinking of CFES Nacional about an education that goes beyond capital. In the case of CFES Nacional, there are limits thwarting the possibility that this experience could be guided towards socialist purposes, among them: the achievement of public policies as a horizon for pedagogical action; the difficulty in contemplating the articulation of workers' struggles in their political training project; the insufficient theoretical deepening in the historical struggles of workers, with the goal of rethinking and guiding the Solidarity Economy movement; and the adherence to terminologies and expressions that translate reformist positions by presupposing coexistence in the capitalist system, such as the concept of *sustainable development*. In view of these stated contradictions, we understand that education practices based on the workers' movement must be problematised in a totalising perspective in view of the context of capital's hegemonic offensive against labour. This approach is a necessary means to explain the complexity involved in the training process without falling into juxtapositions, which should allow us to understand the level of radicalism of workers' educational experiences.

For associated labour to become an educational principle and evolve towards the strengthening of the anti-capital struggle and the exercise of self-management, it must necessarily question the pillars of the current educational model, which is based on the pedagogy of skills and the motto "learning to learn". Thinking about the challenges to be faced in the constitution of an emancipatory education, Mészáros (2005) says that it is necessary to create horizontal workers' organisations—with a view to de-alienating work—linked to an educational process that opposes the internalisation of capital in its various forms. Only a different process of internalisation can contribute to the transcendence of what Mészáros (2002) calls the socio-metabolism of capital, which reproduces itself in all dimensions of life. Thus, the existence of collective ownership of the means of production is not enough, not least because, as Marx (2009) discussed with Proudhon, its private nature within a commodity-producing society remains. The collectivisation of the means of production based on the self-organisation of work presupposes constituting new social processes linked to the broader struggles of workers. The creation of these alternative processes is not achievable without continuous training of workers in self-management. In the words of Mészáros:

> [...] what needs to be confronted and fundamentally changed is the entire internalisation system, with all its dimensions, visible and concealed. Breaking with the logic of capital in education is therefore tantamount to replacing the ubiquitous and deeply rooted forms of mystifying internalisation with a comprehensive concrete alternative. (Mészáros 2005, p. 47)

Only an education that is guided by the principle of workers' autonomy in production and in social life, which faces the revolutionary task of human emancipation through the reorganisation of material and cultural life head-on, can contribute to undermining the capital system.

Final Considerations

In the above lines, we seek to show that, in opposition to the expansionist order of capital, we have an emergence of new democratic ways of organising production by workers, which has associated labour as an educational principle. However, as we have sought to show, organisations that propose self-organisation experiences have quite different intentions, purposes and potential for subversion. In our point of view, being collectively owned does not necessarily mean that there are qualitative changes in the social relations established in production, as well as in steering educational processes towards socialist objectives.

The CFES Nacional, despite some positive aspects, tends to produce and reproduce popular pedagogies within a vision of *sustainable development* and *humanisation of the human being* through dialogue. Its official documents also present an eclectic pedagogical discourse that opens gaps for the reproduction of the new pedagogies of capital.

We believe that educational centres within the World of Associated Labour should rescue some pillars of the pre-Stalin Soviet school, adapting and enriching them with contributions from the body of historical materialism created over the last 80 years. They should rescue the theoretical accumulation of Latin American Marxism, whether in the educational field or in critical social thought, in addition to international Marxism inherited from Marx's thought. Only then will we be able to develop an educational theory and practice beyond capital.

Bibliography

Alaniz, E. P. A política pública de formação para economia solidária no Brasil (2003–2011): análise de um projeto PROESQ/PNQ executado pela Rede Abelha/RN e do CFES nacional. 2012. 371 f. Tese (Doutorado em Educação) – Faculdade de Educação, Universidade de São Paulo, São Paulo, 2012.

Arantes, P. F. Arquitetura Nova – Sérgio Ferro, Flávio Império e Rodrigo Lefèvre, de Artigas aos Mutirões. São Paulo: Editora 34, 2002.

Bernardo, J. Economia dos conflitos sociais. São Paulo: Expressão Popular, 2009.

Bertucci, A. A.; Silva, R. M. 20 anos de Economia Popular Solidária: trajetória da Cáritas brasileira dos PACs às EPS. Brasília: Venâncio, 2003.

Borghetti, R. Limites e possibilidades de uma alternativa de educação: análise do projeto Barracão da Cáritas Diocesana de Marília. 2007. Dissertação (Mestrado em Educação) – Faculdade de Filosofia e Ciências, Universidade Estadual Paulista, Marília, 2007.

Brazilian Forum of Solidarity Economy. Fórum Brasileiro de Economia Solidária. Brasília, 2008.

Centre for Training in Solidarity Economy. Centro de Formação em Economia Solidária. Brasília, 2007.

CFES. Centro de Formação em Economia Solidária. Brasília, 2010.

Chistoffoli, P. I. O desenvolvimento de cooperativas de produção coletiva de trabalhadores rurais no capitalismo: limites e possibilidades. Dissertação de Mestrado. Curitiba: UFPR. 2000.

Christofolli, P. I. A cooperação agrícola nos assentamentos do MST: desafios e potencialidades. In: Rodrigues, F. C.; Novaes, H. T.; Batista, E. L. (orgs.) *Movimentos sociais, trabalho associado e educação para além do capital*. São Paulo: Outras Expressões, 2012.

Cruz, A. C. M. da. A diferença da igualdade: a dinâmica da Economia solidária em quatro cidades do MERCOSUL. 2006. Tese (Doutorado em Economia) – Instituto de Economia, Universidade Estadual de Campinas, 2006.

Dal Ri, N. M.; Vieitez, C. Educação democrática e trabalho associado no Movimento dos Trabalhadores Rurais Sem Terra e nas fábricas de autogestão. São Paulo: Ícone, Fapesp, 2008.

Duarte, N. Vigotski e o "aprender a aprender": críticas às apropriações neoliberais e pós-modernas da teoria Vigotskiana. 3. ed. Campinas: Autores Associados, 2004.

Ewbank, E. G. Autogestão: possibilidade de organização da força de trabalho na construção civil e suas implicações. São Paulo, Dissertação de Mestrado, FAU-USP, 2007.

Ferro, S. Arquitetura e Trabalho Livre. São Paulo: Cosacnaify, 2006.

Fraga, L. Extensão e transferência de conhecimento: As Incubadoras Tecnológicas de Cooperativas Populares. Tese de Doutorado, Instituto de Geociências, Unicamp, 2012.

Luxemburg, R. Reforma ou Revolução? São Paulo: Expressão Popular, 2005.

Mandel, E. Control obrero, consejos obreros, autogestión. Madri: Editora Era, 1974.

Marx, K. A questão judaica. In: Manuscritos econômicos - filosóficos. Lisboa: Edições 70, 1993. pp. 35–76.

Mészáros, I. A educação para além do capital. São Paulo: Boitempo, 2005.

Mészáros, I. Para além do capital. São Paulo: Boitempo, 2002.

MST. Projeto Metodológico: Turma II do curso Técnico em Agroecologia ensino médio integrado. São Miguel do Iguaçu, 2010.

Novaes, H. T. Qual autogestão? São Paulo, Revista da Sociedade Brasileira de Economia Política, n. 22, maio de 2007.

Paiva, V. Paulo Freire e o nacional-desenvolvimento. Rio de Janeiro: Civilização brasileira, 1980.

Pinassi, M. O. Palestra na disciplina "Pedagogia Histórico-crítica e os movimentos sociais". Campinas, Unicamp, 2011.

Rodrigues, F. C. Educação política dos trabalhadores: a centralidade da exploração do trabalho na análise da questão agrária no Brasil - a contribuição de

Octávio Ianni. In: Rodrigues, F. C.; Novaes, H. T.; Batista, E. (orgs.) Movimentos Sociais, Trabalho Associado e Educação para além do capital. São Paulo: Outras Expressões, 2013, vol. II.
Silva, F. A Fábrica como Agência Educativa. Araraquara: Editora Cultura Acadêmica-Unesp, 2005.
Singer, P. Introdução à economia solidária. São Paulo: Editora Fundação Perseu Abramo, 2002.
Tavares, J. C. Universalidade e singularidade do espaço transitório: um estudo a partir de quebradeiras de coco babaçu/MIQCB e trabalhadores rurais sem terra/MST no Maranhão (1990–2000). Tese de Doutorado, Florianópolis, UFSC, 2008.
Training in the Solidarity Economy. Centro de Formação em Economia Solidária. Brasília, 2006.
Tragtenberg, M. Reflexões sobre o socialismo. São Paulo: Moderna, 1986.
USINA. Luta por moradia e autogestão na América Latina - uma breve reflexão sobre os casos do Uruguai, Brasil, Argentina e Venezuela. In: RODRIGUES, F. C.; NOVAES, H. T.; BATISTA, E. (orgs.) Movimentos Sociais, Trabalho Associado e Educação para além do capital. São Paulo: Outras Expressões, 2012.
Wirth, I. Mulheres na Triagem, Homens na Prensa. Questões de Gênero em Cooperativas de Catadores. São Paulo: Annablume, 2013.

CHAPTER 9

"Green Revolution", Agroecology and the MST Agroecology Schools

Introduction

This chapter aims to reflect on the political economy of the "Green Revolution", the debate on agroecology and the MST's agroecology schools. To achieve this objective, in the first section, we present a critical analysis of the so-called Green Revolution fetish, characterised by the concentration of land in the hands of few owners and transnational corporations, control of production and distribution of seeds, tractors, synthetic fertilisers and pesticides by corporations, besides the many socio-environmental problems it caused: cancer, destruction of the immune system, increased unemployment, indebtedness of small farmers, etc.

In the second section, we present the MST's concept of agroecology, a concept that goes beyond the traditional meanings of environmental preservation and/or organic production. Agroecology is a political-economic and cultural concept that mobilises the MST, in the sense of forging new social relations that include: associated work; the appropriate use of agroecosystems; the reconstruction of agriculture through popular agrarian reform, with democratic and participatory management in cooperative and agroecological production systems; gender issues; debates on decommodification and agroecology education. The entry of agroecology into the MST agenda led to the creation of several technical schools, which I will briefly present later in the chapter.

H. Tahan Novaes, *Associated Labor and Production in the Age of Barbarism*, https://doi.org/10.1007/978-3-031-51183-7_9

Capital's Agriculture Campaign and Destructive Production: The Political Economy of the "Green Revolution"

Since the 1960s, capital has been carrying out an offensive to transform agriculture. Its ideologues call it the Green Revolution. Novaes (2012) calls the same phenomenon the political economy of the Green Con. The political economy of the green con is characterised by (a) a new cycle of primitive accumulation (land grabbing and theft, murder of leaders, theft of indigenous knowledge); (b) the growing concentration of land in the hands of transnational corporations[1]; (c) mergers and acquisitions in the seeds and pesticides sector, with a few large corporations from northern countries exercising near-complete domination of the production and distribution of seeds and pesticides; (d) a biotechnological "revolution" (new pesticides and transgenic seeds); (e) the absence of autonomy for small producers, increasingly working for banks and linked to agro-industrial corporations.

According to Costa Neto (1999), over the last 40 years, a drastic restructuring of the input production and industrial transformation sectors took place alongside transformations in financing and credit institutions and mechanisms, commerce circuits and market structures. Educational, research and technical assistance institutions were progressively adapted to follow this model, with a view to training agronomists, researchers, specialists, extension workers and other professionals within the philosophy of the Green Revolution (Serafim 2012).

From a historical perspective, Pinheiro Machado (2009, p. 1) observes that:

> since Liebig, 1848, the capitalist industry has seen in agriculture an excellent source for the reproduction of capital, and, from that point on, agronomy schools around the world do nothing other than teach students to apply synthetic fertilizers, pesticides, and use heavy machinery. (Pinheiro Machado 2009)

Gonçalves (2008, p. 20) defines the Green Revolution as a:

[1] The political economy of agribusiness has significantly altered the land market and the landscape of Brazil through the purchase or lease of land by financialized foreign corporations (Oliveira 2010).

> [...] technological package that resulted in the industrialization of Brazilian agriculture and, consequently, in an increase in agricultural production, an increase in the exploitation of social surplus value, and in concentration of capital in its various parts, especially commercial, agro-industrial, industrial, financial and real estate. The organization and diffusion of the 'Green Revolution' was bountifully 'watered' by significant sums of resources from public, private, and multilateral development agencies. Its implementation attacked and continues to attack so-called 'traditional' economic and organizational logics, including those of peasants, indigenous people, Quilombolas, Faxinalense communities, etc. Thus, elements such as agricultural mechanization (tractors, harvesters, processing machines, plows, harrows, irrigation pumps, sprayers, agricultural aircraft), petrochemical inputs (fertilizers, insecticides, herbicides, maturers, antibiotics, micronutrients, plastics for agricultural use in irrigation and crop protection), 'improved' plants and seeds (hybrid, re-engineered and transgenic), as well as the rise of agro-industrial companies, have become structural elements in a changing agrarian space. [...] In addition, [...] it subjugates the work of rural producers to the dictates of agribusiness companies, increasingly organized and taking part in an oligopolized world agricultural trade dominated by 'tradings companies'. (Gonçalves 2008, p. 20)

The logic of productivism, that is, maximum profit in the shortest possible amount of time, has always been present in capitalism but has been exacerbated over the last 40 years. Guided by the tripod of transgenic seeds, agrochemicals/synthetic fertilisers and heavy machinery, agro-industrial corporations have consolidated a power and domination structure in rural areas.

Shiva (2001) describes this new phase of commodification of capitalism with the terms new colonialism, biopiracy and biocolonialism. To the author, "while biodiversity and indigenous knowledge systems satisfy the needs of millions of people, new patent and intellectual property rights systems" threaten to appropriate "the vital resources and processes of knowledge of peripheral countries and convert them into a monopoly to the advantage of Northern companies". Patents are therefore at the centre of new colonialism. Furthermore, rising productivity in agribusinesses gave rise to diseases such as mad cow disease, avian flu and swine flu, among others.

It is true that the "Green Revolution" offensive is still hegemonic, but it is also true that its advance did not take place without resistance. In Argentina, at the end of 2013, a fight broke out in the small town of

Malvinas, in the province of Córdoba. Monsanto—the American multinational agricultural and biotechnology company and world leader in the production of genetically modified seeds—intends to instal one of the largest transgenic seed production plants in the world in Malvinas. Social movements, NGOs and environmental groups are trying to block the construction of this plant.

The political economy of the Green Con has plenty of consequences: land concentration; increased rural unemployment; soil degradation; compromised quality and quantity of hybrid resources; devastation of forests and other native biomes; impoverished genetic diversity of cultivars,plants and animals; contamination of water and food consumed by the population; increased allergies, deaths and disabilities and increased commodification and proletarianisation of the field, in addition to surges in small farmer debt and rural school closures, among others.

Bayer, Basf, Syngenta, Monsanto and Dow are some of the large corporations that control the market for transgenic seeds and pesticides in Brazil. According to Folgado (2013, p. 1), Brazil has been the largest consumer of pesticides in the world since 2008. "The quantities used are equivalent to about 5.2 litres of poison per inhabitant per year. However, Brazil represents only 5% of the agricultural area among the 20 countries with the largest food production". This means that the country's productivity does not justify its leadership position in the poison use ranking. According to data from the Brazilian Institute of Geography and Statistics (IBGE) and the National Health Surveillance Agency (Anvisa), the inappropriate or excessive use of this type of input can cause serious damage to human health and the environment.

The specificity of the Latin American case lies in the fact that the restructuring of agriculture was implemented during a counter-revolutionary process started by the continent's military dictatorships, which reaffirmed the power of the ruling classes, especially that of the landowning forces of the colonial past in association with foreign capital and sectors among the military and industrialists (Sampaio Jr 2013; Novaes 2012). In other words, large landowners, alongside the military, parts of the industrial bourgeoisie, the middle classes, the Catholic Church and the USA's CIA, led coups that stopped the advance of the workers' struggles in the region.

More generally, the first symptoms of the capital accumulation crisis appeared in the 1970s. In response to this crisis, capital promoted an offensive that could be summarised as follows: (a) pressure for the free movement of financial capital; (b) productive restructuring of the countryside and the city; (c) technological innovations that intensified the production and diversification of goods; (d) expansion towards sectors and fields not yet subject to full commodification, such as health and education, with a wave of privatisation, which took the cycle of commodification to new heights; (e) implementation of processes, including changes in location and outsourcing, that practically dismantled the power of the combative unions of the Taylorist-Fordist eras of capitalism; (f) theft of lands from small producers, indigenous people, Quilombolas, etc.

However, the dynamics of capitalism from the 1970s onwards could be called destructive overproduction, linked to maximum expansion and the corresponding profit, engendering an alienating and ever-expanding self-reproduction (Mészáros 2004). That is, there are profound changes, both in the objective (economic) plane of production, as well as in the subjective reproduction of class relations.[2] In this sense, we can see that any of capital's "civilising" facets, so vigorously promoted by liberals, have been exhausted with capital's own destructive advance. Regarding social movements and political transformations, a crisis of traditional expressions and class representations took place. This culminated in the emergence of the so-called "new social movements", which no longer aim to criticise the destructive logic of capital and the articulation of its specific flags to the overall class struggle, but the demand to expand the statutes of "citizenship".

According to José Paulo Netto (2008), the banners of the "new social movements" are restricted to the struggle for insertion in the bourgeois state, and not overcoming it as an instrument of class oppression. He states:

> Imperialist corporations implement the erosion of state regulations. "Deregulation" is presented as a type "modernization" that values "civil society", releasing it from the tutelage of the "protective State"—and there is a place in this ideological construct for the defence of "freedom", "citizenship", and "democracy". (Netto 2008, p. 17)

[2] For Mészáros: "capitalism, as a mode of social reproduction, is characterized by the irreconcilable contradiction between production for use (corresponding to need) and production for exchange, which at a certain stage of development becomes an end in itself, subordinating all considerations of human use to its completely perverse logic of alienating self-reproduction" (Mészáros 2004, p. 297).

Especially since the 1980s, with the destructive advance of capital and, consequently, the commodification of all spheres of life, several conflicts began to emerge in Latin America around land, water, seeds, electricity, oil, gas, education and labour, among others. In southern Brazil, for example, the destruction of Aracruz's Eucalyptus nurseries and the struggles of the Via Campesina against Syngenta Seeds (a Swiss multinational), can be interpreted as confrontation tactics employed by social movements against a new offensive by capital. These struggles occurred mainly in reaction to the destruction of Creole seeds, to the role that science and technology play in the socio-metabolism of capital and due to the control that multinationals exercise in all dimensions of workers' lives. Because of its contradictions, the political economy of the Green Con, which restructures the field and industrialises it, furthering the accumulation of capital to a new level, gives rise to several social movements that try to point out ways to move forward antagonistically to the paths presented by agribusiness.

Agroecology in the MST: Beyond the Green Agenda

In common sense, agroecology is associated with caring for nature, ecology, environmental protection and small-scale vegetable production. However, this way of understanding social reality tends to be in favour of maintaining relations of domination (Mészáros 2004). For us, the agroecology theorised by the MST is not reduced to an environmental agenda.

Caporal and Costabeber (2002) note that no product will be truly ecological if it is produced at the expense of the exploitation of the workforce, even if it does not use certain inputs, such as pesticides, or if it is using new forms of soil depletion or degradation of natural resources.

For Gonçalves (2008), what mobilises the MST is the denial of the existing agricultural development model in the country, highlighting the need for the preservation and reconstruction of peasant agriculture through agrarian reform, in addition to proposing forms of management and participation of the peasantry in cooperative and agroecological production systems.

Guhur and Toná (2012), members of the Milton Santos MST School of Agroecology (Maringá–PR), note that a more recent and expanded concept of agroecology is in gestation. This school of thought does not see agroecology as a merely technological solution to the structural and contextual crises of the economic and agricultural model. Agroecology is understood as part of the strategy of fighting and confronting agribusiness, the exploitation of workers and the depredation of nature. This way of thinking agroecology includes caring for and defending life, food production and political and organisational awareness, as observed by the Via Campesina and the MST (Guhur and Toná 2012, p. 66).

The authors also state that agroecology is seen as inseparable from the struggle for food and energy sovereignty, for the defence and recovery of territories, for agrarian and urban reform, and for cooperation and alliance between the peoples of the countryside and the city. Thus, agroecology is part of the construction of a society of freely associated producers working to support life, a society in which the final objective ceases to be profit and becomes human emancipation (Mazalla Neto 2013).

The MST's incorporation of the agroecological agenda took place gradually. According to Gonçalves (2008), this renewal of the movement's agricultural technological matrix started catching on starting in the year 2000, when the Movement began to disseminate the idea that squatting and settled families should, first, guarantee the family's food security with a high quality and diversity of products that are, above all, free of agrochemicals and transgenics.[3]

Gonçalves (2008) also states that for the MST, the change in the social, ecological and, above all, technical rationality of families would help to overcome the new dynamics of capitalism in the countryside, based on extremely severe relations of domination, including the presence of transgenic seeds and the schemes of different branches of transnational agro-commercial capital (chemical, food and financial), which put a stranglehold on farmers.

For the MST, agroecology means stimulating the practice

> [...]of an agriculture with no use of external inputs and agrochemical pesticides. Over the years, we should adjust towards this way of producing, avoiding spending money on fertilizers, poisons, and machine-hours. Rather, we should seek to use locally available labour more and in better ways and developing techniques adapted to our reality, so we don't poison ourselves and nature. We should be open to the creativity of our comrades, producing a new technological matrix. (MST 2000, pp. 50–51)

[3] Seeds that in Brazil were grown illegally and procured in Paraguay and Argentina.

In August 2013, the permission to use GMOs in Brazil turned 10 years old. In the 2000s, numerous campaigns were carried out against the use of GMOs and pesticides in the country, which included actions such as the occupation and destruction of nurseries, accusations in the media, production of films and documentaries, occupation of corporation headquarters, dissemination of reports by scientists against GMOs, synthetic fertilisers, heavy machinery and pesticides and campaigns among social movements, researchers from public universities, sectors of Embrapa and NGOs. It is worth noting that the MST conducted or participated in numerous actions described above.

In order to combat the restructuring of the field and the Green Revolution and disseminate the theory and practice of agroecology, the MST has so far held thirteen Agroecology Days, created numerous agroecology technical courses, integrated high school courses, specialisation courses, undergraduate courses and even a master's degree. It is also spreading the gospel of agroecology in elementary and high schools.

The MST's concept of agroecology is complex and differentiated from an analysis that reduces the term to mere environmental protection, as it introduces or covers several related elements. Carter and Carvalho (2004) mention cooperation, gender, education, youth and the environment.

We can raise the hypothesis that the struggle for agroecology is coupled with what Mészáros (2002) calls substantive equality. If capital promotes formal equality, anti-capital social movements are fighting to construct substantive gender, ethnicity and generational equality and, above all, to overcome class exploitation. It is no coincidence that the women of the MST organise struggles for economic independence, not subordination to their husbands. At the same time, class, gender and environmental issues were involved in an interesting and intertwining way (Pinassi and Mafort 2012; Tait 2013).

Despite being part of the Movement, which provides a practice of struggle and political awareness, MST members are still part of general society and, as such, suffer the influences of the hegemonic ideology.

In the specific case discussed here, they also suffer from the influence and pressure exerted by large transnational corporations, which dominate agro-industrial commerce and production. Thus, not all MST settlements are based on agroecology. By direct and indirect mechanisms, such as propaganda, which creates the fetish of the Green "Revolution", the influence of technicians and agronomists, or by means of more subtle instruments, such as linking credit to the acquisition of the Green

Revolution package, capital creates the general conditions for structured production along the lines of the Green "Revolution". This causes the usual form of agricultural production, based on the use of pesticides, synthetic fertilisers, and heavy tractors to be used in a part of the movement's settlements. However, one can see that even in these settlements there is already an effort to progressively move to other forms of production. However, inserted as they are in the capitalist market and under capital's current offensive, it is not easy to oppose the hegemonic model.

The State provides credit with low-interest rates, subsidies, seeds, privileged technical assistance and the development of applied scientific and technological research to agribusiness, among other mechanisms and incentives that maintain the Green Revolution standards (Moura 2014). At the same time, large corporations and the state disfigure and hinder the general conditions for the collective and associated production of healthy foods.

Several studies highlight the difficulties of technical assistance for family farms, which deal with precarious professionals, few technicians per settlement, poor working conditions for technicians, damaged equipment, lack of specific training in agroecology, stimulation of marketing networks, etc. This situation portrays one face of a State that is minimum for workers and maximum for financial capital. In Marx's terms (1996), the state and governments create the general conditions for the production and reproduction of capital and annihilate, subordinate or hinder alternative forms of production that can give rise to a new mode of production.[4]

From the point of view of consumption, despite the existence of agroecological marketing networks, one of the challenges for agroecology is the fact that its products are accessible, mainly, to the middle and upper classes of Brazilian society. According to information provided by the head of the seedling nursery at the Milton Santos School, the costs of producing organic vegetables are not much higher than those cultivated with pesticides. The technician may be right when it comes to small plots. We also need to remember that the final price of food grown with pesticides, transgenics and synthetic fertilisers represents only the tip of the iceberg. If we consider all the costs generated by agribusiness to the Public Health

[4] Sampaio Jr. (2013) makes a good overview of the actions of military governments to strengthen agribusiness, going through the period of "democratization", and even reaching the Lula years in the section "institutionalization of the counterrevolution and liberal adjustment".

System (SUS), to consumers who have to buy medicine in the pharmacy because they have been poisoned, the subsidies given to agribusiness, the final global price of agribusiness products is very expensive, even if on the shelf they appear as "cheaper".

Whatever the case may be, the accusations levelled and pressure exerted by the social movements, combined with greater ecological awareness, ended up resulting in public policies aimed at the purchase of organic food for schools, day care centres, hospitals, sanatoriums, etc. This is the case of the Food Acquisition Program (PAA) and the National School Feeding Program (PNAE). However, even in the municipalities where this policy is applied, the purchase volume does not reach 10% of the total.

Although limited and prone to becoming islands in the capitalist market, the experiences of spreading agroecological and fair-trade practices must be recognised and disseminated by social movements, such as MST's aforementioned Bionatur, based in southern Brazil.[5]

The Creation of the Agroecology Schools

Agroecology reveals a new way of producing, as previously explained. Thus, the MST decided to create schools, alternatives to state schools, that would train technicians, who are not solely technical but also political specialists, according to their needs. To create the schools, the Movement relied on its educational proposal and years of experience, but it was also necessary to count on the involvement of its educators to develop a new curriculum focused on agroecology.

[5] It would also be important to highlight the arrangement that has allowed the genetic improvement of native seeds in Paraná and Santa Catarina. Torres-Rego (2016) and Luzzi (2007) synthesised the work of greater repercussion of AS-PTA (Family Agriculture and Agroecology) of the Contestado and Centro Sul do Paraná: rescue and multiplication of varieties of native seeds of corn, beans, cassava, rice and potato; implementation of a creole germplasm bank in 2003 and a genetic improvement laboratory in 2004 at the State University of Londrina (UEL), subsidizing experiments to evaluate creole cultivars by farmers together with researchers from UEL; holding creole seed fairs; experiments in ecological soil management in partnership with the Paraná Agronomic Institute (IAPAR) and the Brazilian Agricultural Research Company—Agrobiology; organizing agroecological product markets; commercialization of ecological yerba mate with the brand Sombra dos Pinheirais by an association of farmers; creation of a consortium of five community organizations for the processing and commercialisation of ecological grains with the trademark of Alimento Sagrado (Luzzi 2007).

Thus, the incorporation of agroecology into the MST's agenda led to the creation of several Agroecology Schools in different states. There are currently about 30 Agroecology Schools in Brazil, mostly concentrated in the southern region of Brazil, mainly in the State of Paraná. In Paraná, there are five MST training centres and/or schools that present the debate and training for agroecology: Iraci Salete Strozak School, in the municipality of Laranjeiras do Sul and Ireno Alves dos Santos School, in Rio Bonito do Iguaçu, both connected to the Centre for Sustainable Development and Training in Agroecology (CEAGRO); José Gomes da Silva School, located in São Miguel do Iguaçu; Milton Santos School in Maringá and the Latin American Agroecology School, in the municipality of Lapa. In these spaces, Technical Courses in Agroecology are offered in the following modalities: Integrated High School Technician in Agroecology Course; Technician in Agroecology—Youth and Adult Education; Technician in Agriculture with an emphasis on Agroecology; Technologist in Agroecology; Technician in Agroecology with an emphasis on Agroforestry Systems and Technician in Agroecology with Qualification for Milk Production. The courses are held in partnership with public educational institutions, with resources from the National Education Program in Agrarian Reform (PRONERA), certified by the Federal Institute of Paraná (IFPR) and the National Institute of Colonization and Agrarian Reform (INCRA) (Novaes and Santos 2013).

A document crafted by the Paraná chapter of the MST presents the main objectives of the Movement's schools in the State of Paraná.

- To be a training space for working-class organizations;
- To be a space where meetings of the MST and other organizations which seek the same goals of social transformation can take place;
- To be a reference in the development of experiments in the field of agroecological production, presenting concrete results for farmers;
- To be a space for the development of socialist humanist values, matured through collective life;
- To improve methods of technical and political training and schooling since elementary school, as well as in high school and higher education;
- To enable the development of scientific and technological experiments, focused on the peasants' reality;
- To be a space where popular culture is encouraged and experienced, especially peasant culture;
- To be a space where people can live, educate, work, have fun, and build perspectives of the future (MST-PR 2004; Lima 2011, p. 87).

According to Lima et al. (2012), the theoretical and methodological foundations of the MST Agroecology School in Paraná are linked to the Movement's philosophical and pedagogical principles of education and pedagogy, the systematisation of which resulted from reflections on its educational-political praxis, based on three fundamental sources: socialist pedagogy, popular education and dialectical historical materialism (Santos 2015).

Lima et al. (2012, p. 4) also present the Pedagogical Proposal of these schools, including the Milton Santos School, highlighting that it is

> [..] based on the accumulation of work and experience in the training of militants and cadres in the MST, which is based on elements of the Political Pedagogical Project of the Florestan Fernandes National School (ENFF) and the educational experiences carried out at the Josué de Castro Institute of Education (IEJC). For the training of the Militant-Technical-Educator in Agroecology, it is necessary to appropriate the MST's political lines and organizational principles alongside technical-scientific, political, and organizational knowledge.

We observed that, in the pedagogy of the MST, education has a political commitment to social transformation, in line with the organisation's educational practices. Thus, the training of the landless militants and educational practices in agroecology are not limited to activities developed in its schools, but are also forged in the matrices of human formation, among them, "[...] the educational principle of work, social praxis, and history" (Caldart 2004, p. 42; Lima 2011, p. 76) adds that

> Educational practices in Agroecology have the political and pedagogical intentionality of an emancipatory educational project that is associated with the right to school and technical education in the rural reality. The understanding is that, in the settlements conquered by Landless families, collective alternatives can be built within the MST's organizational political praxis that inhibit the reproduction of capitalist social relations.

From the principles and actions of the Movement's agroecological education, seeds of non-capitalist relations can be born. Lima et al. (2012, p. 9) state that "[...] the organic structure and the management process, through the self-organization of the subjects, is the basis that enables the planning, organization and execution of the work, which is developed through cooperative relationships". Thus, agroecology is understood in the MST as an educational principle that guides the subjects to the construction of a societal project beyond capital. Roseli Caldart (2013) points out that today, agroecology is the movement's productive matrix. Along with cooperation, it serves as a guiding principle for all MST schools.

Agroecology in the Curriculum of the MST Vocational Schools

In the same way as in other types of MST-run or -influenced schools, in agroecology schools both the school organisation and the curricula are implemented in a heterogeneous way. The MST Agroecology Schools tend to have an organic curriculum and in the state schools in which the Movement has influence, this agenda may appear in a less substantive way.

Agroecology courses, as well as those of a similar nature, are not only technical, typical of the hard sciences, with a large workload in the exact and biological disciplines. Especially because no course is just technical, not even the lauded state-run technical courses are neutral and free of ideology. Each and every course is political, and every technique carries with it politics, ideology and class interests (Novaes, 2012; Dagnino 2014).

The Agroecology School courses are not different in this way, as they disseminate a certain ideology in the technique they disseminate. They intend to carry out a critique of the Green Revolution and, more generally, the socio-metabolism of capital. At the same time, they criticise the Green Revolution by disseminating research, documents critical of destructive production, and criticism of patents, pesticides, transgenics, etc. The MST courses contribute to the construction of theory and practice, and to the dissemination of the principles and foundations of agroecology.

While the courses of the State and Federal Technical Schools are conservative, with many technical disciplines that do not question the relationship between Science, Technology and Social Classes (Dagnino 2014), they offer little humanistic content and are based on a pedagogical project aimed at training the workforce within the paradigm of flexible skills/accumulation; in the MST Agroecology Schools, despite some contradictions and limits, it is possible to find a curriculum with more integration between social and hard sciences, an attempt to appropriate historical materialism and a fruitful relationship between theory, represented by the scientific foundations of agroecology and scientific criticism of the Green Revolution and practice, through agroecological experimentation.

However, there are also difficulties in the MST Agroecology Schools. Guhur et al. (2012) observed that theoretical appropriation by the students is still low. In addition, Agroecology Schools face many contingencies: not all teachers are organic to the MST, there are problems in integrating disciplines, with relative fragmentation of knowledge, few resources for school maintenance, few researchers from Universities and Research Institutes developing agroecological research and others.

Final Thoughts

Although agroecology for the MST is still an area under construction, we observed that, for them, agroecology is not reduced to preserving the environment. Quite the opposite: the Movement has tried to incorporate other elements and dimensions, such as cooperation; gender issues; decommodification and the rescue and systematisation of knowledge accumulated by peasants, etc. At the same time, the MST Agroecology Schools challenge us to theorise radical criticism of destructive production and alienated labour. Furthermore, they challenge us to think about ways to bring agroecological theory and practice together, experimentations with the democratic management of schools and the educational systems of social movements. They also help us think about creating a curriculum that is both critical and more comprehensive, besides the classic divisions between social and natural sciences.

Agroecology, as a field of comprehensive knowledge which broadens the horizons beyond the epistemological homogeneity of uncritical positivism and postmodernist rejection of any epistemology, seeks to apprehend the historical character of social phenomena and the partial identity between the subject and the object through its practice. That is, theory and practice. However, agroecology, beyond a specific field of knowledge, is also a way of life that aims at an epistemological rupture with the fragmentation of reality and the destructive scientific utilitarianism of the so-called "Green Revolution". In addition to "sustainable development" or variations of "eco-capitalism", the agroecology of social movements helps us to think about agrarian reform, alternative forms of production, commercialisation and education beyond capital in the twenty-first century.

Bibliography

Caldart, R. A pedagogia do Movimento Sem Terra. São Paulo: Expressão Popular, 2004.

Caldart, R. S. Desafios do Vínculo entre Trabalho e Educação na Luta e Construção da Reforma Agrária Popular. Texto apresentado como trabalho encomendado na 36ª Reunião Anual da Anped, GT Trabalho e Educação, Goiânia, 30 set. 2013.

Caporal, F.; Costabeber, J. Análise Multidimensional da Sustentabilidade - uma proposta metodológica a partir da Agroecologia. Revista Agroecologia e Desenvolvimento Rural Sustentável, Porto Alegre, v. 3, n. 3, pp. 70–85, 2002.

Carter, M.; Carvalho, H. M. A luta na terra: fonte de crescimento, inovação e desafio constante ao MST. In: CARTER, M. (org.) Combatendo a desigualdade social. São Paulo: Editora da UNESP, 2004.

Costa Neto, C. P. L. Agricultura sustentável, tecnologias e sociedade. In: Costa, L. F.; Moreira, R. J.; Bruno, R. (Org.). Mundo Rural e Tempo Presente. Rio de Janeiro, 1999, v. 2, pp. 299–321.

Dagnino, R. (org.) Tecnologia Social – ferramenta para construir outra sociedade. Campinas: Instituto de Geociências-Unicamp, 2014.

Folgado, C. Os desafios da campanha contra os agrotóxicos. Curitiba: Brasil de Fato, 2013.

Gonçalves, S. Campesinato, Resistência e Emancipação: o modelo agroecológico adotado pelo MST no Estado do Paraná. 2008. Tese (Doutorado em Geografia) - UNESP, 2008.

Guhur, D. M. P.; Toná, N. *Agroecologia*. In: Caldart, R. S; Pereira, I. B; Alentejano, P; Frigotto, G. (orgs.) Dicionário de educação do campo. Rio de Janeiro, São Paulo: Escola Politécnica de Saúde Joaquim Venâncio, Expressão Popular, pp. 57–66, 2012.

Guhur, D. M. P.; Tardin, J. M. (Org.). Diálogo de Saberes, no encontro de culturas: Caderno de Ação Pedagógica. Maringá: Escola Milton Santos, 2012.

Lima, A. C. Práticas educativas em agroecologia no MST/PR: processos formativos na luta pela emancipação humana. 2011. 321 f. Dissertação (Mestrado em Educação) - Universidade Estadual de Maringá, Maringá, 2011.

Lima, A. Guhur, D. Toná, N.; Noma, A. *Reflexões sobre a educação profissional em agroecologia no MST*: desafios dos cursos técnicos do Paraná. In: Rodrigues, F. C.; Novaes, H. T.; Batista, E. L. (orgs.) Movimentos Sociais, Trabalho Associado e Educação para além do capital. São Paulo: Outras Expressões, 2012.

Luzzi, N. O debate agroecológico no Brasil: uma construção a partir de diferentes atores sociais. 2007. Tese (Doutorado em Ciências Sociais em Desenvolvimento, Agricultura e Sociedade) – Instituto de Ciências Humanas e Sociais, Universidade Federal Rural do Rio de Janeiro, Rio de Janeiro, 2007.

Machado, L. C. P. Carta a Henrique Tahan Novaes. Porto Alegre, 2009.

Marx, K. O capital. São Paulo: Nova Cultural, 1996, volume I.
Mazalla Neto, W. Agroecologia e processamento de alimentos em assentamentos rurais. Campinas: Átomo e Alínea, 2013.
Mészáros, I. Para além do capital. São Paulo: Boitempo, 2002.
Moura, C. As rebeliões no Estado de São Paulo. In: Moura, C. Rebeliões da Senzala. São Paulo: Anita Garibaldi, 2014. 5ª edição.
MST. Reforma Agrária: por um Brasil sem Latifúndio!. Textos para debate do 4 Congresso Nacional do MST. São Paulo: MST, 2000.
Netto, J. P. Introdução. In: Marx, K. Miséria da Filosofia: resposta à Filosofia da Miséria, do sr. Proudhon. São Paulo: Expressão Popular, 2008, pp. 7–16.
Novaes, H. T. Reatando um fio interrompido: a relação universidade-movimentos sociais na América Latina. São Paulo: Expressão Popular-Fapesp, 2012.
Novaes, H. T.; Santos, L. *Produção Destrutiva, Agroecologia e Educação Agroecológica do MST-PR*. V Congresso Teoria Política do Socialismo, Marília, agosto de, 2013.
Oliveira, A. U. A questão da aquisição de terras por estrangeiros no Brasil– um retorno aos dossiês. Agrária, São Paulo, No. 12, 2010.
Pinassi, M. O.; Mafort, K. Os agrotóxicos e a reprodução do capital na perspectiva feminista da Via Campesina In: Rodrigues, F. C.; Novaes, H. T.; Batista, E. L. (Orgs.) Movimentos sociais, trabalho associado e educação para além do capital. São Paulo: Outras Expressões, 2012. pp. 141–158.
Rego, T. T. Formação em agroecologia. Programa do Contestado da AS-PTA. 313f. Tese (Doutorado em Educação), UFSC, 2016.
Sampaio JR., P. Notas críticas sobre a atualidade e os desafios da questão agrária. In: STEDILE, J. P. (org.) Debates sobre a situação e perspectivas da reforma agrária na década de 2000. São Paulo: Expressão Popular, 2013, pp. 189–240.
Santos, S. História da Coopava. In: Novaes, H. T.; Santos, J.; Pires, J. H. (Orgs.) Questão agrária, cooperação e agroecologia, vol II. São Paulo: Outras Expressões, 2015, no prelo.
Serafim, M. P. Agricultura familiar no Brasil: Um panorama sobre a política e as instituições. São Paulo: Annablume, 2012.
Shiva, V. Biopirataria: a Pilhagem da Natureza e do Conhecimento. Petrópolis: Editora Vozes, 2001.
Tait, M. Elas dizem não! Mulheres camponesas e resistência ao cultivo de transgênicos no Brasil e Argentina. 220f. 2013. Tese. (Doutorado em Política Científica e Tecnológica), Universidade Estadual de Campinas.

CHAPTER 10

Notes on Social Movements and Education: Challenges of the Struggle Between Capital and Labour in Brazil

Introduction

This chapter aims to outline the relationship between social movements and education in light of the particularities of Brazilian capitalism. We start from an understanding that social movements are an expression of class struggle. However, there are different theoretical explanations for the existence of these movements and the way they develop. Therefore, we will first present a summary of different theories about social movements. Then, we will work with a specific understanding of social movements as an expression of the contradictions between capital and labour in the capitalist mode of production. Based on this understanding, the third part of the text will discuss the relations formed between social movements and their educational potential in light of the particularities of Brazilian capitalism.

Theories About Social Movements

Professor Maria da Glória Gohn presents a synthesis of the various theories about Social Movements in her work. According to Gohn (2012), the first analyses of social movements are associated with the theory of social action. This line sought to understand collective behaviours. Gohn (2012) calls them classic and categorises them as belonging to a North American paradigm because these approaches first appeared in the USA. This

H. Tahan Novaes, *Associated Labor and Production in the Age of Barbarism*, https://doi.org/10.1007/978-3-031-51183-7_10

line of thinking focuses on socio-psychological aspects. Great importance is attributed to psychological reactions so that adherence to movements would be blind and irrational responses taken by individuals disoriented by the process of change that industrial society generated. Alonso (2009, p. 50) explains:

> [...] in mass society, operated by consumption and in tune with the dominant pattern of individuation, collective mobilisation would break out only as irrationality or, according to Smelser, as a reactive explosion of individual frustrations, which institutions would momentarily be unable to channel. In one way or another, the explanation had psychosocial pillars, based on collective emotions, and a sombre tone, resonating with a context marked by the advance of totalitarian regimes.

Durkheim's thought and his description of the state of anomie and disorder have great influence on this theory. Durkheim saw anomie as being closely linked to the consequences of the disorderly growth of industry, which could create precarious relations, with indefinite, vague rules. In this way, social movements would be created in moments of social unrest, uncertainty and result from frustrations and discomfort. The basis of this analysis is the belief in a static social order which needs to be controlled. A lack of control would lead to the rise of social movements, which would be foreign objects, external to historical subjects.

In the 1960s, Resource Mobilization Theory (RMT) was developed, also in the USA. It expressed a rejection of classical theories regarding their emphasis on feelings and resentments inside collective groups. Psychology was rejected as the explanatory focus of collective actions. The historical context in which this theory appears is linked to the rise of movements in the USA based on civil rights (ethnicity), gender issues (feminism) and life-style choices (pacifism and environmentalism)[1] (Alonso 2009).

RMT builds an approach based on utilitarianism, applying business logic to social movements. The decision to act would start from rational

[1] According to Alonso (2009, p. 51): "McCarthy and Zald (1977) are the foremost names of Resource Mobilization Theory (RMT), which they created in the face of the explanations of collective mobilizations in terms of collective emotions, exacerbating the opposite extreme: their rationality. Against functionalism, they argued that, far from chaotic expression of individual dissatisfactions not channelled by institutions, movements, such the Civil Rights movements in the United States, had meaning and organisation".

calculations of costs and benefits. Thus, collective action would only be possible in the presence of material resources (financial and infrastructure), human resources (activists and supporters) and organisation. This theory exacerbates the rationality of collective mobilizations, seeking to explain the process of mobilisation and not worrying about unravelling its reasons related to the social and political context.

Maria da Glória Gohn (2012) highlights Charles Tilly as one of the most important American scholars of Social Movements. Gohn says Charles Tilly developed historical work on the collective actions that occurred in Europe in different periods between the eighteenth and nineteenth centuries seeking to identify which people, resources and purposes were involved in the movements and pointed out that the basic generating factor of the changes would be in the institutionalised political system, which provided spaces for a democratic political culture that configured modern collective action.[2]

There are two other important theoretical lines on Social Movements. One of them is called the Theory of Political Mobilization (TPM), which also emerged in the USA and the Theory of New Social Movements (TNSM), developed in Europe. These theories stand out because they represent a critique of RMT, because it is restricted to organisational aspects, while also standing apart from Marxist analyses, considered to be too economicist and determinist by TPM and TNSM proponents.

TPM focuses on the development of political processes. One of its most representative authors, Sidney Tarrow, developed the concept of "political opportunity structure" (POS). The POS would be related to the formal and informal dimensions of the political environment, that is, to the channels for the expression of claims that may be more or less permeable to the demands of civil society. According to Tarrow (2009, p. 99):

[2] When emphasizing the historical character of Tilly's studies, Maria da Glória Gohn (2012, pp. 64, 65) explains: "Although many authors include Charles Tilly's work inside Resource Mobilization Theory (and they have their reasons for this), we think that there must be a differentiation, since it has its own characteristics, a style of essentially historical approach that has turned into a school. Other authors, such as Foweraker (1995), relate Tilly's work to the paradigm of the New Social Movements. We disagree with this position because Tilly himself highlights the structural character of his analyses and criticizes approaches focused only on issues of identity and the microsocial perspective. What it shares with the NSM paradigm is the issue of solidarity, particularly communal solidarity."

> Confrontation escalates when people obtain external resources to escape submission and find an opportunity to use them. It also increases when people feel threatened by costs they cannot afford or that offend their sense of justice. Those challenging the status quo find opportunities to present their claims when institutional access is opened, when divisions arise in the elites, when allies become available, and when the state's capacity for repression declines. When this is combined with the perceived high cost of inaction, these opportunities produce episodes of political confrontation.

TNMS, on the other hand, emphasises culture, ideology, daily social struggles and the process of identity created therein. It is a theoretical model based on classless culture and diffuse interests. In TNMS, social movements are seen as pressure groups aiming to change society's general values and customs. In their view, the world of labour would have lost its centrality in contemporary capitalism, so that social movements would no longer focus on redistributive issues but would be engaged in a symbolic struggle around quality of life, personal fulfilment or human rights.

the foremost exponents of this theory we have Alain Touraine (France) and Alberto Melucci (Italy). According to Alonso (2009), Touraine argues that, after 1960, a post-industrial society would have been configured, in which industry and labour would have lost among centrality, so the conflicts around labour would have been diluted and domination would have become markedly cultural. New movements would be related to the struggle for new ways of life, and the new subjects would no longer be classes, but marginalised groups, such as black people, indigenous people, homosexuals, women and young people, would have an attitude of opposition.[3] Melucci dedicated himself to producing a theory

[3] "After the 1960s, a new pattern of society would have been configured, which Touraine initially calls a "programmed society" and then a "post-industrial society", in which industry and labour would have lost centrality. Labor conflicts would have been diluted, processed by democratic institutions, through mechanisms such as the expansion of rights, and by capitalist institutions, with mechanisms like wage increases. Domination would have become eminently cultural, made through the control of information by a technocracy. Technique and culture would interpenetrate, the distinctions between the public and private worlds would be clouded, causing conflicts previously restricted to the economic plane to advance to private life (family, education, sex) and gain symbolic dimensions" (Alonso 2009, p. 60).

of collective identity developed through collective action in which there is communication, production and negotiation of meanings.[4]

Based on the theories presented, from the first theories formulated, which initially saw collective actions as anomalies, the result of irrationality, through RMT, which proposes an approach based on utilitarianism, applying a business logic to social movements, then TMP, which focuses on context-based political opportunities that would determine the actions of the movements until arriving at theories about New Social Movements, we could ask: what is there in common between all these theories?

First, they are not theories that construct comprehensive explanations in view of economic and social totality. It can be said that they are explanations that compartmentalise their analyses and frame social movements within the bourgeois order.

Classical theory completely denies that social movements have a constructive role in society, while others see possibilities for social movements to strengthen democracy. In RMT, the success of social movements is closely linked to the availability of human and material resources. PMT focuses on political opportunities, which can be created by the state itself and can also be hindered by it, since repressive environments could lead to a downturn in social movement activities.

TNMS is based on different authors, such as Touraine and Melucci, who, although they have particular analyses of social movements, have something in common: they argue that we live in a post-industrial society, in which the basic conflict of society would no longer be between capital and labour, but in the cultural sphere. Therefore, the essential contradiction of the capitalist mode of production and the bases of labour exploitation are removed from the agenda. The dominant issue becomes the struggle for new identities and values, thus, identity movements such as feminism, pacifism, environmentalism or citizenship rights are addressed in the foreground.

[4] According to Alonso (2009), in Mellucci's view: "new social movements would then be particularistic forms of resistance, reactive to the directions of socioeconomic development and in search of the reappropriation of time, space and everyday relations. 'Post-materialist' challenges, with symbolic motivations and aimed at the construction or recognition of collective identities".

Social Movements and Class Struggle

In contrast to these approaches, in this chapter, we perceive social movements as an expression of class struggle. Social movements can be understood from what has been conventionally called the "social issue" under the capitalist mode of production. From its beginnings, in its competitive industrial phase, the massive impoverishment of the population constituted one of the immediate expressions of capitalism. Under the capitalist mode of production, the working class, alienated from private property, creates much greater amounts of wealth than it receives in the form of wages, which are only enough to ensure the survival and reproduction of the working class. Unpaid labour is the mechanism behind the accumulation of capital, creating an ever-growing development of the productive forces of society. This process shapes the exploitation of labour and provokes class struggle: on the one hand, those who own and control the means of production and, on the other, those who survive by selling their labour power.

The search for ever greater amounts of surplus value (unpaid labour) is what drives human activity under this mode of production. This drive is fundamentally irrational since truly human needs are denied, while the material conditions to suppress them are increasingly developed.

What makes the exploitation of labour unique in these circumstances is that, at the same time as pauperism grows, it increases the social capacity to produce wealth. This process is outlined by Karl Marx in the twenty-third chapter of "Capital", named *General Law of Capitalist Accumulation* (Marx 2013).

Thus, the "social question" is linked to the characteristic feature of the relationship between capital and labour, which is distinguished by exploitation, and which is a necessary corollary to capitalist development in all its phases. Those who are exploited do not submit passively. At various times in history, they organised themselves collectively in different ways against the situation in which they found themselves. In the nineteenth century, for instance, we could mention the violent actions of the Luddites against productive innovations that drove workers to unemployment and the creation of *trade unions*, which became a real threat to the established social order (Netto 2008).

Therefore, social movements can be understood as an expression of the fundamental contradiction between capital and labour.

This interpretation implies a certain theoretical treatment of the "social issue" that consists of its connection with the problems regarding the foundations of the established economic-social order. The bourgeois order is understood by Marx as a world system, with a historical tendency to encompass everything, from its origins in the classical bourgeois revolutions to the incorporation of all regions of the globe, as described in the Communist Party Manifesto of 1848 (Marx 2009). This does not mean that there is a universal model describing the functioning of the capitalist mode of production in different historical realities.

This universalising historical dynamic is expressed through the rise of bourgeoisies starting with the classical bourgeois revolutions thirsting for new fields of accumulation. In this context, each of the singular objects, which can be, for example, national spaces, is involved in a web of relations of a mode of production that incorporates and subordinates everything. As they are incorporated into this dynamic, these singularities configure particularities, understandable through a set of mediations. Only in this way would it be possible to understand determined, particular economic-social formations.

Thus, due to these methodological theoretical foundations, social movements in Brazil are understood as an expression of the contradiction between capital and labour in a particular reality, characterized by our specific colonial history. Our history has been marked by the interaction between dependence and underdevelopment. Dependence is expressed in external imperialist domination, while underdevelopment is characterised by the maintenance of backwardness, as in the vastly archaic agrarian relations, as Florestan Fernandes (2006) analysed in *The bourgeois revolution in Brazil*.

We can say that the challenges posed to social movements in Brazil are linked to an important educational task that is related, according to Mészáros (2008), to the conscious self-change of individuals called to realise a radically different social order, embodied in the emancipation of human beings from all exploitation. Why is this educational task critical? Because, if we are facing an all-encompassing social order that subjugates everything in its path, the challenges of those who live from their labour can only be understood from a theoretical construction that seeks to understand the problems of our historical particularity, according to the reciprocal relations established with the totality. Thus, proletarian class consciousness consists of the worker's consciousness of his social being as encysted in the structural antagonism of capitalist society:

> An objective theory of class consciousness implies, above all, the evaluation of its issues in terms of the global Marxist conception of capitalism as a real-world system. This means that phenomena such as social conflicts which seem to be purely local must be related to the objective totality of a given stage of socioeconomic development. Without a conscious effort to link specific social phenomena to the general trends and characteristics of capitalism as a global system, the significance of these phenomena remains obscure or seems disproportionately increased, and the same is true of general laws - for example, the law of impoverishment, the decreasing rate of profit, etc., which are valid only in globally qualified terms and which otherwise may seem to be nothing more than speculations and abstractions. (Mészáros 2008, p. 85)

The educational and theoretical challenge of social movements, therefore, would be to transcend the limits of group consciousness, going from determined groups of workers towards a global consciousness of social being.

Social Movements and Political Education in the Brazilian Reality

The 1950s and 1960s were characterised as pre-revolutionary by Octávio Ianni (1981), as we experienced an increase in the organisation and awareness of the exploited classes in the cities and countryside, in the peasant leagues, churches and political parties, among others. In several works of the time, both Marxist and otherwise, the term "Revolution" is used to examine the period. As an example, we could mention: *The Brazilian revolution*, by Caio Prado Júnior (1968) and *The Brazilian pre-revolution* by Celso Furtado (1962). This was the period of intensification of the industrialisation of the country, with the formation of the proletariat and the bourgeoisie.

According to Prado Júnior (1968, p. 2): [...] "Revolution, in its real and profound sense, means a historical process marked by successive economic, social and political reforms and modifications, which, concentrated in a relatively short historical period, will lead to structural transformations of society, and in particular of economic relations and the reciprocal balance of different classes and social categories" (p. 2).

One of the substantial challenges in education was how to teach a large part of the adult population to read and write so that they could vote and participate in political decision-making in the process of building democracy. In *Education as a practice for freedom*, Paulo Freire (2000) follows a similar line to the authors mentioned in the last paragraph and dedicates the first chapter of the book to examining "*Brazilian society in transition*". He describes a closed society, without a people to call its own, contrary to dialogue, backwards, commanded by an elite superimposed on its world and a society in which the people could become participants in all the transformations experienced in the economic, social, political and cultural dimensions:

> An education that would enable man to courageously discuss his problems. Of his insertion in this set of issues. That warned him of the dangers of his time, so that, aware of them, he would gain the strength and courage to fight, instead of being taken and dragged to the perdition of his own "self", subjected to the prescriptions of others. Education that would constantly place him in dialogue with others. That predisposed him to constant revisions. To the critical analysis of their "findings". To a certain rebellion, in the most human sense of the term. To identify it with scientific methods and processes. (Freire, 2000, p. 90)

Paulo Freire develops several experiences of popular education in the aforementioned period, from which he conceives a literacy method embedded in the need to raise awareness of the human being about the social problems in which he is inserted, about his responsibilities and about his role in the cultural climate of the time in transition. It was about working to overcome an intransitivity of consciousness through a method to teach literacy—in which the apprehension of problems is only in the biologically vital sphere. First one would go through a naïve transitivity, still characterised by a limited sphere of apprehension, to later reach a critical transitivity, in which a dialogical and active education could be developed. This stage is characterised by a large depth of interpretation of problems, which would be the basis of true democracy.

Paulo Freire (2000) highlights the close relationship between those who went through their literacy groups and greater engagement in social movements. The relationship makes even more sense if we consider that the population educated by this method was precisely the one that suffered the most from exploitation and the total absence of suitable living conditions. One can point out an intense connection between this pedagogy—which focuses on the subject and his possibilities of knowing and becoming aware of reality—with the struggles around land and better wages and working conditions.

At the beginning of 1964, the Paulo Freire method had become state policy, under the government of President João Goulart. 20,000 culture circles were planned, which would result in 2 million newly literate people by the end of that year. One of the first measures of the military dictatorship when it came to power was to abolish this policy and determine the exile of its creator.

According to Florestan Fernandes (2006), the military dictatorship installed in 1964 represented a bourgeois counterrevolution, halting all possible democratic and economic sovereignty advances in the country. The Brazilian bourgeoisie laid bare its historical character in these so-called "Years of Lead", revealing its subservience to the interests of the countries at the centre of capitalism, reinforcing ties with imperialism while laying claim to omnipotence in their relationship with internally exploited classes.

During this period, the way in which the "social issue" is historically treated in Brazil, that is, as a matter of police repression, intensified. Social movements linked to labour, peasants and student movements were barbarically persecuted. Their leaders were tortured and many were exiled (Novaes 2012). Between 1964 and 1968, the main movement that brought together the forces of opposition to the dictatorship was the student movement. The National Students' Union (UNE) had significant importance because they were able to continue demonstrating, despite the violent scenario that exterminated the possibilities of organising unions. The same would only come to pass for students after the AI-5 in 1968 (Sanfelice 2008).

After the "Years of Lead", the Catholic Church played an important role in organising resistance to the dictatorship. Sectors of the Church were influenced by the Medellín Declaration, coming from the II General Conference of the Latin American Episcopate. According to this statement, "salvation" is announced in the establishment of more humane living conditions and there is an emphasis on denouncing social structures that produce inequalities, exploitation and misery. They also encouraged communities to be formed, which became known as the Ecclesial Base Communities (CEBs). According to Eder Sader (1988), by 1981, more than 80,000 CEBs had been established with over 2 million people involved. These communities congregated groups that, inspired by the

Gospel, began to debate their precarious living conditions, as well as possible proposals to overcome this situation.

The CEBs are at the base of the social movements that emerged in the 1980s. This was the case of some urban movements in Greater São Paulo, such as the Mothers' Club, which fought to reduce the cost of living and the Health Movement of the eastern periphery, which defended more public health posts with quality services. In both cases, these movements played a very significant educational role. The Mothers' Club multiplied popular education activities around the cost of living. The meetings discussed the meanings, causes, and interests involved. Specific topics such as the agrarian issue and foreign debt were discussed.

The Movement for Health is noteworthy for the strength the movement gained with the work of sanitary doctors who carried out activities to teach families about diseases, how they spread and what the state's role in public health care could be. Sader sees these activities as spaces in which men and women contact the reasons that determine their social dramas, becoming aware of their living conditions (Sader 2008).

What happened in the period was a great growth in the number of social movements linked to specific agendas, based on the struggle for rights that somehow fed the popular struggles around the 1988 Constitution. On the one hand, the narrowness of the demands is justified by the violent context and the dismantling of the political organisations of the pre-dictatorial period. On the other, we have an element related to theoretical issues regarding social movements.

Virginia Fontes (2010) states that at the end of the 1970s, there was a return of many intellectuals from exile. They had been influenced by international sociological production on the "new social movements", which in turn established a strong criticism of the approaches that related structures to social classes, considering them as not backed by the immediate experience of the subjects, and so were not sufficiently empirical. Thus, there would have been a disdain for any reference to the totality and historical mode of the constitution of the subjects.

In this sense, there is a confluence of two aspects that contribute to the compartmentalization of struggles. First, we have the concrete reality of the subjects who engage in struggle during this period. They were intensely restricted in their political organisations and were blocked from thinking in terms of social classes. Then, we have the strong influence of the theoretical model related to the "new social movements", which consolidated a view that saw popular sectors as thinking in immediate, short-term goals.

During that same period, the Landless Rural Workers Movement, MST, was formally created in 1984 under the powerful influence of the CEBs, from which most of its key leaders came. The MST put agrarian reform back on the country's agenda—it had been intensely debated and was the aim of many struggles in the period before the coup. Their struggle focused on the occupation of huge unproductive tracts of land in the hands of large landowners. According to Roseli Caldart (2004), these land occupations became one of the primary tactics of the struggle and one of the foundations of their pedagogy. To carry out the occupations, there was an intense effort by the movement towards the political formation of its base, clarifying the legal bases that made the struggle an occupation and not an invasion of land, strongly based on the Land Statute (1964), which provided for agrarian reform measures to take place in large unproductive tracts of land, as well as pointing to the need for land to fulfil its social function (Rodrigues 2013).

The MST has become the largest social movement in the country, a nation-wide organisation with a very relevant concern about education, seen as a primary aspect to deal with the challenges posed by a social movement of this size. First, because the social base of the MST, which is excluded from access to land, is also historically excluded from access to education, so from the establishment first occupations there was a need to think about school and education for the children in these camps.

The MST touches on one of the pillars Brazil's particular brand of capitalism: land concentration, which underpins the extreme exploitation of the workforce in the countryside and in the cities. Because of this, the MST faces all kinds of violence, whether ideological, perpetrated by the media, or physical, by police forces or private militias. The organisation of this movement requires a very good understanding of all parties and policies involved in the dispute, hence the relevance of education in all its forms, from the dimension of schools to political training.

One of the consistent characteristics of the MST since the early 1980s is the struggle for public schools within settlements, camps and other areas. According to Kolling, Vargas and Caldart, "[...] Organising this struggle was the main objective of the creation of an education sector within the Movement" (Kolling et al. 2014, p. 95). Throughout its history, the Movement's thinking on education has become more complex, and the struggle's guiding principles have been established. They can be summarized as follows: (a) development and implementation of the Movement's own educational project; (b) criticism and/or denial of official state education; (c) implementation of democratic management in schools; (d) training of educators within the Movement; (e) establishing links between teaching and productive work (Dal Ri 2004).

In addition to the struggle for public schools, there is a concern with the political formation of the Movement's cadres. In the 1980s, there was a strong connection between the MST, the Pastoral Land Committee (CPT) and the PT, which played a central role in training militants in the struggle for land. In the 1990s, the Movement idealised its own training schools, capable of giving it greater autonomy. This culminated in the creation of the Florestan Fernandes National School (ENFF) in Guararema, in the state of São Paulo, in the 2000s. It was designed to host lectures and political training courses for militants from various parts of the world, especially Latin America, as well as courses with less autonomy, in partnership with portions of the left from universities.

To improve political formation, we must highlight the creation of Editora Expressão Popular, under the control of the MST. Producing cheap books with a critical bias, many of them in the Marxist field, Expressão Popular has been fundamental for the formation of many activists of the MST and other social movements. In the educational field, we could highlight the publication of some books by Anton Makarenko, Moisey Pistrak and Viktor Shulgin. In the field of political science, we have the publication of books by Karl Marx, Antonio Gramsci and Friedrich Engels, among others. Likewise, it is possible to have access to numerous agroecology classics, such as Albert Howard, Francis Chaboussou, Andre Voisin, Miguel Altieri, Sevilla Guzmán and Pinheiro Machado, among others.

Likewise, many of the so-called "místicas"[5] carried out by the movement have enormous educational potential, insofar as they help peasants to understand our capitalism, the exploitation of workers and peasants, the contradictions of youth in the countryside, the role of the capitalist state in class society, among other topics approached during the events.

In the 1990s, training courses for Technicians in Cooperative Administration (TAC) emerged, focused on the production and commercialisation

[5] The MST's "mistícas", literally mystiques, are collective ceremonies imbuing a sense of belonging, used as tools for organizing and political action.

of agrarian reform products. In the 2000s, in the context of resistance to the advance of corporations producing pesticides, transgenics, etc., agroecology entered the MST agenda. It was at this time that numerous professional education courses and non-school workshops on knowledge socialisation among peasants emerged, in view of the agroecological transition and self-organisation of students (Novaes et al. 2015; Caldart 2013).[6]

It is also worth mentioning the bachelor's degrees in Pedagogy, History, Agronomy and Veterinary Medicine offered by public universities, among others, which allowed many peasants to enter public universities, influencing and being influenced by the theoretical-ideological currents found in that environment (Lerrer 2010). In this sense, the training of educators themselves has been vital for the MST. We could mention the case of Paraná, where there was a combination of training carried out through a degree in Pedagogy from UNIOESTE and numerous training courses at the Zumbi dos Palmares Itinerant School (Cascavel).

In all these courses, the official history, eminently pacifying, is put in check, with different degrees of radicalism and contact with materialism. Workers' struggles are brought to the forefront of history. Dates commemorating the assassination of leaders are remembered to keep the flame of the struggle burning. The forces of labour appear as the guide of history, in contrast to the history of successful entrepreneurs, emperors or presidents.

In Rodrigues's doctoral dissertation (Rodrigues 2013), the theme of political formation in the MST in the 1980s was explored, highlighting the links that were established with the strategic guidelines arising from the Workers' Party.

The PT was created in 1981, and, as Virginia Fontes (2010) pointed out, this party played a very important role in the 1980s as a reference for a significant set of social movements in struggle. The PT acted as a connection between various popular movements, as a basis for expanding the content and scope of social struggles.

If, on the one hand, the PT had this unifying role, the 1980s also saw the consolidation and growth of NGOs, which were a form of organisation strongly supported by sources of international financing and related

[6] This theme was developed in the chapters of João Henrique de Souza Pires and Lais dos Santos in this collection.

to specific demands. Within NGOs, a professionalisation of advisory services provided to popular movements was developed. Thus, there was a significant dilution of social engagement and the possibilities of perceiving the real dimension of the struggle that is taking place, contributing to the makeup of class society.

NGOs grew in the 1980s and began to play an even more significant role in the 1990s with the adoption of neoliberal policies and the decrease in adherence to social movements throughout the country. The transformative potential of these organisations is very limited. There is little possibility of linking their specific agendas with the contradictions of classes installed in the Brazilian reality, and this seems to be one of the great challenges posed to us at this historical moment (Montaño 2002).

Final Thoughts

The economic and social challenges imposed on the country in the mid-1950s put the structures of class society and the correlation of forces between capital and labour on the agenda. These items were especially evident in union struggles, as well as in land struggles. The military dictatorship crushed the set of Brazilian social movements, leaving little space for organisation and resistance, which from the 1970s took place in the left-leaning sectors of the Catholic Church. The 1980s were the scene of a reality rife with contradictions. On the one hand, we have a rise of social struggles, in various spheres, unified in the struggle for direct elections and in the emergence and growth of the PT. On the other hand, there's an intense compartmentalization of struggles, making it difficult to have a more comprehensive view of the challenges imposed on Brazilian capitalism, and in this scenario, the struggle for Agrarian Reform cools down.

The most recent theories about social movements, such as the Theory of Political Mobilisation and the Theory of New Social Movements, have the characteristic of not carrying out more comprehensive analyses that relate the existence of movements to structural and organic causalities of the current order. These theories, as Virginia Fontes (2010) pointed out, get significant acceptance in the Brazilian intellectual scenario from the 1980s on. Together with the fragmentation of struggles contesting the established order, as a result of the dictatorship, they contributed to the difficulty of agglutination of all organisations according to a classist base.

In Brazil, the MST, with its origins in that same period, became the most important social movement in Latin America. With historical origin in land occupations in the south of the country in direct contestation of the agrarian policies of authoritarian governments, the MST, throughout its historical trajectory, increasingly realised that its struggle could not be restricted only to access to land, also including the educational issue, both within the scope of public schooling and the political formation of its militancy (Rodrigues 2013). The MST has made explicit in its current writings on the Popular Agrarian Reform project the need to perceive the Brazilian agrarian issue as one that touches the entire Brazilian working class, in several ways, from those that concern working conditions in the countryside and in the city, as well as the quality of the food that is commercialised (MST 2014). Therefore, the MST emphasises the importance of the struggle for agrarian reform being taken up by the entire Brazilian working class.

While the theoretical discussion of the MST has gone in the direction described above, the concrete reality has been of extreme difficulties in fighting effectively, which can be verified by the significant decrease in the number of land occupations in recent years.

The downturn of social movements' power is a reality, especially since the 2000s. In parallel, the State, taken by neoliberal policies, reduces the protection of the basic needs of the population, with recurring budget cuts that increasingly make health, education and other public services increasingly precarious.

Therefore, the challenges to be faced by social struggles intensify while conditions of organisation and political education worsen. These are necessary to understand Brazilian problems from a perspective that includes an analysis of the totality and places the class struggle in our reality as central,

Bibliography

Alonso, A. As teorias dos movimentos sociais: um balanço do debate. In: Lua Nova Revista de Cultura e Política, n.76, pp. 49–86, 2009.

Caldart, R. A pedagogia do Movimento Sem Terra. São Paulo: Expressão Popular, 2004.

Caldart, R. S. Desafios do Vínculo entre Trabalho e Educação na Luta e Construção da Reforma Agrária Popular. Texto apresentado como trabalho encomendado na 36ª Reunião Anual da Anped, GT Trabalho e Educação, Goiânia, 30 set. 2013.

Dal Ri, N. Vieitez, C. A educação do movimento dos sem-terra. Revista brasileira de educação, 2004, n. 26.

Fontes, V. O Brasil e o Capital imperialismo – teoria e história. Rio de Janeiro: Escola Politécnica de Saúde de São Joaquim Venâncio, Universidade Federal do Rio de Janeiro, 2010.

Foweraker, J. Theorizing Social Movements. Pluto Press (UK), 1995.

Freire, P. Educação como prática da liberdade. 24ª ed. Rio de Janeiro: Paz e Terra. 2000.

Furtado, C. A pré-revolução brasileira. Rio de Janeiro: Fundo de Cultura, 1962.

Gohn, M. da G. Teoria dos Movimentos Sociais. Paradigmas Clássicos e contemporâneos. 10ed. São Paulo: Loyola, 2012.

Ianni, O. A ditadura do grande capital. Rio de Janeiro: Civilização Brasileira, 1981.

Kolling, E. J.; Vargas, M. C.; Caldart, R. MST e educação. In: MST, Boletim da Educação n. 12. – II Encontro Nacional de Educadores e Educadoras da Reforma Agrária, Dez. 2014.

Lerrer, D. Preparar gente: a educação superior dentro do MST. Revista Estudos Sociedade e Agricultura, 2010.

Marx, K. A miséria da filosofia. São Paulo: Expressão Popular, 2009.

Marx, K. O capital. Crítica da Economia Política. Livro I. São Paulo: Boitempo, 2013.

McCarthy, J.; Zald, M. Resource Mobilization and Social Movements: A Partial Theory. American Journal of Sociology, Vol. 82, No. 6 (May, 1977), pp. 1212–1241.

Meszáros, I. Filosofia, ideologia e ciência social. São Paulo: Boitempo, 2008.

Montaño, C. Terceiro Setor e Questão Social. São Paulo: Cortez, 2002.

Netto, J. P. Introdução. In: Marx, K. Miséria da Filosofia: resposta à Filosofia da Miséria, do sr. Proudhon. São Paulo: Expressão Popular, 2008, pp. 7–16.

Novaes, H. T. Reatando um fio interrompido: a relação universidade-movimentos sociais na América Latina. São Paulo: Expressão Popular-Fapesp, 2012.

Novaes, H.; Mazin, D.; Santos, L. (Orgs.) Questão Agrária, Cooperação e Agroecologia. São Paulo: Outras Expressões, 2015.

Prado JR., Caio. A revolução brasileira. São Paulo: Brasiliense, 1968.

Rodrigues, F. C. Educação política dos trabalhadores: a centralidade da exploração do trabalho na análise da questão agrária no Brasil - a contribuição de Octávio Ianni. In: Rodrigues, F. C.; Novaes, H. T.; Batista, E. (orgs.) Movimentos Sociais, Trabalho Associado e Educação para além do capital. São Paulo: Outras Expressões, 2013, vol. II.

Sader, E. Quando novos personagens entram em cena: experiências, falas e lutas dos trabalhadores da Grande São Paulo (1970–1980). Rio de Janeiro: Paz e Terra, 1988.

Sader, E. Quando novos personagens entram em cena. Rio de Janeiro: Paz e Terra, 2008.

Sanfelice, J. L. Movimento Estudantil. A UNE na resistência ao golpe de 1964. Campinas: Alínea, 2008.

Tarrow, S., O poder em movimento. Movimentos Sociais e Confronto Político. São Paulo: Vozes, 2009.

Bibliography

Aarão Reis, D. A. A revolução faltou ao encontro: os comunistas no Brasil. São Paulo: Brasiliense, 1990.

Agacino, R. Chile In: Rodrigues, F. C.; Novaes, H. T.; Batista, E. (orgs.) Movimentos Sociais, Trabalho Associado e Educação para além do capital. São Paulo: Outras Expressões, 2013, vol II.

Agazzi, D. L. Trabalho e alienação no paradigma marxiano: uma discussão teórica e uma reflexão sobre a sua aplicação no capitalismo contemporâneo. 2000, 317 f. Tese (Doutorado em Economia), FEA – USP, São Paulo, 2000.

Aiziczon, F. In: Rodrigues, F. C.; Novaes, H. T.; Batista, E. (orgs.) Movimentos Sociais, Trabalho Associado e Educação para além do capital. São Paulo: Outras Expressões, 2013, vol II.

Alaniz, E. P. *Qualificação Profissional: um estudo das práticas educacionais em uma empresa de autogestão.* São Paulo: Editora da Unesp, 2007.

Alaniz, E. P. A política pública de formação para economia solidária no Brasil (2003–2011): análise de um projeto PROESQ/PNQ executado pela Rede Abelha/RN e do CFES nacional. 2012. 371 f. Tese (Doutorado em Educação) – Faculdade de Educação, Universidade de São Paulo, São Paulo, 2012.

Alonso, A. As teorias dos movimentos sociais: um balanço do debate. In: Lua Nova Revista de Cultura e Política, n.76, pp. 49–86, 2009.

Altieri, M. *Agroecología:* bases científicas para una agricultura sustentable. Montevidéu: Nordan–Comunidad, 1999.

Antunes, C. A concepção de educação na obra de István Mészáros. In: Batista, E.; Novaes, H. T. (orgs.) Trabalho e reprodução social. Bauru/Marília: Canal 6/Praxis, 2013, 2ª edição.

H. Tahan Novaes, *Associated Labor and Production in the Age of Barbarism*, https://doi.org/10.1007/978-3-031-51183-7

Antunes, R. A rebeldia do trabalho: o confronto operário no ABC paulista: as greves de 1978/80. Campinas, SP: Editora da Unicamp, 1992.

Antunes, R. Os sentidos do trabalho – ensaios sobre a afirmação e negação do trabalho. São Paulo: Boitempo, 2000.

Antunes, R. Os sentidos do trabalho: ensaios sobre a afirmação e negação do trabalho. São Paulo: Boitempo, 2002.

Antunes, R. O caracol e sua concha – ensaios sobre a nova morfologia do trabalho. São Paulo: Boitempo editorial, 2005.

Antunes, R. (org.) *Riqueza e Miséria do trabalho no Brasil*. São Paulo: Boitempo Editorial, 2006.

Antunes, R. Adeus ao trabalho? 15. ed. São Paulo: Cortez, 2008.

Antunes, R. *Palestra*. VI Colóquio Internacional Marx e Engels. Unicamp, IFCH, outubro de, 2010.

Antunes, R. Apresentação da coleção *Trabalho e Emancipação*. São Paulo: Expressão Popular, s/d.

Anweiler, O. Os conselhos na Revolução Húngara de 1956. In: Pinheiro, M.; Martorano, L. (orgs). Teoria e prática dos conselhos operários. São Paulo: Expressão Popular, 2013, pp. 201–212.

Arantes, P. F. Arquitetura Nova – Sérgio Ferro, Flávio Império e Rodrigo Lefèvre, de Artigas aos Mutirões. São Paulo: Editora 34, 2002.

Assis, M. O Alienista e outros contos. São Paulo: Moderna, 1995.

Azevedo, J.; Thomaz Júnior, A; Oliveira, A. M. S. A nova ofensiva do capital canavieiro e os desdobramentos para o trabalho no Pontal do Paranapanema e Alta Paulista (SP). Geografia em Atos (Online), v. 1, pp. 10–17, 2006.

Azpiazu, D.; Basualdo, E. *Concentración econômica y regulación de los servicios públicos. 2001.* Obtido em: www.wilsoncenter.org/topics/docs/concentració n%20economica.doc. Retirado em junho de 2007.

Baravelli, J. O cooperativismo uruguaio na habitação social de São Paulo Das cooperativas FUCVAM à Associação de Moradia Unidos de Vila Nova Cachoeirinha. USP, Faculdade de Arquitetura e Urbanismo, Dissertação de Mestrado, 2005.

Barreto, M. J. Territorialização das agroindústrias canavieiras na Região do Pontal do Paranapanema e os desdobramentos para o trabalho. 2012. Dissertação (Mestrado em Geografia) - Universidade Estadual Paulista Júlio de Mesquita Filho.

Barriguelli, J. C. Subsídios à história das lutas no campo em São Paulo (1870–1956). São Carlos: UFSCAR, Arquivo de História Contemporânea, 1981. 3v.

Barros, F. *Capítulo 2 – a Escola Madre Celina Polci*. Dissertação de Mestrado, FAU, USP, São Paulo, 2012.

Batista, E. Terceirização no Brasil e suas implicações para os trabalhadores. Campinas: Pontes, 2013. 2ª edição.

Behring, E. R; Boschetti, I. Política social: fundamentos e história. 9 ed. São Paulo: Cortez, 2011.v.2.

Benini, E. Sistema orgânico do trabalho. Rio de Janeiro: Ícone, 2012.

Benini, E.; Faria, M. S.; Novaes, H. T.; Dagnino, R. Gestão Pública e Sociedade: fundamentos e políticas públicas de economia solidária. São Paulo: Outras Expressões, 2011, vol. I. Disponível em: gestaopublicaesociedade.blogspot.com/

Benini, E.; Faria, M. S.; Novaes, H. T.; Dagnino, R. (orgs.) *Gestão Pública e Economia Solidária*. São Paulo: Outras expressões, 2012.

Benini, E.; Novaes, H. T. *As lutas por uma educação para além do capital na América Latina e a criação do curso de especialização "Gestão Pública e Sociedade"*. In: Benini, E.; Sales, A. L.; Novaes, H. T.; Silva, M.R. Gestão Pública e Sociedade: balanço e resumos dos trabalhos da 3ª edição do curso de especialização. São Paulo: Outras Expressões/Cromosete, 2013.

Bensaid, D. Sobre a questão judaica. In: Marx, K. A questão judaica. São Paulo: Boitempo Editorial, 2009.

Bernardo, J. "A autonomia das lutas operárias". In: Bruno, L. e Saccardo, C. (coordenadoras). Organização, trabalho e tecnologia. São Paulo: Atlas, 1986.

Bernardo, J. Apresentação. In: Pedreira Filho, V. Comissões de Fábrica – um claro enigma. São Paulo: Editora Entrelinhas, 1997.

Bernardo, J. A Autogestão da Sociedade Prepara-se na Autogestão das Lutas. Revista Piá Piou, 2006a.

Bernardo, J. Economia dos conflitos sociais. São Paulo: Expressão Popular, 2006b.

Bernardo, J. Economia dos conflitos sociais. São Paulo: Expressão Popular, 2009.

Bernardo, J. MST e agroecologia: uma mutação decisiva. Passa Palavra, 2012. Disponível em: http://passapalavra.info/2012/03/97517.

Bernardo, J.; Pereira, L. *Capitalismo Sindical*. São Paulo: Xamã, 2008.

Bertucci, A. A.; Silva, R. M. 20 anos de Economia Popular Solidária: trajetória da Cáritas brasileira dos PACs às EPS. Brasília: Venâncio, 2003.

Bionatur, cooperativa de produção de sementes agroecológicas. Disponível em http://www.mst.org.br/video-bionatur. Obtido em 14 de junho de, 2010.

Bionatur. 2013. [online] Disponível em: http://www.youtube.com/watch?v=wGTmm9xU7LA. Acesso em: 14 de junho de 2010.

Bonduki, N. Origens da habitação social no Brasil. 2 ed. São Paulo: Estação Liberdade, 1999.

Borghetti, R. Limites e possibilidades de uma alternativa de educação: análise do projeto Barracão da Cáritas Diocesana de Marília. 2007. Dissertação (Mestrado em Educação) – Faculdade de Filosofia e Ciências, Universidade Estadual Paulista, Marília, 2007.

Braverman, H. Trabalho e capital monopolista. Rio de Janeiro: LTC, 1987.

Brazilian Forum of Solidarity Economy. Fórum Brasileiro de Economia Solidária. Brasília, 2008.

Brie, M. Prefácio. In: Loureiro, I. M. *Rosa Luxemburg:* os dilemas da ação revolucionária. São Paulo: UNESP: Fundação Perseu Abramo, 2004.

Bruno, L. E. B. N. O que é autonomia operária. 3. ed. São Paulo: Brasiliense, 1990.

Bruno, L. Estudos sobre poder político, ideologia, trabalho e educação. 2004. 512 f. Tese (Livre-Docência), FE – USP, São Paulo, 2004.

Cabral, F. Arte para pensar a vida e educar os sentidos. In: Mendonça, S. G. L. et al. (Orgs.). Marx, Gramsci e Vigotski: aproximações. Araraquara, SP: Junqueira & Marin, 2012. pp. 377–398.

Caldart, R. A pedagogia do Movimento Sem Terra. São Paulo: Expressão Popular, 2004.

Caldart, R. S. (org). *Caminhos para a transformação escolar*. São Paulo: Expressão Popular, 2009.

Caldart, R. Desafios do vínculo entre trabalho e educação na luta e construção da Reforma Agrária Popular. Goiânia, 36ª Reunião Anual da Anped, GT Trabalho e Educação, 2013.

Campos, F. A arte da conquista: o capital internacional no desenvolvimento capitalista brasileiro (1951–1992). Tese de Doutorado, Instituto de Economia, Unicamp, 2009.

Cano, W. As raízes da concentração industrial do Estado de São Paulo. São Paulo: Unesp, 2005.

Caporal, F.; Costabeber, J. Análise Multidimensional da Sustentabilidade - uma proposta metodológica a partir da Agroecologia. Revista Agroecologia e Desenvolvimento Rural Sustentável, Porto Alegre, v. 3, n. 3, pp. 70–85, 2002.

Cardoso, E. Trabalho coletivo nos assentamentos de reforma agrária. Revista da Associação Brasileira de Reforma Agrária, vol. 4, n° 3, p.140–153, set/dez, 1994.

Carone, E. Movimento Operário no Brasil. São Paulo: Difel, 1981.

Carter, M.; Carvalho, H. M. A luta na terra: fonte de crescimento, inovação e desafio constante ao MST. In: CARTER, M. (org.) Combatendo a desigualdade social. São Paulo: Editora da UNESP, 2004.

Castro, M. Aprendendo a construir um mundo novo: feminismo, agroecologia e trabalho associado na experiência da Rede Xique-Xique. Marília, mimeo (impresso), 2012.

Castro, M. E. et. al. Extensão e Autogestão na Construção Civil: reflexões sobre a experiência junto à Cooperativa União. Campinas, Incubadora Tecnológica de Cooperativas Populares, Unicamp, 2012.

Castro, Mariana Pereira de. Em busca de uma pedagogia da produção associada. In: Édi A. Benini; Maurício Sardá de Faria; Henrique T. Novaes; Renato Dagnino. (Org.). Gestão pública e sociedades: fundamentos e políticas de economia solidária. 1ed. São Paulo: Outras Expressões, 2015, v. 1, p. 125–166.

Centre for Training in Solidarity Economy. Centro de Formação em Economia Solidária. Brasília, 2007.

Cerioli, P. Educação para a cooperação: experiência do curso técnico em Administração de cooperativas do MST. São Leopoldo, UNISINOS-RS, 1997 (Especialização).

Cerioli, P.; Martins, A. Caderno de Cooperação Agrícola - Sistema Cooperativista dos Assentados. n. 5. São Paulo: MST, n. 5, 1999.

CFES. Centro de Formação em Economia Solidária. Brasília, 2010.

Chesnais, F. (org.) A finança mundializada. São Paulo: Boitempo Editorial, 2005.

China Blue. Direção de Micha X. Peled. Estados Unidos: Teddy Bear. 2005. Dvd.

Chistoffoli, P. I. O desenvolvimento de cooperativas de produção coletiva de trabalhadores rurais no capitalismo: limites e possibilidades. Dissertação de Mestrado. Curitiba: UFPR. 2000.

Christoffoli, P. I. A cooperação agrícola nos assentamentos do MST – desafios e potencialidades. In: Benini, E.; Faria, M. S.; Novaes, H. T.; Dagnino, R. Gestão Pública e Sociedade: fundamentos e políticas públicas de economia solidária. São Paulo: Outras Expressões, 2011, vol. I. Disponível em: gestaopublicaesociedade.blogspot.com/

Christofolli, P. I. A cooperação agrícola nos assentamentos do MST: desafios e potencialidades. In: Rodrigues, F. C.; Novaes, H. T.; Batista, E. L. (orgs.) *Movimentos sociais, trabalho associado e educação para além do capital*. São Paulo: Outras Expressões, 2012.

Ciavatta, M. Formação integrada: entre a cultura da escola e a cultura do trabalho. In: Ciavatta, M. (org.) Memória e Temporalidades do trabalho e da educação. Rio de Janeiro: Lamparina/Faperj, 2007.

Cleaver, H. Leitura política do capital. Rio de Janeiro: Zahar, 1981.

Conterrâneos velhos de guerra. Direção de Vladimir Carvalho. Rio de Janeiro: Vertovisão, 1984. Videocassete.

Costa Neto, C. P. L. Agricultura sustentável, tecnologias e sociedade. In: Costa, L. F.; Moreira, R. J.; Bruno, R. (Org.). Mundo Rural e Tempo Presente. Rio de Janeiro, 1999, v. 2, pp. 299–321.

Couto, A. M. M. (2003) Greve na Cobrasma: uma história de luta e resistência. São Paulo: Annablume, 2003.

Cruz, A. C. M. da. A diferença da igualdade: a dinâmica da Economia solidária em quatro cidades do MERCOSUL. 2006. Tese (Doutorado em Economia) – Instituto de Economia, Universidade Estadual de Campinas, 2006.

Dagnino, R. Neutralidade da ciência e determinismo tecnológico. Campinas: UNICAMP, 2008.

Dagnino, R. (org.) Tecnologia Social – ferramenta para construir outra sociedade. Campinas: Instituto de Geociências-Unicamp, 2009.

Dagnino, R.; Novaes, H. T. "As forças produtivas e a transição ao socialismo: contrastando as concepções de Paul Singer e István Mészáros". Revista Organizações & Democracia, Unesp, Marília, v. 7, 2007.

Dagnino, R. (org.) Tecnologia Social – ferramenta para construir outra sociedade. Campinas: Instituto de Geociências-Unicamp, 2014.

Dal Ri, N. M.; Vieitez, C. Educação democrática e trabalho associado no Movimento dos Trabalhadores Rurais Sem Terra e nas fábricas de autogestão. São Paulo: Ícone, Fapesp, 2008.

Dalmagro, S. 25 de maio: vida e luta de uma escola do campo. In: Alternativas de escolarização dos assentamentos e acampamentos do MST. Veranópolis, 2003.

Del Roio, M. Os prismas de Gramsci. A fórmula política da frente única. São Paulo: Xamã, 2004.

Delgado, G. C. Capital financeiro e agricultura no Brasil. São Paulo/Campinas: Ed. Ícone/ Ed. da Unicamp, 1985.

Diamante de sangue. Direção de Edward Zwick, 2006.

Dieese. Relatório sobre o mundo do trabalho. 2012.

Dória, F. O nordeste: 'problema nacional' para a esquerda. In: QUARTIM DE MORAES, J.; DEL ROIO, M. (orgs.) História do Marxismo no Brasil – Visões do Brasil. Campinas: Unicamp, vol. VII.

Dos Santos, T. Teoria da dependência: balanço e perspectivas. Rio de Janeiro: Civilização Brasileira, 2000.

Dowbor, L. *O que acontece com o trabalho?* São Paulo, agosto de 2001. Disponível em http://ppbr.com/ld. Obtido em novembro de 10/10/2001.

Dreifuss, R. 1964: A Conquista do Estado – ação política, poder e golpe de classe. Petrópolis: Vozes, 1981.

Duarte, N. Vigotski e o "aprender a aprender": críticas às apropriações neoliberais e pós-modernas da teoria Vigotskiana. 3. ed. Campinas: Autores Associados, 2004.

ELISALDE, R.; AMPUDIA, M. "Movimientos sociales y escuelas populares de jóvenes y adultos. Notas sobre la construcción de un proyecto de educación popular". Marília, Mimeo (impresso), 2011.

Engels, F. A situação da classe trabalhadora na Inglaterra. São Paulo: Boitempo Editorial, 2006.

Essays. [Edited with an introduction by Warren Dean]. Armonk, N. Y.; M. E. Sharpe.

Ewbank, E. G. Autogestão: possibilidade de organização da força de trabalho na construção civil e suas implicações. São Paulo, Dissertação de Mestrado, FAU-USP, 2007.

Faria, J. H. Comissões de fábrica: poder e trabalho nas unidades produtivas. Curitiba: Criar, 1987.

Faria, M. "Autogestão, Cooperativa, Economia Solidária: avatares do trabalho e do capital". Tese de doutorado. Florianópolis, UFSC, Sociologia Política, 2005.

Faria, M. S.; Novaes, H. T. Brazilian recovered factories: the constraints of worker control. In: Azzellini, D.; Ness, I. (Org.). Ours to máster and to own – workers control from the Comunne to the Present. 1ed.Chicago: Haymarket Books, 2010, v. 1, pp. 350–372.

Faria, M. S. Autogestão, cooperativa, economia solidária: avatares do trabalho e do capital. Florianópolis: Editora em Debate, 2011.

Faria, José Henrique de. Economia Política do Poder. Curitiba: Juruá, 2004. Volume 2.

Fernandes, F. Nova república? São Paulo: Zahar, 1986.

Fernandes, F. A Revolução burguesa no Brasil: ensaio de interpretação sociológica. São Paulo: Global, 2006a.

Fernandes, F. O circuito fechado. Rio de Janeiro: Globo, 2006b.

Fernandes, F. Poder e contrapoder na América Latina. São Paulo:, Zahar, 1981.

Ferreira, E. B.; Garcia, S. R. O. O ensino médio integrado à educação profissional: um projeto em construção nos estados do Espírito Santo e do Paraná. In: Frigotto, G.; Ciavatta, M.; Ramos, M. (orgs.) Ensino Médio Integrado: concepções e contradições. São Paulo: Cortez, 2010. 2ª Ed.

Ferro, S. Arquitetura e Trabalho Livre. São Paulo: Cosacnaify, 2006a.

Ferro, S. (Entrevista). Arquitetura: Uma construção coletiva e livre. Brasil de Fato n. 161, 2006b. Retirado em http://www.brasildefato.com.br/v01/impresso/anteriores/161/cultura/materia.2006-04-06.1810849998. Obtido em 20/11/2006.

Folgado, C. Os desafios da campanha contra os agrotóxicos. Curitiba: Brasil de Fato, 2013.

Fontes, V. O Brasil e o Capital imperialismo – teoria e história. Rio de Janeiro: Escola Politécnica de Saúde de São Joaquim Venâncio, Universidade Federal do Rio de Janeiro, 2010.

Foster, J. B. *A ecologia de Marx*. Rio de Janeiro: Civilização Brasileira, 2006.

Foweraker, J. Theorizing Social Movements. Pluto Press (UK), 1995.

Fraga, L. Extensão e transferência de conhecimento: As Incubadoras Tecnológicas de Cooperativas Populares. Tese de Doutorado, Instituto de Geociências, Unicamp, 2012.

Fraga, L.; Novaes, H. T.; Dagnino, R. Educação em Ciência, Tecnologia e Sociedade para as engenharias: obstáculos e propostas. In: Dagnino, R. (org.) Estudos Sociais da Ciência e Tecnologia e Política de Ciência e Tecnologia – abordagens alternativas para uma nova América Latina. João Pessoa: EDUEPB, 2010.

Freire, P. Educação como prática da liberdade. 24ª ed. Rio de Janeiro: Paz e Terra. 2000.

Freire, P. Pedagogia do oprimido. Rio de Janeiro: Paz e Terra, 2002.

Freitas, L. C. A luta por uma pedagogia do meio: revisitando o conceito. In: Pistrak, M. M. A escola-comuna. São Paulo: Expressão Popular, 2009, pp. 8–100.

Frigotto, G. Educação e crise do capitalismo real. 5ª ed. São Paulo: Cortez, 2003.

Furtado, C. A pré-revolução brasileira. Rio de Janeiro: Fundo de Cultura, 1962.

Gennari, A. M. Réquiem ao capitalismo nacional: lei de remessas de lucros no Governo Goulart. São Paulo: Cultura Acadêmica Editora, 1999.

Gohn, M. da G. Teoria dos Movimentos Sociais. Paradigmas Clássicos e contemporâneos. 10ed. São Paulo: Loyola, 2012.

Gonçalves, S. Campesinato, Resistência e Emancipação: o modelo agroecológico adotado pelo MST no Estado do Paraná. 2008. Tese (Doutorado em Geografia) - UNESP, 2008.

Guhur, D. M. P.; Toná, N. *Agroecologia*. In: Caldart, R. S; Pereira, I. B; Alentejano, P; Frigotto, G. (orgs.) Dicionário de educação do campo. Rio de Janeiro, São Paulo: Escola Politécnica de Saúde Joaquim Venâncio, Expressão Popular, pp. 57–66, 2012.

Guimaraes, V. N. et al. Autogestão como estratégia de sobrevivência das organizações e dos trabalhadores: estudos multisetoriais no Estado de Santa Catarina. Relatório de Pesquisa CNPq. Florianópolis, UFSC, 2004.

Guhur, D. M. P.; Tardin, J. M. (Org.). Diálogo de Saberes, no encontro de culturas: Caderno de Ação Pedagógica. Maringá: Escola Milton Santos, 2012.

Guillerm, A.; Bourdet, Y. Autogestão: uma visão radical. Rio de Janeiro: Zahar, 1976.

Habermas, J. "Autonomy and Solidarity". Entrevistas; edição e introdução de Peter Dews. London: Verso, 1986.

Hardman, F. F. (2002) Nem pátria nem patrão! Memória operária, cultura e literatura no Brasil. São Paulo: Editora da Unesp. 3ª Ed.

Harvey, D. *O Novo Imperialismo*. São Paulo: Loyola, 2004.

Harvey, D. A produção capitalista do espaço. São Paulo: Annablume, 2005.

Henriques, F. C. Empresas Recuperadas por Trabalhadores no Brasil e na Argentina. Doutorado (Planejamento urbano e regional). UFRJ, Rio de Janeiro, 2013a.

Henriques, F. C. O Engenheiro na Assessoria a Empreendimentos de Autogestão. In: Schmidt, C.; Novaes, H. T. (orgs.) Economia Solidária e Transformação Social: rumo a uma sociedade para além do capital? Porto Alegre: Ed. da UFRGS, 2013b.

Henriques, F.; Faria, M. S.; Novaes, H. T. "Os distintos caminhos das fábricas recuperadas no Brasil e na Argentina" In: Rodrigues, F. C.; Novaes, H. T.;

Batista, E. (orgs.) Movimentos Sociais, Trabalho Associado e Educação para além do capital. São Paulo: Outras Expressões, 2012.
Henriques, F. C. et al. *Empresas recuperadas pelos trabalhadores*. Rio de Janeiro: Multifoco, 2013.
Hilsenbeck, Filho A. O MST e o Teatro – potencialidades pedagógicas. 2012. Obtido em: http://passapalavra.info/2012/11/66247. Retirado em 15/11/2012.
Hilsenbeck Filho, A.O MST no fio da navalha – dilemas, desafios e potencialidades da luta de classes. Tese de Doutorado, IFCH, Unicamp, 2013.
Hirao, F. H.; Lazarini, K.; Arantes, P. F. Metodologia de projeto arquitetônico participativo em empreendimentos habitacionais autogeridos em São Paulo –a experiência recente da assessoria técnica Usina junto aos movimentos populares de sem-teto (UMM) e sem-terra (MST). Córdoba (Argentina), 5° Seminário Latino-Americano de Ciência e Tecnologia para o Habitat, 2010.
Hirata, H. Transferência de tecnologia de gestão: o caso dos sistemas participativos. 1994.
Hirata, H. Nova divisão sexual do trabalho? São Paulo: Boitempo, 2002.
Holyoake, G. Os vinte oito tecelões de Rochdale. Rio de Janeiro: GB, 1933.
Ianni, O. Estado e capitalismo, estrutura social e industrialização no Brasil. Rio de Janeiro, Civilização Brasileira, 1965.
Ianni, O. A ditadura do grande capital. Rio de Janeiro: Civilização Brasileira, 1981.
Ianni. O. O declínio do Brasil-nação. Estudos Avançados, 2000.
Ianni, O. Estado e Planejamento econômico no Brasil. Rio de Janeiro: Ed. da UFRJ, 2009.
Iasi, M. Ensaios sobre consciência e emancipação. São Paulo: Expressão Popular, 2006.
Iasi, M. Educação, consciência de classe e estratégia revolucionária. Revista Universidade e Sociedade, Distrito Federal, n. 48: 122–130. July 2011. (Transcrita a partir da palestra no 5° EBEM – Encontro Brasileiro de Educação e marxismo – Florianópolis, abril de 2011).
IBGE. www.ibge.gov.br, 2012.
Ibrahim, J. O que todo cidadão precisa saber sobre comissões de fábrica. São Paulo: Global, 1986.
Ilha Das Flores. Direção de Jorge Furtado. Porto Alegre: Casa de cinema de Porto Alegre, 1989.
Infranca, A. Trabajo, individuo, historia: el concepto de trabajo em Lukács. Buenos Aires: Herramienta, 2005.
Jinkings, Ivana. Nobile, Rodrigo. (Org.). István Mészáros e os desafios do tempo histórico. São Paulo: Boitempo Editorial, 2011.

Kapp, S. et al. Architecture as Critical Exercise: Little Pointers Towards Alternative Practices, 2008. Obtido em: http://www.field-journal.org/uploads/file/2008%20Volume%202%20/Architecture%20as%20Critical%20Exercise_MOM.pdf

Kolling, E. J.; Vargas, M. C.; Caldart, R. MST e educação. In: MST, Boletim da Educação n. 12. – II Encontro Nacional de Educadores e Educadoras da Reforma Agrária, Dez. 2014.

Konder, L. Marxismo e Alienação. São Paulo: Expressão Popular, 2009.

Korsch, K. O que é socialização? Um programa de socialismo prático In: Pinheiro, M.; Martorano, L. (orgs). Teoria e prática dos conselhos operários. São Paulo: Expressão Popular, 2013, pp. 141–170.

Koury, A. P. (2004) Grupo Arquitetura Nova: Flávio Império, Rodrigo Lefèvre, Sérgio Ferro. São Paulo: Edusp.

Kuenzer, A. Z. Pedagogia da fábrica: as relações de produção e a educação do trabalhador. São Paulo: Cortez: Autores Associados, 1985.

Kuenzer, A. Z. As mudanças no mundo do trabalho e a educação: novos desafios para a gestão. In: Ferreira, N. S. C. Gestão democrática da educação: atuais tendências, novos desafios. São Paulo: Cortez, 1998, pp. 33–58.

Lamosa, R.; Loureiro, C. Agronegócio e educação ambiental: uma análise crítica. [Obtido na Internet] 2013.

Leandro, J. B. Curso técnico em administração de cooperativas do MST: a concepção de educação e a influência no assentamento Fazenda Reunidas de Promissão-SP. Dissertação de Mestrado, Faculdade de Educação, Unicamp, 2003.

Lefébvre, Henri. Critique de la vie quotidienne. Paris: Arhc, 1968.

Leher, R. Reforma Universitária de Córdoba, noventa anos. Um Acontecimento Fundacional para a Universidade Latino-americanista. In: Sader, E.; Gentili, P.; Aboites, H. (compiladores). La reforma universitaria: desafíos y perspectivas noventa años después. - 1a ed. - Buenos Aires: CLACSO, 2008.

Lerrer, D. Preparar gente: a educação superior dentro do MST. Revista Estudos Sociedade e Agricultura, 2010.

Lima Filho, P. A. Os devoradores da ordem: exclusão social no capitalismo incompleto. In: Galeazzi, M. A. (Org.). Segurança alimentar e cidadania: a contribuição das universidades paulistas. Campinas, SP: Mercado das Letras, 1996. pp. 45–77.

Lima Filho, P. A. O Projeto Universidade Popular. São Paulo, impresso (mimeo), 1999.

Lima Filho, P. A. Carta sobre a Universidade Federal da Grande Fronteira Sul. Campinas, Impresso, outubro de 2008.

Lima Filho, P. A.; Macedo, R. A poeira dos mitos: Revolução e contrarrevolução nos capitalismos da miséria. In: Benini, É.; Sardá De Faria, M. S.; Novaes, H.

T.; Dagnino, R. Gestão pública e sociedade: fundamentos e políticas públicas de economia solidária. São Paulo: Outras Expressões, 2011. pp. 150–182.

Lima Filho, P. A. et al. O Projeto Universidade Popular: um marxismo para o Século XXI. In: II Encontro Brasileiro de Educação e Marxismo: "Concepção e Método". Curitiba: UFPR, 2006.

Lima Filho, Paulo A. Sobre as revoluções burguesas radicais. In: NOVAES, H. T.; DAL RI, N. (orgs.) Movimentos Sociais e Crises Contemporâneas à luz dos clássicos do materialismo crítico. Uberlândia: Navegando, 2017, volume 2.

Lima, A. C. Práticas educativas em agroecologia no MST/PR: processos formativos na luta pela emancipação humana. 2011. 321 f. Dissertação (Mestrado em Educação) - Universidade Estadual de Maringá, Maringá, 2011.

Lima, A. Guhur, D. Toná, N.; Noma, A. *Reflexões sobre a educação profissional em agroecologia no MST*: desafios dos cursos técnicos do Paraná. In: Rodrigues, F. C.; Novaes, H. T.; Batista, E. L. (orgs.) Movimentos Sociais, Trabalho Associado e Educação para além do capital. São Paulo: Outras Expressões, 2012.

Lima, A. S. A Militância Comunista e as Lutas Camponesas no Interior Paulista (1945–1958). Dissertação de mestrado. UNESP, Marília, 2009.

Lima, M. A.; Vargas, M. T. Teatro operário em São Paulo. In.: Prado, A. (org.) Libertários no Brasil: memória, lutas, cultura. São Paulo: Brasiliense, 1986.

Linhart, D. A desmedida do capital. São Paulo: Boitempo, 2007.

Linhart, R. O acúçar e a fome. Rio de Janeiro: Paz e Terra, 1980.

Lombardi, J. C. Educação e ensino na obra de Marx e Engels. Campinas: Alínea, 2011.

Lopes, J. M.; Rizek, C. O mutirão autogerido como procedimento inovador na produção da moradia para os pobres: uma abordagem crítica. Rio de Janeiro, Revista da Finep, 2005. Obtido em: http://www.habitare.org.br/doc/docs_revista/artigoFinep_usina.pdf. Retirado em 25/07/2009.

Lukács, G. The process of democratization. Albany: State University of New York, 1991.

Lukács, G. História e consciência de classe. São Paulo: Martins Fontes, 2003.

Lukács, G. Socialismo e Democratização. Rio de Janeiro: UFRJ, 2008.

Lukács, G. Prolegômenos para uma ontologia do ser social. São Paulo: Boitempo, 2010.

Lukács, G. Para uma ontologia do ser social II. São Paulo. Boitempo, 2013.

Luxemburg, R. Reforma ou Revolução? São Paulo: Expressão Popular, 2005.

Luxemburgo, Rosa. Reforma ou Revolução? São Paulo, Ed. Expressão Popular, 1999.

Luzzi, N. O debate agroecológico no Brasil: uma construção a partir de diferentes atores sociais. 2007. Tese (Doutorado em Ciências Sociais em

Desenvolvimento, Agricultura e Sociedade) – Instituto de Ciências Humanas e Sociais, Universidade Federal Rural do Rio de Janeiro, Rio de Janeiro, 2007.
Machado, L. C. P. Carta a Henrique Tahan Novaes. Porto Alegre, 2009.
Macedo, R. O governo Lula e a miséria brasileira. Tese de Doutorado. Araraquara, FCL, UNESP, 2012.
MAMANI, P. *Destotalización Del poder colonial/moderno - Rotación del poder y la economía otra - El caso de El Alto-Bolivia.* Mimeo, 2012.
Mamani, P. El poder anti-liberal. In: Rodrigues, F. C.; Novaes, H. T.; Batista, E. (orgs.) Movimentos Sociais, Trabalho Associado e Educação para além do capital. São Paulo: Outras Expressões, 2013, vol II.
Mandel, E. Control obrero, consejos obreros, autogestión. Madri: Editora Era, 1974.
Mandel, E. O lugar do marxismo na história. São Paulo: Xamã, 2001.
Manfredi, S. M. Educação profissional no Brasil. São Paulo: Cortez, 2002.
Mariátegui, J. C. Sete ensaios de interpretação da realidade peruana. São Paulo: Expressão Popular, 2008.
Maricato, E. A política habitacional durante o regime militar. Petrópolis: Vozes, 1987.
Martins, A. Potencialidades transformadoras dos movimentos camponeses no Brasil contemporâneo: as comunidades de resistência e superação no MST. Dissertação de Mestrado, PUC-SP, São Paulo, 2004.
Martins, J. S. O cativeiro da Terra. 9 ed. 1 reimpressão. São Paulo: Contexto, 2013.
Marx, K. A Guerra civil na França. São Paulo: Global, 1986.
Marx, K. O Capital. 3. ed. São Paulo: Nova Cultural, 1988. v. III e IV.
Marx, K. A questão judaica. In: Manuscritos econômicos - filosóficos. Lisboa: Edições 70, 1993. pp. 35–76.
Marx, K. O capital. 3. ed. São Paulo: Abril Cultural, 1983, volume I.
Marx, K. O capital. São Paulo: Nova Cultural, 1996, volume I.
Marx, K. A miséria da filosofia. São Paulo: Expressão Popular, 2009a.
Marx, K. *A questão judaica.* São Paulo: Boitempo Editorial, 2009b.
Marx, K. Crítica do programa de Gotha. São Paulo: Boitempo, 2012.
Marx, K. Manuscritos econômicos-filosóficos de 1844. Lisboa: Avante, 1994.
Marx, K. Manuscritos Econômico-Filosóficos. São Paulo: Boitempo Editorial, 2004.
Marx, K. O capital. Crítica da Economia Política. Livro I. São Paulo: Boitempo, 2013.
Marx, K.; Engels, F. Manifesto do Partido Comunista. São Paulo: Expressão Popular, 2008.
Mateus, D. Entrevista a Henrique Novaes, João Henrique Pires e Douglas Silva. Agudos, maio de 2015.

Mazalla Neto, W. Agroecologia e processamento de alimentos em assentamentos rurais. Campinas: Átomo e Alínea, 2013.

McCarthy, J.; Zald, M. Resource Mobilization and Social Movements: A Partial Theory. American Journal of Sociology, Vol. 82, No. 6 (May, 1977), pp. 1212–1241.

Medeiros, L. S. História dos movimentos sociais no campo. Rio de Janeiro: Fase, 1989.

Mello, I. J. Sob o domínio do medo: controle social e criminalização da miséria no neoliberalismo. Tese de doutorado, Unicamp, 2008.

Mélo, C. Estado e Educação pela imprensa: o debate de Florestan Fernandes ante a lei de Diretrizes e Bases da Educação Nacional (1959–1961). 2009. Dissertação de Mestrado, Universidade Estadual de Maringá.

Menezes Neto, A. J. Além da terra: a dimensão sociopolítica do projeto educativo do MST. Tese de Doutorado. Faculdade de Educação, USP, 2001.

Mészáros, I. La Rivolta Degli Intellettuali in Ungheria. Turim: Einaudi, 1958.

Mészáros, I. Marx: a teoria da alienação. 4. ed. Rio de Janeiro: Zahar, 1981.

Mészáros, I. A necessidade do controle social. São Paulo: Ensaio, 1987.

Mészáros, I. Filosofia, ideologia e controle social. São Paulo: Ensaio, 1993.

Mészáros, I. Para além do capital. São Paulo: Boitempo, 2002.

Mészáros, I. O poder da ideologia. São Paulo: Boitempo Editorial, 2004a.

Mészáros, I. Marxismo e direitos humanos. In: Mészáros, I. Filosofia, ideologia e ciência social. Ensaios de negação e afirmação. São Paulo: Boitempo, 2004b, pp. 157–168.

Mészáros, I. A educação para além do capital. São Paulo: Boitempo, 2005.

Mészáros, I. A teoria da alienação em Marx. São Paulo: Boitempo Editorial, 2006.

Mészáros, I. O desafio e o fardo do tempo histórico. São Paulo: Boitempo, 2007.

Meszáros, I. Filosofia, ideologia e ciência social. São Paulo: Boitempo, 2008.

Mészáros, I. O conceito de dialética em Lukács. São Paulo: Boitempo, 2015.

Mészáros, I. A montanha que devemos conquistar. São Paulo: Boitempo, 2016.

Minto. L. W. A educação da "miséria": particularidade capitalista e educação superior no Brasil. Tese de Doutorado, Faculdade de Educação, Unicamp, Campinas, 2011.

Molina, M.; Arelaro, L.; Wolf, S. Resumo do 2° Encontro do Residência Agrária, Brasília, agosto de 2015.

Monbeig, P. Pioneiros e fazendeiros de São Paulo. São Paulo: Hucitec, 1984.

Moniz BANDEIRA, L. A. O governo João Goulart: as lutas sociais no Brasil, 1961–1964. 7ª ed. Rio de Janeiro: Revan; Brasília: Ed. UnB, 2001.

Montaño, C. Terceiro Setor e Questão Social. São Paulo: Cortez, 2002.

Morais, C. S. Elementos sobre a teoria da organização no campo. Caderno de Formação, n° 11. São Paulo: MST, 1986.

Morissawa, M. A História da luta pela terra e o MST. São Paulo: Expressão Popular, 2001.

Moura, C. As rebeliões no Estado de São Paulo. In: Moura, C. Rebeliões da Senzala. São Paulo: Anita Garibaldi, 2014.

MST. Reforma Agrária: por um Brasil sem Latifúndio!. Textos para debate do 4 Congresso Nacional do MST. São Paulo: MST, 2000.

MST. Projeto Metodológico: Turma II do curso Técnico em Agroecologia ensino médio integrado. São Miguel do Iguaçu, 2010.

MST Organização. *Movimento dos Trabalhadores Rurais Sem Terra*. Pagina eletrônica. [São Paulo]: 02 nov. 2012. Disponível em: http://www.mst.org.br/taxonomy/term/330. Acesso em novembro 2012.

MST. Assentados conquistam 1° agroindústria do Terra Forte em SP. http://www.mst.org.br/2014/09/25/assentados-conquistam-1-agroindustria-do-terra-forte-em-sp.html, Obtido em 20/01/2015.

Musto, M. Revisitando a concepção de alienação em Marx. In: DEL ROIO, M. (org.) Marx e a dialética da sociedade civil. Marília: Oficina Universitária, 2014, pp. 61–94.

Nascimento, C. A oposição sindical no exílio: sindicalismo e autonomia. [Mimeo], s/d.

Nascimento, C. Do "Beco dos Sapos" aos canaviais de Catende. (Os "ciclos longos" das lutas autogestionárias). SENAES, April 2005. www.mte.senaes.gov.br, 2005.

Nascimento, C. *Autogestão: Economia Solidária e Utopia*. Revista eletrônica Otra Economía, 2008, pp. 27–40.

Nascimento, C. Do Beco dos Sapos aos Canaviais de Catende. Marília: Lutas anticapital, 2019

Nascimento, C. Do Beco dos Sapos aos canaviais de Catende. Porto Alegre, 2023.

Nascimento, C. Experimentação autogestionária: autogestão da pedagogia e pedagogia da autogestão. In: Batista, E. L.; Novaes, H. T. (Orgs.). Educação e reprodução social: as contradições do capital no século XXI. Bauru, SP: Canal 6; Londrina: Praxis, 2011, pp. 130–166.

Ness, I. Azzellini, D. (eds). Ours to Master and to Own: Workers' Control from the Commune to the Present. Chicago: Haymarket, 2011.

Netto, J. P. Uma face contemporânea da barbárie. Disponível em: http://pcb.org.br/portal/docs/umafacecontemporaneadabarbarie.pdf Acesso em jan.

Netto, J. P.; Braz, M. Economia política: uma introdução crítica. São Paulo: Cortez, 2008.

Netto, J. P. Introdução. In: Marx, K. Miséria da Filosofia: resposta à Filosofia da Miséria, do sr. Proudhon. São Paulo: Expressão Popular, 2008, pp. 7–16.

Netto, J. P. Capitalismo e reificação. São Paulo: ICP, 2014.

Netto, J. P. Marx em Paris. In: Marx, K. Cadernos de Paris e Manuscritos econômico-filosóficos de 1844. São Paulo: Expressão Popular, 2015, pp. 9–178.

Novaes, H. T. Qual autogestão? São Paulo, Revista da Sociedade Brasileira de Economia Política, n. 22, maio de 2007.

Novaes, H. T. Qual autogestão? São Paulo, Revista da Sociedade Brasileira de Economia Política, n. 22, maio de, 2008.

Novaes, H. T. Peasant Leagues. In: Azzellini, D.; Ness, I. International Encyclopedia of Revolution and Protest - 1500 to the Present, 2009.

Novaes, H. T. O fetiche da tecnologia – a experiência das fábricas recuperadas. São Paulo: Expressão Popular, 2010a, 2ª edição.

Novaes, H. T. (Org.). O retorno do caracol à sua concha: alienação e desalienação em associações de trabalhadores. São Paulo: Expressão Popular, 2010b.

Novaes, H. T. A Autogestão como Magnífica Escola: notas sobre a educação no trabalho associado. In: Batista, E. L.; Novaes, H. T. (orgs.) Educação e reprodução social: as contradições do capital no século XXI. Bauru: Canal 6/ Praxis, 2011.

Novaes, H. T.; Faria, M. S. . ? Para dónde van las Empresas Recuperadas por los Trabajadores brasileños?. In: Ruggeri, A.; Novaes, H. T.; Faria, M. S.. (Org.). Crisis y autogestión en el siglo XXI - cooperativas y empresas recuperadas en tiempos de neoliberalismo. 1ed.Buenos Aires: Continente, 2015, v. 1, p. 75-91.

Novaes, H. T. Reatando um fio interrompido: a relação universidade-movimentos sociais na América Latina. São Paulo: Expressão Popular-Fapesp, 2012.

Novaes, H. T.; Castro, M. Em busca de uma pedagogia da produção associada. In: Benini, É.; Sardá De Faria, M.; Novaes, H. T.; Dagnino, R. (Org.). Gestão pública e sociedade: fundamentos e políticas públicas de economia solidária. São Paulo: Outras Expressões, 2011. pp. 153–188.

Novaes, H. T.; Benini, É. Quem controla o Estado Brasileiro: o capital rentista e a dívida pública. In: Benini, E. A.; Faria, M. S.; Novaes, H. T.; Dagnino, R. (orgs.) *Gestão Pública e Sociedade: fundamentos e políticas públicas de Economia Solidária*. São Paulo: Outras Expressões, 2012.

Novaes, H. T. A miséria ideológica da política educacional paulista. Marília, mimeo, 2013.

Novaes, H. T. A decadência ideológica da política educacional do Estado de São Paulo – notas sobre a precarização estrutural do trabalho docente. Marília – XIV Jornada Pedagógica, 2014.

Novaes, H. T. O trabalho associado como princípio educativo e a educação escolar: notas a partir das fábricas recuperadas brasileiras e argentinas. Revista HisterBr online, 2013a.

Novaes, H. T. Os 8 pilares do Trabalho Associado. Palestra proferida na UNESP – Franca, outubro de, 2013b.

Novaes, H. T.; Christoffoli, P. I. As contradições da auto-educação no trabalho associado: reflexões a partir da experiência das fábricas recuperadas brasileiras. In: Marañon, B. (org.) Economia Solidária. Buenos Aires: Clacso, 2013.

Novaes, H. T.; Santos, L. *Produção Destrutiva, Agroecologia e Educação Agroecológica do MST-PR*. V Congresso Teoria Política do Socialismo, Marília, agosto de, 2013.

Novaes, H. T.; Nemirovsky, G. Gyrogy Lukács e István Mészáros no Levante Popular Húngaro de 1956. Marília, mimeo, 2016.

Novaes, H.; Mazin, D.; Santos, L. (Orgs.) Questão Agrária, Cooperação e Agroecologia. São Paulo: Outras Expressões, 2015.

Oliveira, A. U. A questão da aquisição de terras por estrangeiros no Brasil– um retorno aos dossiês. Agrária, São Paulo, No. 12, 2010.

Oliveira, A. U. Os Agrocombustíveis e a Produção de Alimentos. In: Simonetti, M. L. (Org.). A (in) sustentabilidade do desenvolvimento: meio ambiente, agronegócio e movimentos sociais. 1ª ed. São Paulo/Marilia: Cultura Acadêmica/Oficina Universitária, 2011, v. 1, pp. 159–180.

Oliveira, F. Crítica à razão dualista - O ornitorrinco. São Paulo: Boitempo Editorial, 2003.

Oliveira, F. Noiva da revolução. São Paulo: Boitempo, 2004.

Oliveira, E. Toyotismo no Brasil. São Paulo: Expressão Popular, 2006.

Oliveira, F. Noiva da Revolução – Elegia para uma re(li)gião. São Paulo: Boitempo editorial, 2008.

Oliveira, F. O ornitorrinco. Crítica a razão dualista. São Paulo: Boitempo, 2014.

Oliveira, S. B. Espaços sociais contra-hegemônicos: organização e autonomia de trabalhadores na comuna urbana do MST a partir de suas relações de produção. Trabalho de Conclusão do Curso e Especialização em Economia Solidária e Tecnologia Social na América Latina – 2009/2010. Unicamp, Campinas, 2010.

Oliveira, S. B. Repensando a (re)produção social do espaço – um estudo de caso da Comuna Dom Hélder Câmara - MST. Dissertação de Mestrado, UNIFESP, São Paulo, 2013.

Paiva, V. Paulo Freire e o nacional-desenvolvimento. Rio de Janeiro: Civilização brasileira, 1980.

Pagenotto, M. Elizabeth Teixeira uma camponesa marcada pela resistência. Curitiba: Brasil de Fato, 2020.

Panzieri, R. The capitalist use of machinery: Marx versus the 'Objectivists'. In: SLATER, P. (org) Outlines of a critique of technology. Londres: Ink Links, 1980.

Panzieri, R. Mais-valia e Planejamento. In: Tronti, M. et al. (Org.) Processo de trabalho e estratégias de classe. Rio de Janeiro: Zahar editores, 1982.

Pateo, F. V. Economia solidária: limites e avanços dos trabalhadores sob o controle do processo e do sentido do produto do seu trabalho. In: Rodrigues, F.

C.; Novaes, H. T.; Batista, E. (orgs.) Movimentos Sociais, Trabalho Associado e Educação para além do capital. São Paulo: Outras Expressões, 2013, vol. II, no prelo.

Pedreira Filho, V. Comissões de Fábrica – um claro enigma. São Paulo: Editora Entrelinhas, 1997.

Pereira, V. A. Terra e poder – formação histórica de Marília. Marília: Unesp, 2005.

Pinassi, M. O. Da miséria ideológica à crise do capital – uma reconciliação histórica. São Paulo: Boitempo, 2009.

Pinassi, M. O. Palestra na disciplina "Pedagogia Histórico-crítica e os movimentos sociais". Campinas, Unicamp, 2011.

Pinassi, M. O. Prefácio. Rodrigues, F. C.; Novaes, H. T.; Batista, E. L. (orgs.) Movimentos sociais, trabalho associado e educação para além do capital. São Paulo: Outras Expressões, 2012. pp. 7–14.

Pinassi, M. O.; Mafort, K. Os agrotóxicos e a reprodução do capital na perspectiva feminista da Via Campesina In: Rodrigues, F. C.; Novaes, H. T.; Batista, E. L. (Orgs.) Movimentos sociais, trabalho associado e educação para além do capital. São Paulo: Outras Expressões, 2012. pp. 141–158.

Pinassi, M. O.; Cruz Neto, R. G. La minería y la lógica de la producción destructiva en la Amazonia brasileña. Herramienta (Buenos Aires), v. 51, pp. 121–134, 2012.

Pinassi, M. O.; Mafort, K. Os agrotóxicos e a reprodução do capital na perspectiva feminista da Via Campesina. In: Rodrigues, F. C.; Novaes, H. T.; Batista, E. (Org.). Movimentos sociais, Trabalho Associado e Educação para além do capital. 1ª ed. São Paulo: Outras Expressões, 2013.

Pinheiro M.; L. C. Correio eletrônico enviado para Henrique Novaes. 10/10/2009.

Pinheiro, M.; Martorano, L. (orgs). Teoria e prática dos conselhos operários. São Paulo: Expressão Popular, 2013.

Pinheiro, S. A máfia dos alimentos no Brasil. Rio de Janeiro: 2005.

Pistrak, M. Fundamentos da Escola do Trabalho. São Paulo: Expressão Popular, 2002.

Pistrak, M. M. (org.) A escola-comuna. São Paulo: Expressão Popular, 2009.

Prado JR, C. A revolução Brasileira. São Paulo: Brasiliense, 1977.

Puigrós, A.; Gagliano, R. La fábrica del conocimiento – los saberes socialmente productivos en América Latina. Rosario: Homo Sapiens, 2004.

Quijano, A. Sistemas alternativos de produção? In: Santos, B.S. (org.) Produzir para viver, os caminhos da produção não capitalista. Rio de Janeiro: Civilização Brasileira, pp. 300–345.

Rago, L. M O controle da fábrica: os anarquistas e a autogestão. In: Rago, L. M. Do cabaré ao lar: a utopia da cidade disciplinar: Brasil 1890–1930. Rio de Janeiro: Paz e Terra, 1985.

Ramos, M. Trabalho, educação e correntes pedagógicas no Brasil. Rio de Janeiro: EPSJV/ UFRJ, 2010.

Ranieri, J. A câmara escura: alienação e estranhamento em Marx. São Paulo: Boitempo, 2001.

Rede Xique Xique. Disponível em: http://redexiquexique.blogspot.com.br/p/instituicao.html. Acesso em 10/04/2013.

Rego, T. T. Formação em agroecologia. Programa do Contestado da AS-PTA. 313f. Tese (Doutorado em Educação), UFSC, 2016.

Ribas, A. D. MST, Cooperativismo e território: dinâmica e contradições. In: Thomaz JR., A. (Org.). Geografia e Trabalho no Século XXI. Presidente Prudente: Centelha, 2004, v. 1, pp. 8–40.

Ribeiro, D. Confissões. São Paulo: Companhia das Letras, 1996.

Rocha, G. (2004) Revolução do cinema novo. São Paulo: Cosac Naify.

Rodrigues, F. C. Educação política dos trabalhadores: a centralidade da exploração do trabalho na análise da questão agrária no Brasil - a contribuição de Octávio Ianni. In: Rodrigues, F. C.; Novaes, H. T.; Batista, E. (orgs.) Movimentos Sociais, Trabalho Associado e Educação para além do capital. São Paulo: Outras Expressões, 2013, vol. II.

Rodrigues, F. C. MST - Formação Política e Reforma Agrária nos anos de 1980. Tese (Doutorado em Educação). UNICAMP, Campinas, 2013.

Rodrigues, F. C.; Novaes, H. T.; Batista, E. L. (orgs.) Movimentos sociais, trabalho associado e educação para além do capital. São Paulo: Outras Expressões, 2012. v. I.

Rodrigues, F. C.; Novaes, H. T.; Batista, E. L. (Orgs.). Movimentos sociais, trabalho associado e educação para além do capital. São Paulo: Outras Expressões, 2014. v. II.

Rolo, M. Ocupando os latifúndios do saber: subsídios para o ensino da ciência na perspectiva politécnica da educação. 2012. 382f. Tese (Doutorado em Educação). Rio de Janeiro, UERJ, 2012.

Rosar, M. F. Centros de Ensino Médio Integrados na região da Baixada Maranhense: pontos de desenvolvimento territorial? In: Lombardi, J. C.; Saviani, D. (orgs.) História, Educação e Transformação: tendências e perspectivas para a educação pública no Brasil. Campinas: Autores Associados, 2011.

Ruggeri, A. (org.) La economía de los trabajadores - Autogestión, cooperativas y empresas recuperadas en tiempos de crisis global. Buenos Aires: Continente/ Peña Lillo, no prelo.

Ruggeri, A. Que son las empresas recuperadas por sus trabajadores? Buenos Aires: Continente, 2014.

Ruschel, V. B. Pedagogia da organização coletiva: a cooperativa dos estudantes da Escola Agrícola 25 de Maio. In: Vendramini, C. R. (Org.). Educação em movimento na luta pela terra. Florianópolis, SC: UFSC-CED, 2002.

Sachs, I. Espaços, tempos e estratégias de desenvolvimento. São Paulo: Vértice, 1986.
Sader, E. (1988) Quando novos personagens entram em cena: experiências, falas e lutas dos trabalhadores da Grande São Paulo (1970–1980). Rio de Janeiro: Paz e Terra.
Sader, E. Quando novos personagens entram em cena. Rio de Janeiro: Paz e Terra, 2008.
Sampaio JR. P. A. *Entre a Nação e a Barbárie*. Rio de Janeiro: Vozes, 1996.
Sampaio JR., P. Notas críticas sobre a atualidade e os desafios da questão agrária. In: STEDILE, J. P. (org.) Debates sobre a situação e perspectivas da reforma agrária na década de 2000. São Paulo: Expressão Popular, 2013, pp. 189–240.
Sampaio JR, P. A. Notas críticas sobre a atualidade e os desafios da questão agrária. In: Stedile, J. P. (Org.) A questão agrária no Brasil: debate sobre a situação e perspectiva da reforma agrária na década de 2000. 1 ed. São Paulo: Expressão Popular, 2013.
Sanfelice, J. L. Movimento Estudantil. A UNE na resistência ao golpe de 1964. Campinas: Alínea, 2008.
Sanfelice, J. L. A política educacional do Estado de São Paulo: apontamentos. Nuances (UNESP Presidente Prudente), v. 18, pp. 145–160, 2010.
Santos, S. Aparecida dos. A trajetória do Assentamento Reunidas: o que mudou? 133f. (Dissertação de Mestrado). Instituto de Economia, Unicamp, 2007.
Santos, S. História da Coopava. In: Novaes, H. T.; Santos, J.; Pires, J. H. (Orgs.) Questão agrária, cooperação e agroecologia, vol II. São Paulo: Outras Expressões, 2015, no prelo.
Saviani, D. Escola e Democracia. (Edição Comemorativa). Campinas: Autores Associados, 1998.
Saviani, D. O legado educacional do "longo século XX" brasileiro. In: Saviani, D. et al. (org.) O legado educacional do século XX. 2ª ed. Campinas, SP: Autores Associados, 2006, pp. 9–57.
Saviani, D. História das Idéias Pedagógicas no Brasil. Campinas: Autores Associados, 2007.
Saviani, D. Escola e Democracia. (Edição Comemorativa). Campinas: Autores Associados, 2008a. 20ª Edição.
Saviani, D. Pedagogia histórico-crítica: primeiras aproximações. Campinas, SP: Autores Associados, 2008b.
Saviani, D. Pedagogia histórico-crítica: primeiras aproximações. Campinas, SP: Autores Associados, 2012.
Schaff, A. La alienación como fenómeno social. Barcelona: Crítica, 1979.
Schimidt, C. Regulação econômica e transformação social: discussão sobre as possibilidades de uma sociedade para além do capital. ORG & DEMO, v. 13, 2008, p. 5–2.

Schiochet, V. Da democracia à autogestão: Economia Solidária no Brasil. In: Benini, E.; Faria, M. S.; Novaes, H. T.; DAGNINO, R. (orgs.) Gestão Pública e Trabalho Associado. São Paulo: Outras Expressões, 2012.

Schwarz, R. Cultura e Política – 1964–1969. Rio de Janeiro: Paz e Terra, 2007.

Scopinho, R. Controle do trabalho e condições de vida em assentamentos rurais: possibilidades e limites da cooperação autogestionária. Controle do Trabalho e Condições de Vida em Assentamentos Rurais: Possibilidades e Limites da Cooperação Autogestioária. In: VII Congreso Latino Americano de Sociología Rural, 2006, Quito-Equador. VII Congreso Latino Americano de Sociología Rural. Quito-Equador: ALASRU, 2006.

Serafim, M. P. Agricultura familiar no Brasil: Um panorama sobre a política e as instituições. São Paulo: Annablume, 2012.

Sevá Filho, O. Populações e territórios espoliados pela ampliação recente da infraestrutura industrial capitalista: focos de luta política e ideológica na América do Sul. In: Rodrigues, F. C.; Novaes, H. T.; Batista, E. L. (Orgs.). Movimentos sociais, trabalho associado e educação para além do capital. São Paulo: Outras Expressões, 2013. v. II, pp. 24–50.

Sevá Filho, A. Populações e Territórios espoliados pela ampliação recente da infraestrutura industrial capitalista: focos de luta política e ideológica na América do Sul. Marília: Lutas anticapital, 2019.

Sève, L. Aliénation et émancipation. Paris: Éditions La Dispute, 2012.

Shelley, M. Frankestein. Porto Alegre: L&PM, 2000.

Shiva, V. Biopiratária: a Pilhagem da Natureza e do Conhecimento. Petrópolis: Editora Vozes, 2001.

Shulgin, V. Rumo ao politecnismo. São Paulo: Expressão Popular, 2013.

Silva, F. A Fábrica como Agência Educativa. Araraquara: Editora Cultura Acadêmica-Unesp, 2005.

Simão, A. (1966) Sindicato e Estado: suas relações na formação do proletariado de São Paulo. São Paulo: Dominus Editora.

Singer, P. A recente ressurreição da Economia Solidária. In: Santos, B.S. (org.) Produzir para viver, os caminhos da produção não capitalista. Rio de Janeiro: Civilização Brasileira, 2002, pp. 81–129.

Singer, P. Introdução à economia solidária. São Paulo: Editora Fundação Perseu Abramo, 2002.

Sodré, N. A farsa do neoliberalismo. Rio de Janeiro: Graphia, 1995.

Sodré, N. W. Evolução Social do Brasil. Porto Alegre: Editora da Universidade – UFRGS, 1988.

Souza, R. B. A mística no MST: mediação da praxis formadora de sujeitos históricos. 320f. Doutorado em Sociologia. UNESP – Araraquara, 2012.

Souza, S. M. R. A emergência do discurso do agronegócio e a expansão da atividade canavieira: estratégias discursivas para a ação do capital no campo.

2011. Tese (Doutorado em Geografia) - Universidade Estadual Paulista Júlio de Mesquita Filho.
Stédile, J. P. A questão agrária no Brasil. São Paulo: Atual (Espaço e debate), 1999.
Stédile, J. P.; Fernandes, B. M. Brava Gente: a trajetória do MST e a luta pela reforma agrária no Brasil. São Paulo: Perseu Abramo, 1999.
Storch, S. Discussão da Participação dos Trabalhadores na Empresa. In: Fleury, M. T. e Fischer, R. M. (Org.) Processo e Relações de Trabalho no Brasil. São Paulo: Ed. Atlas, 1985.
Svampa, M., Pereyra, S. Entre la ruta y el barrio: la experiência de lãs organizaciones piqueteras. 1° ed. Buenos Aires: Biblos, 2003
Tait, M. Elas dizem não! Mulheres camponesas e resistência ao cultivo de transgênicos no Brasil e Argentina. 220f. 2013. Tese. (Doutorado em Política Científica e Tecnológica), Universidade Estadual de Campinas.
Tardin, J. M. Brasil não tem política para agroecologia [Entrevista]. Obtido em: http://www.mst.org.br/node/1863. 10/03/2013.
Tarrow, S., O poder em movimento. Movimentos Sociais e Confronto Político. São Paulo: Vozes, 2009.
Tauile, J. R. Do socialismo de mercado à economia solidária. Revista Economia Contemporânea, Rio de Janeiro, 2002, p. 107–122.
Tauile, J. R.; Rodrigues, H. "Economia Solidária e autogestão: a criação e recriação de trabalho e renda". Revista Mercado de Trabalho, Brasília, IPEA, n. 24, agosto de 2004.
Tavares, J. C. Universalidade e singularidade do espaço transitório: um estudo a partir de quebradeiras de coco babaçu/MIQCB e trabalhadores rurais sem terra/MST no Maranhão (1990–2000). Tese de Doutorado, Florianópolis, UFSC, 2008.
Theis, I. M.; Meneghel, S. M. *Universidade, desenvolvimento e meio ambiente.* In: Wulf, C.; Bryan, N. P. (Org.). Desarrollo sustenible: conceptos y ejemplos de buenas prácticas en Europa y América Latina. Münster: Waxmann Verlag GmbH, 2006, v. 22, pp. 85–97.
Tiriba, L. Pedagogia(s) da produção associada. Ijuí: Ed. da Unijuí, 2001.
Tiriba, L; Fischer, M.C.B. Saberes do trabalho associado. In: Cattani, A. D.; Laville, J. L.; Gaiger, L. I.; HESPANHA, P. Dicionário Internacional da Outra Economia. São Paulo/Coimbra, Almedina Brasil Ltda/Edições Almedina S.A., 2009, pp. 293–298.
Tolentino, C. O farmer contra o Jeca - O projeto de revisão agrária do Governo Carvalho Pinto. Marília: Oficina Universitária, 2011.
Toná, N. Elementos de Balanço do Processo de construção da Agroecologia no MST – PR. In: Queiroz, J. G; Toná, N. Nossa História: Agroecologia e as Escolas de Formação do Paraná. Curitiba: Acap., 2011.

Training in the Solidarity Economy. Centro de Formação em Economia Solidária. Brasília, 2006.

Tragtenberg, M. Marxismo Heterodoxo. São Paulo: Brasiliense, 1981.

Tragtenberg, M. Reflexões sobre o socialismo. São Paulo: Moderna, 1986.

Tragtenberg, M. Administração, poder e ideologia. 3. ed. São Paulo: Editora da UNESP, 2005.

Tragtenberg, M. Sobre educação, política e sindicalismo. 2ª Ed. São Paulo: Editora da Unesp, 2006.

Tragtenberg, M. Reflexões sobre Socialismo. São Paulo: Editora da Unesp, 2008.

Tragtenberg, M. Autonomia operária. São Paulo: Unesp, 2011.

USINA. Luta por moradia e autogestão na América Latina - uma breve reflexão sobre os casos do Uruguai, Brasil, Argentina e Venezuela. In: RODRIGUES, F. C.; NOVAES, H. T.; BATISTA, E. (orgs.) Movimentos Sociais, Trabalho Associado e Educação para além do capital. São Paulo: Outras Expressões, 2012.

USINA. Obtido em: http://www.usinactah.org.br/index.php?/apresentacao/. Retirado em 5/11/2013.

Varsavsky, O. Por uma Política Científica Nacional. Rio de Janeiro: Paz e Terra, 1976.

Varsavsky, O. Ciencia, Política y Cientificismo. Caracas: Monte Ávila, 2007 [1969].

Vasapolo, L. Trabalho atípico e precariedade. São Paulo: Expressão Popular, 2005.

Vazquez, A. S. As ideias estéticas de Marx. São Paulo: Expressão Popular, 2009.

Vazzoler. M. R. Cooperativismo em assentamentos de reforma agrária: a sobrevivência de cooperativas do MST no contexto capitalista. 2004. Tese (Doutorado em Engenharia de Produção) - Programa de Pós-graduação em Engenharia de Produção, Universidade Federal de São Carlos, São Carlos, 2004.

Vendramini, C. R.; Machado, I. F. (Orgs.). Escola e movimento social: experiências em curso no campo brasileiro - reimpressão. 2. ed. São Paulo: Expressão Popular, 2013.

Venturelli, R. M. Terra e poder – as disputas entre agronegócio e resistência camponesa no sudoeste paulista – uma abordagem do uso das terras públicas. Dissertação de mestrado. São Paulo, USP, 2013.

Vieitez, C.; Dal Ri, N. Trabalho associado. Rio de Janeiro: DP&A, 2001.

Vieitez, C.; Dal Ri, N. M. Trabalho associado. Rio de Janeiro: DP&A, 2001.

Viola, S. Palestra no Seminário de Direitos Humanos. Marília, Unesp, out. 2012.

Wallerstein, I. Uma política de esquerda para o século XXI ? ou teoria e práxis novamente. In: Loureiro, I.; Leite, J.C.; CEVASCO, M. (orgs.) O espírito de Porto Alegre. São Paulo: Paz e Terra, 2002.

Welch, C. A. A semente foi plantada – as raízes paulistas do movimento sindical camponês no Brasil, 1924–1964. São Paulo: Expressão Popular, 2010.
Wirth, I. G.; Fraga, L.; Novaes, H. T. Educação, Trabalho e Autogestão: limites e possibilidades da Economia Solidária. In: Batista, E. L.; Novaes, H. T. (orgs.) Educação e reprodução social: as contradições do capital no século XXI. Bauru: Canal 6/Praxis, 2011.
Wirth, I. Mulheres na Triagem, Homens na Prensa. Questões de Gênero em Cooperativas de Catadores. São Paulo: Annablume, 2013.

Films

A classe operária vai ao paraíso. Direção: Elio Petri. Roma: 1976.
A corporação. 2002. Direção de Jeniffer Abbott e Mark Achbar. 2002. Canadá. Dvd.
A terceira morte de Joaquim Bolivar. Diretor: Flávio Candido, 1999.
ABC da Greve. Diretor: Leon Hirszman, 1979.
Acervo (Tempo Glauber), http://www.tempoglauber.com.br/english/.
Barravento. Diretor: Glauber Rocha, 1962.
Bolivianos. Diretor. Kiko Goifmann. Sesctv, dezembro de, 2012.
Braços Cruzados Máquinas Paradas. Diretores: Roberto Gervitz e Sergio Toledo, 1978.
Capitalismo – uma estória de amor. Michael Moore, 2009.
China Blue. Direção: Micha X. Peled, 2005
Cidadão Boilesen. Diretor: Chaim Litewski, 2009.
Conterrâneos velhos de guerra. Direção: Vladimir Carvalho. Rio de Janeiro, 1984.
Conterrâneos velhos de guerra. Vladimir Carvalho, 1984.
Deus e o Diabo na terra do Sol. Diretor: Glauber Rocha, 1964.
Entre os muros da escola. Laurent Cantet, 2006.
Entrevista com Daniel Becker. www.canalsaude.fiocruz.com.br. TVNBR, 12/02/2013.
Escola Nacional Florestan Fernandes.
Ilha das Flores. Direção: Jorge Furtado. Porto Alegre, 1989.
Macunaíma. Diretor. Joaquim Pedro de Andrade, 1969.
Me matam se não trabalho e se trabalho me matam. Direção de Raymundo Gleyzer. Buenos Aires, 1974. Videocassete.
Notícias de uma guerra particular. Diretor: João Moreira Salles, 2002.
O Som ao redor. Diretor: Kleber Mendonça, 2012.
O veneno está na mesa. Diretor: Silvio Tendler. Ano, 2008.
Os companheiros. Direção: Mario Monicelli. Roma, 1964.
Os Fuzis. Diretor: Ruy Guerra, 1964.
Ou tudo ou nada. Diretor: Peter Cattaneo. Londres, 1998.

Os companheiros. Direção de Mario Monicelli. Roma, 1964. Videocassete.
Precários inflexíveis. Diretor: Giovanni Alves, 2012.
Pro dia nascer feliz. Diretor: João Jardim, 2005.
Rio 40 graus. Diretor: Nelson Pereira dos Santos, 1957.
Segunda feira ao sol. Direção: Fernando Leon de Aranoa. Madrid, 2002.
Sickso – SOS Saúde. Michael Moore, 2006.
Terra em Transe. Diretor: Glauber Rocha, 1967.
Vidas Secas. Diretor: Nelson Pereira dos Santos, 1963.

Index

H. Tahan Novaes, *Associated Labor and Production in the Age of Barbarism*, https://doi.org/10.1007/978-3-031-51183-7

The manufacturer's authorised representative in the EU is Springer
Nature Customer Service Centre GmbH, Europaplatz 3, 69115 Heidelberg,
Germany. If you have any concerns regarding our products, please
contact ProductSafety@springernature.com

Printed and bound by CPI Group (UK) Ltd, Croydon, CR0 4YY
01/10/2026
02225854-0006